IFIP Advances in Information and Communication Technology 477

Editor-in-Chief

Kai Rannenberg, Goethe University Frankfurt, Germany

Editorial Board

IFIP – The International Federation for Information Processing

IFIP was founded in 1960 under the auspices of UNESCO, following the first World Computer Congress held in Paris the previous year. A federation for societies working in information processing, IFIP's aim is two-fold: to support information processing in the countries of its members and to encourage technology transfer to developing nations. As its mission statement clearly states:

IFIP is the global non-profit federation of societies of ICT professionals that aims at achieving a worldwide professional and socially responsible development and application of information and communication technologies.

IFIP is a non-profit-making organization, run almost solely by 2500 volunteers. It operates through a number of technical committees and working groups, which organize events and publications. IFIP's events range from large international open conferences to working conferences and local seminars.

The flagship event is the IFIP World Computer Congress, at which both invited and contributed papers are presented. Contributed papers are rigorously refereed and the rejection rate is high.

As with the Congress, participation in the open conferences is open to all and papers may be invited or submitted. Again, submitted papers are stringently refereed.

The working conferences are structured differently. They are usually run by a working group and attendance is generally smaller and occasionally by invitation only. Their purpose is to create an atmosphere conducive to innovation and development. Refereeing is also rigorous and papers are subjected to extensive group discussion.

Publications arising from IFIP events vary. The papers presented at the IFIP World Computer Congress and at open conferences are published as conference proceedings, while the results of the working conferences are often published as collections of selected and edited papers.

IFIP distinguishes three types of institutional membership: Country Representative Members, Members at Large, and Associate Members. The type of organization that can apply for membership is a wide variety and includes national or international societies of individual computer scientists/ICT professionals, associations or federations of such societies, government institutions/government related organizations, national or international research institutes or consortia, universities, academies of sciences, companies, national or international associations or federations of companies.

More information about this series at http://www.springer.com/series/6102

Maria Cecilia Calani Baranauskas · Kecheng Liu
Lily Sun · Vânia Paula de Almeida Neris
Rodrigo Bonacin · Keiichi Nakata (Eds.)

Socially Aware Organisations and Technologies

Impact and Challenges

17th IFIP WG 8.1 International Conference
on Informatics and Semiotics in Organisations, ICISO 2016
Campinas, Brazil, August 1–3, 2016
Proceedings

 Springer

Editors
Maria Cecilia Calani Baranauskas
University of Campinas
Campinas
Brazil

Kecheng Liu
University of Reading
Reading
UK

Lily Sun
University of Reading
Reading
UK

Vânia Paula de Almeida Neris
Federal University of São Carlos
São Carlos
Brazil

Rodrigo Bonacin
Center for Information Technology Renato
  Archer
Campinas
Brazil

Keiichi Nakata
University of Reading
Reading
UK

ISSN 1868-4238   ISSN 1868-422X (electronic)
IFIP Advances in Information and Communication Technology
ISBN 978-3-319-82498-7   ISBN 978-3-319-42102-5 (eBook)
DOI 10.1007/978-3-319-42102-5

Printed on acid-free paper

This Springer imprint is published by Springer Nature
The registered company is Springer International Publishing AG Switzerland

Preface

The 17th International Conference on Informatics and Semiotics in Organisations (ICISO 2016) is an IFIP WG 8.1 Working Conference and part of a series of international events devoted to the latest research and practice in informatics and organizational semiotics. As a pioneer event in the discussion of organizations and technologies from an integrated perspective, this edition of ICISO was especially concerned with the social context in which they exist. This focus is especially important at a time where social responsibility is no longer a differential but a mandatory characteristic of organizations, of their products and processes, as well as of their staff.

Organizational semiotics (OS) is a discipline that studies the nature, characteristics, function, and effect of information and communication in organizational contexts, supporting the understanding and articulation of relevant technical, formal, and social issues. The contribution of this discipline to the understanding, analysis, modelling, design, and implementation of organizational and technical information systems has attracted the attention of researchers and practitioners from many subject areas. The ICISO conferences have become the key focal point for participants from multidisciplinary backgrounds to exchange the development and the state of the art of their theoretical and practical work (see www.orgsem.org for earlier conferences since 1995).

In 2006, the ICISO conference was held for the first time in Brazil, discussing the interface between society, technology, and organizations. Ten years later, for the second time in Brazil, the conference promoted the debate on "Socially Aware Organizations and Technologies: Impact and Challenges," bringing renowned researchers and professionals from different parts of the world, fostering partnerships, and joining different interested parties in the community. Organizational semiotics, as a study of sign, information, and human communication in organized contexts, will provide a holistic and comprehensive approach with which to examine the issues of the theme from scholarly and practical views. A semiotic perspective can accommodate the individual and the social, the human and the technical demands, at a level of detail that is required for studying, modelling, designing, and engineering organizational and technical systems. Research and practice in the increasingly complex contexts of a society mediated by information and communication technology urge us to rethink and revisit our theories, methods, and techniques, dealing with the challenges of the present and anticipating the questions of the near future.

We received 39 paper submissions from 15 countries, which demonstrates the global dimension of this conference. From these, 16 (41 %) were accepted for presentation as full papers. Moreover, nine manuscripts were accepted as short papers and six as posters. These numbers show the intention of preserving a high level of quality for future editions of this conference, at the same time welcoming new participants with work in progress in the field. The papers are organized into five topics: digital business ecosystems; knowledge management and engineering; organizational semiotics theory and research; semiotics of interactions and socially aware user interface design; trends challenges and new issues in education, health, and eScience systems. Besides the presentation of scientific papers that show the trends and state of the art on the conference's topics, the event hosted a panel to discuss the future of organizations and technology, and a hands-on workshop in which participants were introduced to and put into practice a socially aware view on the understanding and design of contemporary systems.

The high quality of the papers demanded especial effort from the Program Committee, whose members are highly qualified researchers in the conference topic areas, performing two rounds of paper review. Moreover, ICISO also featured a number of keynote lectures delivered by internationally recognized experts, namely: Prof. Maria Lucia Santaella Braga, from São Paulo Catholic University, director of the Center of Research in Digital Media, one of the honorary presidents of the Latin-American Federation of Semiotics; and Prof. Jeffrey Bardzell, from HCI/Design and new media at the School of Informatics in the Indiana University, USA. We are also very pleased to have a special contribution from Prof. Ronald Stamper and the participation of Prof. Clarisse S. de Souza from PUC-Rio in the conference panel. These special contributions were significant highlights of the conference.

Building an interesting and successful program for the conference required the dedicated effort of many people. We would like to express our thanks to all authors including those whose papers were not included in the program. We would also like to express our gratitude to all the members of the Program Committee and additional reviewers, who helped us with their expertise and valuable time. Furthermore, we thank the invited speakers for their invaluable contribution and for taking the time to prepare their talks. Moreover, we thank the other ICISO 2016 chairs, Roberto Pereira, Heiko H Hornung, and Weizi Li, whose contribution to the conference organization was essential, as well as the valuable work of the student volunteers.

Finally, we gratefully acknowledge the funding agencies supporting the event (CNPq, Capes and FAPESP), and the professional and organizational support from the Institute of Computing, the Nucleus of Informatics Applied to Education, University of Campinas UNICAMP, Brazil, and Informatics Research Centre, Henley Business School, University of Reading, UK.

May 2016

M. Cecília C. Baranauskas
Kecheng Liu
Lily Sun
Vânia P.A. Neris
Rodrigo Bonacin
Keiichi Nakata

Organization

Conference Chairs

M. Cecilia C. Baranauskas   University of Campinas, Brazil
Kecheng Liu   University of Reading, UK

Program Chairs

Keiichi Nakata   University of Reading, UK
Vânia Neris   Federal University of Sao Carlos, Brazil

Publication Chairs

Lily Sun   University of Reading, UK
Rodrigo Bonacin   CTI and FACCAMP, Brazil

Publicity Chair

Roberto Pereira   University of Campinas, Brazil

Organizing Chairs

Heiko Hornung   University of Campinas, Brazil
Weizi Li   University of Reading, UK

Conference Secretariat

Shixiong Liu   University of Reading, UK
Siwen Liu   University of Reading, UK
Vanessa Maike   University of Campinas, Brazil

Program Committee

Leonelo Almeida   Federal University of Technology - Paraná, Brazil
Alessandro Arpetti   University of Campinas, Brazil
Simone D.J. Barbosa   Pontifical Catholic University of Rio de Janeiro, Brazil
Joseph Barjis   Delft University of Technology, The Netherlands
Adrian Benfell   University of Portsmouth, UK
Ig Ibert Bittencourt   Federal University of Alagoas, Brazil
Marcos A.F. Borges   University of Campinas, Brazil
Clodis Boscarioli   State University of West Paraná, Brazil

Yinshan Tang	University of Reading, UK
Christina Tay	Chinese Culture University, Taiwan
George Tsaramirsis	King Abulaziz University, Saudi Arabia
Jose Armando Valente	University of Campinas, Brazil
Hans Weigand	Tilburg University, The Netherlands
Martin Wheatman	Reading University, UK
Pornpit Wongthongtham	Curtin University, Australia
Mohammad Yamin	King Abdelaziz University, Saudi Arabia
Zhijun Yan	Beijing Institute of Technology, China
Kevin Yang	Chinese Academy of Sciences, China
Changrui Yu	Shanghai Jiao Tong University, China
Yunchuan Zhang	Wuhan University of Science and Technology, China

Additional Reviewers

Tatiana de Alencar	Federal University of Sao Carlos, Brazil
Aron Lopes	Federal University of Mato Grosso, Brazil
Kamila Rios da Hora Rodrigues	University of Sao Paulo, Brazil

Sponsors

In Co-operation with

Abstract of Keynotes

Signification, Design, and Inquiry

Jeffrey Bardzell

Faculty of the Kinsey Institute for Sex, Gender, and Reproduction
Indiana University School of Informatics and Computing, Indiana, USA
jbardzel@indiana.edu

Abstract. As the design of technology has increasingly become implicated in our personal lives, our social worlds, and our physical environments, innovative design methodologies have emerged to take on these challenges. One of these is research through design, which uses design processes not to develop traditional end-user products, but instead to contribute to theory and knowledge about human-computer interaction (HCI) and interaction design. As an emerging practice, research through design faces questions about how it works, what constitutes a good research outcome, how practitioners can build on each other's work, and how it can be made legible to other areas of HCI and interaction design, such as user-centered design. I will present work that seeks to develop epistemological resources for research through design practitioners, including those who are intrigued about it but don't know where to begin. Like other design researchers, I will argue that research through design is best not pursued as a scientific practice. My contribution to this debate is to consider research through design in relation to humanistic knowledge practices, including criticism and aesthetics. I will explore these themes through a dialogue between critical concepts and concrete examples, drawn from the maker movement, critical design, and social computing. And I will argue that research through design, among other things, is distinguished by its modes of signification, with implications for its uptakes into the broader HCI and interaction design communities.

What Is OS? Where did it Come from? How to Proceed? Where Is it Going?

Ronald Stamper[1,2,3]

[1] Oxford OX3 7SL#38, UK
[2] London School of Economics, London, UK
[3] University of Twente, Enschede, The Netherlands
stamper.measur@gmail.com

Abstract. I address these questions within my experience of investigating organisations as information systems. Gathering and analysing data were of little use without a clearer terminology. Even "information" was embarrassingly vague until recognised as a jumble of diverse properties of signs. Thus, "organisational semiotics" became our conceptual framework. Clarifying terminology for empirical investigations remains an important aspect of research. Collecting and analysing data may be only a popular research ritual unless it is justified within a carefully chosen scientific method: Popper's refutationist method in our case. Popper emphasises the role of imagination in formulating hypotheses that combine clarity, novelty, conciseness and boldness with the precision that exposes them to empirical refutation. The researcher must not take for granted the orthodox theory but discover and question its dominant metaphor. In our case it was a century-old "information flow" metaphor that focuses attention on technology and bureaucracy, leaving the human and social aspects of information unaddressed. This observation revealed the paucity of useful the invariants whose discovery is characteristic of good science. We adopted a "knowledge field" paradigm, leading to previously unknown organisational invariants with huge potential for engineering better organisations. Wide reading, inter-disciplinary interests and sheer delight in ideas motivate research work.

Is Artificial Consciousness Possible?

Lucia Santaella

São Paulo Catholic University (PUCSP),
Rua Monte Alegre, 984, São Paulo - SP, 05014-901, Brazil
lbraga@pucsp.br

Abstract. Against all the arguments that deny the possible simulation of consciousness, there are already numerous computer architectures able to emulate if not all, at least some of the skills of a conscious mind. Taking into account that the goal of a cognitive architecture is to summarize the various results of psychic cognition in a comprehensive computer model, there are already several different architectures, for example, and without any intention of completeness: Qubic (Quantum and Bio-inspired cognitive Architecture for machine Consciousness); Global Workspace, by Baars; CLARION, by Ron Sun, an architecture capable of simple reactive activities to complex cognition. In the connectionist matrix there are several proposals, including still as an example, Penti Haikonen's architecture that instead of rules, ambitiously proposes to reproduce perceptual processes, internal images, inner speech, pain and pleasure with their internal cognitive functions. Whatever these architectures may be, they still come up against the crucial question whether machines can emulate creativity, emotions and free will. This is where I justify the input of C.S. Peirce's semiotic theory of consciousness not as a solution to the thorny problems that still exist, but as an original vision that can bring us new data on the two issues more finely defining human consciousness: self-consciousness, on the one hand, and the unconscious, on the other.

Contents

Knowledge Management and Engineering

Trends, Challenges and New Issues in Education, Health and eScience Systems

Poster Papers

Organisational Semiotics:
Theory and Research

An X-ray of ICISO Portrayed Through the Lens of Actor-Network Theory

Alysson Bolognesi Prado[(✉)] and Maria Cecilia Calani Baranauskas

Institute of Computing, State University of Campinas,
Campinas, São Paulo, Brazil
{aprado,cecilia}@ic.unicamp.br

Abstract. Any scientific community relies on a shared set of concepts and methods that, when well established and known, can guide its members to better solving research problems. Actor-Network Theory states that human and non-human entities – such as scientific literature – work together when a scientific fact is constructed. We applied this viewpoint as social network analysis technique, to assess the bibliographical data from the last two ICISO proceedings. The resulting graphs highlighted persons and publications acting as points of convergence for each conference edition. These findings lead to a recurring structure cored on Ronald Stamper and his publications, and the book Semiotics in Information Systems Engineering.

Keywords: Scientific communities · Actor-Network Theory · ICISO

1 Introduction

Kuhn [8] defines a scientific community as a group of persons who study a specific subject sharing a common *paradigm*, that is, a set of methods, values, language, principles and concepts. This shared viewpoint allows the proposition of problems and the acceptance of the respective solutions by the members of the community. Scientific literature plays a twofold role, either providing for the novice the stabilized facts widely accepted by the community, and communicating the newer theories, under development by the experts [3]. The actual paradigm is formalized, spread out and evolved through the literature.

As part of his work on Social Studies of Science and Technology, Latour [9] proposes, as a methodological principle, that the study of science should not be restricted to the analysis of its final products; instead, it should start from the discussions that evolve to the inception and refinement of such outcomes. By observing the science while it is produced, it is possible to witness the involved entities acting upon one another, making possible to understand how the resultant of the combined interests and possibilities shapes the path towards scientific discoveries.

The International Conference on Informatics and Semiotics in Organizations – ICISO – is the most traditional event to reunite periodically the community devoted to the research on Organizational Semiotics, reaching its 17th edition in 2016. It is also part of a series of international conferences aiming to study the role and effects of information and communication in organizational contexts.

© IFIP International Federation for Information Processing 2016
Published by Springer International Publishing Switzerland 2016. All Rights Reserved
M.C.C. Baranauskas et al. (Eds.): ICISO 2016, IFIP AICT 477, pp. 3–12, 2016.
DOI: 10.1007/978-3-319-42102-5_1

In this work, our goal is to provide an understanding of the current structure of the Organizational Semiotics community as expressed through the papers published in the last two editions of ICISO. We draw upon methods of Social Studies of Science and Technology to grasp the broader social context in which the more technical and methodical work of researchers is immersed. We expect to contribute to the self-knowledge about how the community is arranged, in an alternative way, complementary to common widely available scientometrics.

This paper is organized as follows: Sect. 2 presents the chosen theoretical framework to support scrutinizing the structure of associations that compose ICISO. In Sect. 3 we detail the data sources and methodological steps applied, followed by Sect. 4 presenting and discussing the results of such procedure. In Sect. 5 we discuss the findings, and concluding in Sect. 6.

2   Theoretical Background

The study of science-making from the viewpoint of the sociology is the root of the Actor-Network Theory (ANT) a theoretical and methodological framework that understands social phenomena as the result of entities, or actors, capable of influencing the behavior of the others; these actors are tied together by relationships of mutual benefit, constituting a network. Moreover, ANT claims that the role of actors in social phenomena is not restricted to humans, but can also be played by non-humans.

One of the non-human participants of the collaborative construction of scientific facts is the scientific literature. Using another piece of literature in a paper may help building the adopted theoretical background, showing related results for the sake of positive or negative comparison, manifesting affiliation to a certain group or trend of opinion, or expressing the acceptance of a previous result taking it for granted and using it for further research. As an allegation of one publication is accepted by others in the form of citations, it progressively gains the status of scientific fact.

Only when it becomes tacit knowledge, the citation is no longer required. To give an example, Latour [9] asks "Who refers to Lavoisier's paper when writing the formula H_2O for water?" The stabilized fact of water being composed of hydrogen and oxygen becomes incorporated into tacit knowledge, with no mark of being produced by anyone [11].

When a scientific publication P refers to another one R, authors of P are benefited by the previous results and statements provided by the other, since much of the content of R might be – at least partially – accepted by the target audience. On the other hand, the more R is cited, the more its authors are benefited by the acknowledgement of the relevance of their work and the spreading of R's content among P's readers. This relationship, shown in Fig. 1, provides mutual benefit for the human actors, being mediated by the non-human entities P and R. Even whether authors of P and R do not know each other, they become associated.

Tracing and analyzing these networks of relationships, one can understand how a scientific community is arranged, what are the sources of its adopted paradigm, how convergent are its interests, and if there is any pattern over time. Unlike other methods of bibliometric analysis, as the co-authorship [6] or co-citation [15] graphs, which

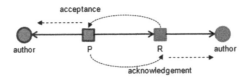

Fig. 1. Relationship of mutual benefit established between authors of a paper P referencing another publication R. Solid arrows denote reference, dashed ones the provided benefit

focus only on the persons or the publications, the ANT approach does not privilege participants of any specific nature. It allows highlighting main scientists and important bibliography contributing to the subject of a conference, and the whole structure that emerges from their relationships.

3 Procedures of Data Gathering and Summarization

Considering the editions of ICISO conference as samples of the Organizational Semiotics community, we chose to apply ANT's point of view to its bibliographic data freely available on the internet. Springer provides the proceedings of 2014 and 2015 occurrences of ICISO, along with the list of references for each published paper. This data were fed into a software originally intended to support systematic bibliographic reviews [13], but that proved suited for our purpose, managing the publication list, the relations to references and authors, and generating the visualizations.

Not all references could be used. For instance, web pages are not considered references since their authors – human actors – are not defined. Other papers have duplicate references that were accounted only once. Some similar author names were disambiguated using an automatic algorithm [10]. Whenever available, DOI is applied to retrieve additional information about the references and to solve duplications due to typos or divergences in credited titles.

Once the automatic procedure was finished, we carried out a manual inspection of the results and performed minor corrections by hand when necessary. This includes splitting nodes representing distinct persons with the same name abbreviation, and merging references with misspelled titles, using additional data sources and search engines when necessary. Not all nodes required manual inspection: possible splitting was checked only by the ones representing authors and with degree >1 (177 of 3599, or about 5%); similarly, candidates for merging were screened using a Levenshtein distance <3 prior to manual procedures. The final dataset is summarized in Table 1.

Table 1. Summary of data retrieved for each conference edition

	ICISO 2014	ICISO 2015
Published papers	49	21
Number of references as shown at Springer.com	857	427
Identified references	763	396
Identified authors of papers	133	57
Identified authors of references	1568	724

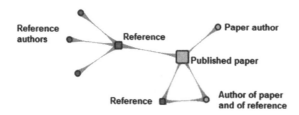

Fig. 2. Adopted representation for the actor-network graph (Color figure online)

The visualization of the graph of bibliographic references is based on the proposal of Prado and Baranauskas [12]. They applied the betweenness centrality measure [2] to calculate the size of the vertices, representing the importance that each vertex has to keep the network together. They also used a spring forces layout algorithm [5], to obtain an automatic arrangement of vertices, what they argue is well aligned with ANT's view of a social group as a balance between the forces generated by authors through associations, bringing together the ones they are interested but keeping apart from the others. In comparison to the most commonly used graphs of co-authorship containing only human actors, this representation provides a better view of the conference edition as a single social phenomena, since the number of connected components is significantly smaller.

The final representation of the graph is exemplified in Fig. 2: papers published in the conference are represented as blue square vertices and their authors as blue circles; while the references and their authors are red squares and circles, respectively. If an author of a paper has also authored a reference, that first condition prevails. The size of each vertex is proportional to the logarithm of its betweenness centrality. We can use it to identify the relevant actors for each network and understand the main contributors to the shared theoretical background. When authors and publications are marked relevant in more than a single conference edition, we can suspect their importance are not due to the specific topic of that particular edition, but instead it is part of the community's adopted paradigm. Besides the full graphs, smaller versions were obtained by applying an intensive graph pruning algorithm [7]. This succinct preview allows knowing the main actors that compose the backbone of the graph, before we drill down into the details of the whole network.

Buchdid and Baranauskas [4] analyze conferences using word clouds [14] extracted from the titles of papers published in conference editions. Word clouds provided visual clues to the essence of the studied conferences at a glance. We believe that this high-level representation complements the lower level structural analysis of ANT and both together provide a better understanding of the work of the social group.

To support the study in relation to the particularities of each conference edition, we recovered their proposed topics of interest. ICISO 2014 called for papers about "Service Science and Knowledge Innovation", a young discipline that has attracted great attention by academy and industry because of the increasing need for a scientific approach to guide the study of services. ICISO 2015 tackled "Information and Knowledge Management in Complex Systems", such as large-scale projects, network of networks, and dynamic and evolving enterprises.

4 Analysis of Results

Using the titles of the papers published in each conference edition, we built the word clouds shown in Fig. 3. The 2014 edition is well aligned with that conference motto, as the words "service", "based" and "approach" are the most frequent, followed by "method" and "architecture". For 2015, however, the topics become more generic, and "information" becomes highlighted, followed by "semiotics", "systems", and as in the previous year, "based" and "approach", aligning the community production more to its roots of semiotics and information systems.

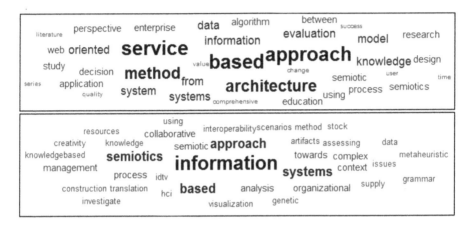

Fig. 3. Word clouds generated from the titles of papers published in ICISO 2014 and 2015 – above and below, respectively

From the graph data structures, some metrics were obtained, as shown in Table 2. Not all published papers share a path with the others, thus creating insulated groups of vertices, that is, distinct connected components [1]. Papers published in 2014 are aggregated in 11 components while the 2015 edition produced 10. However, there is always a major connected component gluing most of the vertices. In both years, this component comprises more than half of the whole graph, showing the convergence of the community persisting along the 2 years, despite of the different themes and scales of each conference edition.

Figure 4 shows the simplified versions of the actor-networks, composed only by the main actors and their associations for each conference edition, including published

Table 2. General graph measures for each conference edition

	ICISO 2014	ICISO 2015
Graph's connected components	11	10
Graph's total number of vertices	2440	1159
Size of major connected component (vertices)	1994	661
Coverage of major connected component	81%	57%

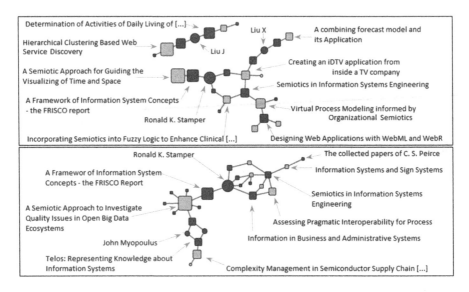

Fig. 4. Simplified graphs showing main actors for ICISO 2014 and 2015 – above and below, respectively

papers, references and authors with higher betweenness. Although papers published at each edition and well aligned to its theme are included, e.g., "Hierarchical Clustering Based Web Service Discovery" for 2014, and "A Semiotic Approach to Investigate Quality Issues of Open Big Data Ecosystems" for 2015 – our analysis will focus on the references they draw upon to make their claims, as the basis of the community.

Considering the complete dataset, given the greater number of published papers in 2014, it is not feasible to print the whole graph in a single picture; therefore, we cropped it to show the central portion of the main connected component, producing Fig. 5. For the 2015 edition, having less than half of the features, it was possible to build Fig. 6 depicting the complete graph. Some of the actors cited in the text are pointed out.

In both years, the most relevant reference author is "Ronald K. Stamper" and the most relevant reference is "A Framework of information system concepts - The FRISCO Report". The nodes representing them are well positioned in the two generated layouts, at the center of the main connected component. Both constitute a path between two large blocks of published papers and their related references. Another reference worth noting is "Semiotics in Information Systems Engineering", being placed in the middle of dense clusters of papers in the two graphs, what led the analysis to its author, "Kecheng Liu", who provided more used references and authored some of the published papers in each conference edition.

Regarding well-positioned references and authors that appear in a single conference edition, we can cite for 2014 the "Review of web service discovery technology" by "Liu J. et al."; and "Measuring and Comparing Effectiveness of Data Quality Techniques" by "John Mylopoulos *et al.*". Their titles suggest they are aligned to each

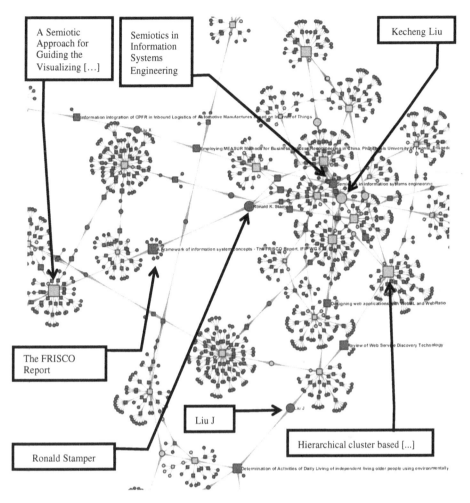

A Semiotic Approach for Guiding the Visualizing [...]

Semiotics in Information Systems Engineering

Kecheng Liu

The FRISCO Report

Ronald Stamper

Liu J

Hierarchical cluster based [...]

Fig. 5. Detail of the main connected component of ICISO 2014 actor-network. The references and authors with higher betweenness centrality are labeled

conference theme, what adds proof to the relative relevance calculated to them, inside the subject of that particular edition.

5 Discussion of the Outcomes

There seems to be a recurring pattern of associations of the published papers and their references along with the studied conference editions, as sketched in Fig. 7. Stamper's publications and himself are connecting distant clusters of papers, as a broader source of concepts. On the other hand, "Semiotics in Information Systems Engineering" appears inside a cluster of papers with several inner connections. This may be extrapolated as the current general pattern that creates a solid structural basis for the O.S. community.

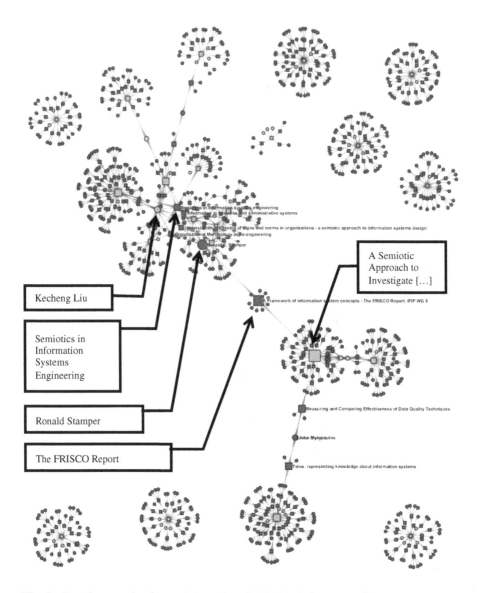

Fig. 6. Complete graph of associations for ICISO 2015. Some smaller components were repositioned for better fitting on the page

During the manual inspection of data, some limitations of the used tool were detected. The person "Taylor A", pointed out as author of two references used in 2015, is in fact the abbreviated name of two distinct researchers: Alex Taylor, author of "On the naturalness of touchless" and Alva Taylor, author of "Superman or the Fantastic Four?". An additional node was created for each one, removing the original. This kind of interventions did not reshape significantly the graph as a whole, but created one of

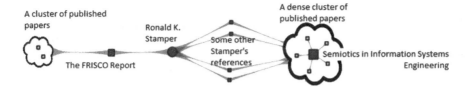

Fig. 7. General pattern found in both conference editions

the minor connected components. In another situation, author "Liu J." could not have his identity checked: he is credited as "Jiajun Liu" at IEEE for authoring "Determination of Activities of Daily Living of independent living older people using environmentally placed sensors", but the authorship of "Review of Web service discovery technology" could not be verified. In case of splitting, this node would have its relevance recalculated as a lower value.

To a brief comparison to a purely quantitative bibliometric analysis, we ranked the number of cited publications and authors among the conference papers. The most used bibliography are "Semiotics in Information Systems Engineering" (12 citations) and "Information in Business and Administrative Systems" (4 citations). Comparing to ANT's results, both have also a relatively high betweenness, particularly for the 2015 edition, what makes them indubitably important for the community. However, the second one is cited only by papers of the same two groups of researchers, making it more localized into the community. Authors most often cited are Kecheng Liu (37 citations), followed by John Krogstie (23 citations), reputed scientists in the field of Information Systems. However, the citations for the latter come mostly from a single paper published at ICISO 2015; therefore, his publications cannot be seen as common ground for the community. There is a contrast between the good results obtained by "Ronald K. Stamper" and "The FRISCO report" using ANT and their lower citation count; we interpret this as if the ideas contained therein are becoming tacit knowledge within the members of the O.S. community. The major weakness of the used method is the dependence to the availability of data, as a relevant subset of the publications' bibliographical references is required to provide a representative outcome. The unavailability of full proceedings of a conference edition hinders a longer-term analysis.

6   Conclusion

Scientific communities evolve around a set of concepts and assumptions, drawn from distinct bibliographic references and authors. Some of these become tacit knowledge among the researchers and practitioners, and therefore are not always captured by the most traditional scientometric methods. In this paper, we applied an alternative approach to analyze the relationships between researches within a scientific community mediated by scientific literature, as proposed by ANT. Based on the ICISO 2014 and 2015 proceedings available online, we were able to construct graphs representing such associations, and apply algorithms to build visualizations of the core structures that keep this community standing up as an X-ray.

Our analysis highlights the very foundational work of Ronald Stamper towards defining a common ground for the Organizational Semiotics researchers through the "FRISCO Report" and other papers. Besides, the book "Semiotics in Information Systems Engineering" also appears as a central source of tools and methods enabling many other related scientific projects, while its author Kecheng Liu remains an active member of the community. These results corroborate ANT's choice of keeping human and non-human together and trace their relationships for the study of scientific communities.

Acknowledgments.   We thank the Brazilian Research Foundation CNPq (Grant # 308618/ 2014-9). The opinions expressed in this work do not necessarily reflect those of the funding agencies.

References

1. Bondy, J.A., Murty, U.S.: Graph Theory with Applications. Elsevier, Amsterdam (1976)
2. Brandes, U.: A faster algorithm for betweenness centrality. J. Math. Soc. **25**(2), 163–177 (2001)
3. Brorson, S., Andersen, H.: Stabilizing and changing phenomenal worlds: Ludwik Fleck and Thomas Kuhn on scientific literature. J. Gen. Philos. Sci. **32**(1), 109–129 (2001). doi:10. 1023/A:1011236713841
4. Buchdid, S., Baranauskas, M: IHC em context, o que as palavras relevam sobre ela. In: 11th Brazilian Symposium on Human Factors in Computer Systems. ACM (2012)
5. Eades, P.: A heuristic for graph drawing. Congressus Numerantium **42**, 149–160 (1984)
6. Glanzel, W., Schubert, A.: Analysing scientific networks through co-authorship. In: Moed, H.F., Glänzel, W., Schmoch, U. (eds.) Handbook of Quantitative Science and Technology Research. Springer, Heidelberg (2005)
7. Hennessey, D., Brooks, D., Fridman, A., Breen, D.: A simplification algorithm for visualizing the structure of complex graphs. In: Information Visualisation (2008)
8. Kuhn, T.: The Structure of Scientific Revolutions. University of Chicago Press, Chicago (1962)
9. Latour, B.: Science in Action: How to Follow Scientists and Engineers Through Society. Harvard University Press, Massachusetts (1987). ISBN 0-674-79291-2
10. Levin, F.H., Heuser, C.A.: Evaluating the use of social networks in author name disambiguation in digital libraries. J. Inf. Data Manag. **1**, 183 (2010)
11. Linton, J.: What is Water? The History of a Modern Abstraction. UBC Press, Vancouver (2010)
12. Prado, A.B., Baranauskas, M.C.C.: Representing scientific associations through the lens of actor-network theory. In: Proceedings of the Fourth International Conference on Computational Aspects of Social Networks – CASoN (2012)
13. Prado, A.B., Baranauskas, M.C., Bittencourt, I.I., Goncalves, F.M.: Expandindo revisões bibliográficas sistemáticas pela análise de redes sócio-técnicas científicas. In: XLI Seminário Integrado de Software e Hardware, SEMISH (2014)
14. Rivadeneira, A.W., Gruen, D.M., Muller, M.J., Millen, D.R.: Getting our head in the clouds: toward evaluation studies of tagclouds. In: Proceeding of the SIGCHI Conference on Human Factors in Computing Systems. ACM Press (2007)
15. Small, H.: Co-citation in the scientific literature: a new measure of the relationship between two documents. J. Am. Soc. Inf. Sci. **24**, 265–269 (1973)

Studies in Organisational Semiotics:
A Systematic Literature Review

Maria Carolina de Souza Santos, Bruna da Silva Magalhães Bertãozini,
and Vânia Paula de Almeida Neris[✉]

Department of Computer Science, Federal University of São Carlos,
Rod Washington Luiz, Km 235, São Carlos, Brazil
`mariasantoshci@gmail.com`, `magalhaes.bruna.b@gmail.com`,
`vania@dc.ufscar.br`

Abstract. Organizational Semiotics (OS) is a discipline that supports analyzing and modeling organizations as Information Systems (IS). This paper investigates the use of OS theories in studies published in the last five years, aiming to identify how researchers have been employing the OS theory and the current approaches derived from OS. In this sense, we conducted a systematic review in four scientific databases. Starting with an initial set of 91 papers, we selected 53 for this review. The results suggest almost twenty new modeling approaches using OS artifacts and ideas. Moreover, the number of publications has been increasing and publications have occurred in several different journals and conference proceedings.

Keywords: Organizational semiotics · Semiotics · Systematic literature review

1 Introduction

Organizational Semiotics (OS) is a discipline that emerged around 1973, and it aimed at analyzing and modeling organizations as Information Systems (IS). The pioneers of this discipline, such as Stamper [55] and Liu [34], have developed methods, techniques and approaches grounded in Peircean Semiotics [49] focused on organizations. Therefore, they have inspired other authors to adopt these methods, techniques, and approaches in different IS and to develop new approaches based on OS theories.

This paper investigates the use of OS theories in studies published in the last five years, aiming to identify how researchers have been employing the OS theory and the current approaches derived from OS. To achieve this aim, we searched first the main methods, techniques, frameworks grounded on OS theories and published before 2011, and we named them as OS approaches. Thus, we have followed a systematic literature review process that consists of three key stages: planning, conducting, and reporting the review. In addition, we have defined and applied the inclusion and exclusion criteria. Afterward, we have extracted the data and synthesized them to answer the research questions.

Published by Springer International Publishing Switzerland 2016. All Rights Reserved
M.C.C. Baranauskas et al. (Eds.): ICISO 2016, IFIP AICT 477, pp. 13–24, 2016.
DOI: 10.1007/978-3-319-42102-5_2

2   Research Method

This research follows a systematic review process adopted by [7, 28, 31]. Therefore, we developed a study protocol, a data extraction strategy to ensure a systematic search and review process.

2.1   Research Question

The performed literature review aimed to summarize the current studies that adopt OS approaches, to identify how researchers employ the methods and techniques derived from various OS approaches and the current approaches grounded on OS theories. We raised four central questions in order to address the research objectives:

- *RQ1*. How do researchers employ OS theory?
- *RQ2*. What are new OS approaches developed by researchers?
- *RQ3*. Where are these studies published?
- *RQ4*. How many papers using OS has been published since 2011 per year?

2.2   Search Strategy

Concerning the adoption of Organizational Semiotics approaches, we searched for papers in four web-based scientific databases: ACM digital library, IEEE Explorer digital library, ScienceDirect, and Springer Link. The search string used for retrieving study materials was as follows: "Organizational Semiotics" OR "Organisational Semiotics" (in title, abstract, or keywords). In relation to the study sources, we made sure that our search covered conferences, journals, and book chapters published over the last 5 years (from January 1st, 2011 to December 31st, 2015). Further, we established inclusion and exclusion criteria. Consequently, we included full papers in English or in Portuguese. Therefore, we excluded duplicated papers and irrelevant papers based on title, abstract or keywords.

2.3   Data Extraction Strategy

This review considered few important considerations to extract the specific kinds of data to reach the review goals. We decomposed these considerations into nine questions to provide effective answers to the research questions stated above. The data extracted (DE) from each study were:

- *DEQ 1*. What is the research problem?
- *DEQ 2*. What are the research objectives?
- *DEQ 3*. What are the OS approaches used by researchers?
- *DEQ 4*. How do researchers adopt the OS approaches?
- *DEQ 5*. Do the authors present a new approach derived from OS? What are the proposal and OS basis of the new approach?

- *DEQ 6.* What is the journal or conference where it has been published?
- *DEQ 7.* What is the publication year?

2.4   Conducting the Review

With respect to searching, selecting, as well as reviewing the papers, we conducted the activities during December 2015 to January 2016. The preliminary searching returned 91 papers. Following, we describe the number of hits in each database: ACM retrieved two papers, IEEEXplorer retrieved three papers, ScienceDirect retrieved three papers, and SpringerLink retrieved 83 papers. Applying the inclusion and exclusion criteria, we excluded 36 hits in the first review of titles, abstracts and keywords. Further, we did not find duplicated papers. However, we excluded two non-full papers. Consequently, we considered 53 papers to extract data.

3   Results

We summarized the data by tabulating results against stated questions. Due to space limitation, the complete set of extracting data for each question is not included in this paper.

3.1   How Do Researchers Employ OS Theory?

Concerning the data extraction question numbers 3 and 4, we describe summarily how authors adopted OS theory:

Semiotic Onion (SO): The majority of the authors used the SO to identify the informal, formal and technical norms, and to represent and comprehend the information systems, the rules and stakeholders' needs [15, 16, 18, 19, 21, 26, 29, 30, 45, 46, 49]. For instance, SO helped to identify socio-technical barriers that arise in the domain of integrated digital television (iDTV) [12]. Concerning the design solutions, [47] shows the development of a model to suggest solutions through artifacts which analyze, synthesize and evaluate the informal, formal and technical layers, respectively. In addition, Liu et al. [36] used the SO as a dimension of the Pragmatic Interoperability Measurement Model. Furthermore, this dimension illustrates how an integrated system works. Concerning human values, [48] presents a way to identify values according to SO levels.

Semiotic Framework (SF): It usually supports the elicitation and formalization of the requirements of each SF level [9, 29, 42]. Furthermore, researchers developed frameworks (e.g. Semiotic interoperability framework [32]) and proposed a set of methods (e.g. NormEST [40]) that deal with the six levels of SF in an information system. Additionally, the authors used SF to bring social aspects into smart manufacturing [62], and to support the understanding, design, and analysis of Web systems [21]. Also, they used the six levels of the SF as criteria to compare the existing evaluation frameworks for information systems integration [37]. Concerning the data lifecycle, [27] showed a way to use the six layers in the different stages of the data lifecycle and with different stakeholders, consequently they could map design issues or questions that make the data lifecycle more explicit. Regarding the interoperability, [35] developed the concepts of semiotic interoperability ground on the SF.

Semantic Analysis Method (SAM): It assists the identification of ontological dependence on information systems and the generation of ontology charts [8, 22, 41, 50, 52, 54, 61]. For instance, researchers could represent the possible patterns of behaviors in Clinical Pathway and their relationships in an OC, which delineates the boundary of concern in the analysis and defines the meaning of terminology used in the clinical pathway model [60]. In addition, researchers used the SAM to produce a stable ontology of the context that describes the semantic aspects of the signs shared in a Social Network Services (SNS) [53].

Norm Analysis Method (NAM): The authors usually use NAM to eliciting and formalizing norms [8, 16, 18, 33, 41, 42, 50, 61]. For instance, [60] used NAM to extract and analyze patterns of care activities and informal safety norms that affect patient safety outcomes. Researchers also adopted NAM to identify norms of the production and consumption of Web content [22]. In [42], the authors elicited different interface representations through NAM and participatory practices. Consequently, they defined and implemented several norms that represent the system tailorable behavior. Likewise, NAM helped to identify substantive activities in the university's postgraduate admission process [19].

Problem Articulation Methods (PAM): The authors used PAM to reduce the complexity of the system and to clarify the problem [24, 59]. For instance, PAM artifacts, such as Stakeholder Analysis, Evaluation Framing, and Semiotic Framework, helped to elicit interested parties in the prospective Learning Design software tool, and anticipate possible problems and propose solutions [1].

Evaluation Frame (EF): Researchers usually used the Evaluation Framing to identify the interests, questions, and problems of each stakeholder according to the three problem levels, based on SO, in participatory practices [9, 21]. For instance, Buchdid et al. [9] proposed to participants to fill in the EF artifact in order to think about possible important issues related to the different stakeholders and the way they could affect the project.

Stakeholder Analysis (SA): It supported researchers to elicit stakeholders, their roles, responsibilities and their impact on the different organizations organization [30, 42].

Stakeholder Identification Diagram (SID): The authors used SID because different stakeholders bring different perspectives to the innovation being proposed, and have different interests, views, needs, values, and culture [46, 47]. In [9], participants filled in the SID artifact in participatory workshops. As a result, the SID allowed researchers to observe that only people immersed in the situated context can measure the importance of some stakeholders.

Authors of other papers have mentioned the adoption of OS theories. However, these authors did not explicitly specify the employed artifacts [5, 6, 10, 11, 13, 14, 17, 20, 23, 38, 39, 51, 56–58].

3.2   What are New Approaches Derived from OS?

Considering *DE5*, we briefly present new methods, artifacts, and frameworks based on OS concepts.

eValue [43]: This artifact aims to evaluate interactive systems or their prototypes through a value-oriented and culturally aware. The authors developed this artifact on the grounds of OS theory [34] and the Building Blocks of Culture [25].

Value-Oriented and Culturally Informed Approach (VCIA) [47]: This approach supports the design of interactive systems and involves a set of artifacts (e.g. SID and eValue). The authors developed it on the grounds of the OS theory [34], the Building Blocks of Culture [25], and the Socially Aware Computing view for design [2–4].

Web Ontology Design Aided by Semiotics (WODAS) [52]: This method supports the construction of representative Web ontologies. The authors developed it on the grounded of Semantic Web technologies (Web ontology) combined with OS concepts and methods to identify the users' profile and language.

Decision Making Method for SAAS Adoption (DEMSA) [59]: This method supports the decision making process for Software as a Service (SaaS) adoption. The method adopts PAM.

InDIE [29]: This method supports the production and validation of the design solutions with end-users in an interactive and iterative process. The authors adopted OS theory such as SA and SF.

Pragmatic Interoperability Analysis Framework and Pragmatic Interoperability Measurement Model [36]: The approaches help to measure pragmatic interoperability from two dimensions including six aspects (informal, formal, technical, substantive, communication, and control). The authors adopted the SO and the organization morphology.

A Semiotic-Based Approach for Search Personalization in SNS [53]: This approach provides means to discover as well to distinguish the meanings used by people at the SNS through the agents represented into Ontology Charts.

PLuRaL [42]: This framework supports the design of tailorable applications. It adopts a sociotechnical approach and a comprehensive view of interaction requirements. The authors included OS approaches in the pillars of PLuRaL such as SA, SF, SAM, and NAM.

SCPS-Based Manufacturing Framework [62]: This framework integrates the social, cyber, and physical systems as a whole, and allows producers/customers/users to collaborate on product design and development. The authors propose a framework from the SF.

Semiotically Inspired Fuzzy Clinical decision support systems (CDSSs) Framework [15]: This framework allows describing medical domain concepts contextually and reasoning with vague knowledge. The authors adopted the SO and SF.

Valuation Framing for Social Software (VF4SS) [44]: This artifact supports designers in the identification and understanding of the cultural dimensions of a product. The authors developed it based on Valuation Frame.

NormEST [40]: This tool provides an intuitive development interface that makes it easy to create Knowledge-Based Systems. It also provides deep considerations of the SF levels that permitted to relate the system user interface to the processes and social practices of the users.

Semiotic Interoperability Framework [32]: This framework supports the assessment of organization's interoperability level to identify organization's requirement towards comprehensive interoperation. The authors developed this framework based on SF.

Semantics-Oriented Method for Generation of Clinical Pathways (SOG-CP) [60]: This method supports the generation of clinical pathways, and adopts SAM and NAM.

NOrmative Modelling of Information Systems (NOMIS) [17]: This approach aims to improve modeling objectivity and precision. The authors adopt a new ontology named Human Relativism, proposing a new vision of IS composed of different views inspired by ideas from OS, and defining a new modeling notation and a set of diagrams to represent NOMIS vision and views.

A Framework for Conceptualizing Dynamic Knowledge [5]: This framework supports an exchange of human "messy" knowledge into shared useful information. The research explored two scenarios: *VilanaRede* (a SNS) and *Yahoo! Answers*. The authors adopted NAM.

Value Pie [49]: This artifact supports designers to identify values in the context of social software. The authors created Value Pie based on OS and Building Blocks of Culture [25].

Semiotic Cockpit Evaluation Method (SCoEM) [41]: This method consists of a checklist where each affordance and norm is evaluated with the artifacts that support the agent's action. In the development, the authors adopted NAM and SAM.

Value Identification Frame (VIF) [46]: This artifact aims to identify the values related to different stakeholders. The authors use SID to help the system that is being designed.

3.3   Where Have These Studies Been Published?

In response to *DE6*, the systematic review results (Table 1) showed that authors published almost all papers (88 %) in conference proceedings. In addition, the authors published more in conferences that focus on information systems such as ICISO (20 %) and ICEIS (13 %).

Table 1. Number of papers by journals and conferences proceedings.

Conference/Journal	Acronym	No. of papers
IFIP WG 8.1 Int. Conf. on Inform. and Semiotics in Organ.	ICISO	11
Int. Conf. on Enterprise Information Systems	ICEIS	7
Int. Conf. on Human-Comp. Interaction	HCII	5
Int. Symp. on Business Modeling and Software Design	BMSD	3
Int. Conf. on Design, User Experience, and Usability	DUXU	3
Int. Conf. on Information Society	i-Society	3
Int. Conf. on Logistics, Informatics and Service Science	LISS	3
European Conf. on Technology Enhanced Learning	EC-TEL	2
J. Health Policy and Technology	HPT	2
Brazilian Symp. on Hum. Factors in Comp. Systems	IHC	2
Int. Conf. on Universal Access in Human-Comp. Interaction	UAHCI	2
J. Universal Access in the Information Society	UAIS	2
Int. Conf. on Advanced Information Systems Engineering	CAiSE	1
IFIP WG 6.11 Conf. on e-Business, e-Services, and e-Society	I3E	1
Int. Joint Conf. on K. Discov., K. Engin. and K. Manag.	IC3K	1
Int. Conf. Software Engineering and Comp. Systems	ICSECS	1
The Int. Journal of Advanced Manufacturing Technology	IJAMT	1
Int. Journal of Human-Comp. Studies	IJHCS	1
Journal of the Brazilian Comp. Society	JBCS	1
Int. Conf. Online Communities and Social Computing	OCSC	1

Table 2. Number of papers published per year

	Year				
	2011	2012	2013	2014	2015
No. of papers	6	7	12	13	17

3.4 How Many Papers Using OS Have Been Published Since 2011 Per Year?

In response to *DE7*, Table 2 presents the number of papers published each year since 2011. It is possible to notice that the number of publications that use OS concepts has almost increased three times in the last five years.

4 Discussion and Conclusion

The results suggest that slightly more than a quarter of the papers (15 out of 53) employed the SO in order to identify and comprehend the three levels of norms within an information system. Moreover, it was possible to note that 23 % of papers (12 out of 53) employed NAM due to eliciting, analyzing and formalizing norms in different types of ISs. Besides, less than one-fifth of the papers employed Semiotic Framework (10 out of 53) and SAM (9 out of 53). In addition, we noticed that few studies employed PAM, Evaluation Frame, Stakeholder Identification Diagram (all, 3 out of 53), Stakeholder Analysis (2 out of 53), Valuation Frame and Semio-Participatory framework (both, 1 out of 53). However, less than one-third of the papers (15 out of 53) do not explicitly describe the OS approach used. Thus, we could not determine which Organizational Semiotic methods and artifacts those researchers have employed.

Somewhat more than one-third of the papers (19 out of 53) describe a new approach derived from OS ideas. In general, these new approaches support the design process and the evaluation of a product, the assessment of the interoperability in an IS, and the identification and understanding of the cultural dimensions of a product. Therefore, researchers have been engaged in creating new approaches based on organizational semiotics to find solutions in different natures of IS.

Regarding to the number of publications in the last five years, we found that the number of publications that use OS concepts has been increasing.

For practice, this review showed the significance of OS to improve the business process, elicit requirements for interface design, understand the nature of different IS, and to create an appropriate approach to design, implement and evaluate IS. In addition, we consider this paper as the basic starting step for future researchers interested in understanding the concepts and applicability of OS, its traditional approaches, and the most current approaches. Furthermore, this review suggests to the research community a small picture of current advances in the OS studies.

References

1. Arpetti, A., Baranauskas, M.C., Leo, T.: Eliciting requirements for learning design tools. In: Rensing, C., de Freitas, S., Ley, T., Muñoz-Merino, P.J. (eds.) EC-TEL 2014. LNCS, vol. 8719, pp. 1–14. Springer, Heidelberg (2014)
2. Baranauskas, M.C.C.: Social awareness in HCI. Interactions **21**(4), 66–69 (2014)
3. Baranauskas, M.C.C.: Socially aware computing. In: Proceedings of the 6th International Conference on Engineering and Computer Education, Buenos Aires, Argentina, pp. 1–5 (2009)
4. Baranauskas, M.C.C., Bonacin, R.: Design - indicating through signs. Des. Issues **24**(3), 30–45 (2008)
5. Bonacin, R., Hornung, H., Reis, J.C.D., Pereira, R., Baranauskas, M.C.: Pragmatic aspects of collaborative problem solving: towards a framework for conceptualizing dynamic knowledge. In: Cordeiro, J., Maciaszek, L.A., Filipe, J. (eds.) ICEIS 2012. LNBIP, vol. 141, pp. 410–426. Springer, Heidelberg (2013)
6. Bonacin, R., Dos Reis, J.C., Hornung, H., Pereira, R., Baranauskas, M.C.: Understanding pragmatic aspects with social values in web-mediated collaborative systems. In: Yamamoto, S. (ed.) HCI 2014, Part I. LNCS, vol. 8521, pp. 471–482. Springer, Heidelberg (2014)
7. Borg, J., et al.: Accessibility to electronic communication for people with cognitive disabilities: a systematic search and review of empirical evidence. Univ. Access Inf. Soc. **14** (4), 547–562 (2014)
8. Buchdid, S.B., Hornung, H.H., Pereira, R., Baranauskas, M.C.: Clarifying the situational context of a TV company towards the design of iDTV applications. In: Liu, K., Nakata, K., Li, W., Galarreta, D. (eds.) ICISO 2015. IFIP AICT, vol. 449, pp. 70–79. Springer, Heidelberg (2015)

9. Buchdid, S.B., Pereira, R., Baranauskas, M.C.: Creating an iDTV application from inside a TV company: a situated and participatory approach. In: Liu, K., Gulliver, S.R., Li, W., Yu, C. (eds.) ICISO 2014. IFIP AICT, vol. 426, pp. 63–73. Springer, Heidelberg (2014)

10. Buchdid, S.B., Pereira, R., Baranauskas, M.C.C.: Designing an IDTV application in a situated scenario: a participatory approach based on patterns. In: Cordeiro, J., Hammoudi, S., Maciaszek, L., Camp, O., Filipe, J. (eds.) ICEIS 2014. LNBIP, vol. 227, pp. 341–360. Springer, Heidelberg (2015)

11. Buchdid, S.B., Pereira, R., Baranauskas, M.C.: Designing iDTV applications from participatory use of patterns. In: Marcus, A. (ed.) DUXU 2013, Part I. LNCS, vol. 8012, pp. 459–468. Springer, Heidelberg (2013)

12. Buchdid, S.B., Pereira, R., Hornung, H.H., Cecília, M., Baranauskas, C.: Socio-technical barriers induced by the design of emerging technologies. In: Antona, M., Stephanidis, C. (eds.) UAHCI 2015, Part I. LNCS, vol. 9175, pp. 34–45. Springer, Heidelberg (2015)

13. Buchdid, S.B., Pereira, R., Baranauskas, M.C.: You can interact with your TV and you may like it an investigation on persuasive aspects for an iDTV application. In: Marcus, A. (ed.) DUXU 2014, Part IV. LNCS, vol. 8520, pp. 208–219. Springer, Heidelberg (2014)

14. de Carvalho Correia, A.C., Brizolara, P.L.S., de Miranda, L.C., Marciano, J.N.: Syntactic/semantic formalizations and metrics of residential applications based on gestural interface. In: Marcus, A. (ed.) DUXU 2014, Part II. LNCS, vol. 8518, pp. 521–532. Springer, Heidelberg (2014)

15. Chen, X., Gao, H., Liu, K., Zhang, Y.: Incorporating semiotics into fuzzy logic to enhance clinical decision support systems. In: Liu, K., Gulliver, S.R., Li, W., Yu, C. (eds.) ICISO 2014. IFIP AICT, vol. 426, pp. 97–106. Springer, Heidelberg (2014)

16. Chidzambwa, L.: The social considerations for moving health services into the home: a telecare perspective. Health Policy Technol. 2(1), 10–25 (2013)

17. Cordeiro, J.: A new way of modelling information systems and business processes – the NOMIS approach. In: Shishkov, B. (ed.) BMSD 2014. LNBIP, vol. 220, pp. 102–118. Springer, Heidelberg (2015)

18. Effah, J.: Virtual process control modelling in organisational semiotics: a case of higher education admission. In: Liu, K., Nakata, K., Li, W., Galarreta, D. (eds.) ICISO 2015. IFIP AICT, vol. 449, pp. 51–59. Springer, Heidelberg (2015)

19. Effah, J., Liu, K.: Virtual process modelling informed by organisational semiotics: a case of higher education admission. In: Liu, K., Gulliver, S.R., Li, W., Yu, C. (eds.) ICISO 2014. IFIP AICT, vol. 426, pp. 42–51. Springer, Heidelberg (2014)

20. Ferreira, A.L.S., et al.: Interfaces cérebro-computador de sistemas interativos: estado da arte e desafios de IHC, vol. 5138, pp. 239–248 (2012)

21. Ferreira, M.A.M., Bonacin, R.: Analyzing barriers for people with hearing loss on the web: a semiotic study. In: Stephanidis, C., Antona, M. (eds.) UAHCI 2013, Part II. LNCS, vol. 8010, pp. 694–703. Springer, Heidelberg (2013)

22. Ferreira, M.A.M., Bonacin, R.: Eliciting accessibility requirements for people with hearing loss: a semantic and norm analysis. In: Kurosu, M. (ed.) HCI 2014, Part III. LNCS, vol. 8512, pp. 277–288. Springer, Heidelberg (2014)

23. Gonçalves, V.P., et al.: Providing adaptive smartphone interfaces targeted at elderly people: an approach that takes into account diversity among the elderly. Univ. Access Inf. Soc. 1–21 (2015)

24. Gulliver, S., et al.: Changing building user attitude and organisational policy towards sustainable resource use in healthcare. Health Policy Technol. 2(2), 75–84 (2013)

25. Hall, E.T.: The Silent Language. Doubleday, New York (1959)

26. Hayashi, E.C.S., Martins, M.C., Baranauskas, M.C.C.: Introducing new technology in educational contexts: schools as organizations. In: Cordeiro, J., Maciaszek, L.A., Filipe, J. (eds.) ICEIS 2012. LNBIP, vol. 141, pp. 340–357. Springer, Heidelberg (2013)

27. Hornung, H., Pereira, R., Baranauskas, M.C., Liu, K.: Challenges for human-data interaction – a semiotic perspective. In: Kurosu, M. (ed.) Human-Computer Interaction. LNCS, vol. 9169, pp. 37–48. Springer, Heidelberg (2015)

28. Islam, M.N.: A systematic literature review of semiotics perception in user interfaces. J. Syst. Inf. Technol. 15(1), 45–77 (2013)

29. Jensen, C.J., Dos Reis, J.C., Bonacin, R.: An interaction design method to support the expression of user intentions in collaborative systems. In: Kurosu, M. (ed.) Human-Computer Interaction. LNCS, vol. 9169, pp. 214–226. Springer, Heidelberg (2015)

30. Ketabchi, S., et al.: A pattern for structuring the information system architecture -introducing an EA framework for organizing tasks. J. Chem. Inf. Model. 263–273 (2011)

31. Kitchenham, B.A.: Procedures for Undertaking Systematic Reviews. Eveleigh, Los Angeles (2004)

32. Li, W., et al.: Semiotics in interoperation for information systems working collaboratively. In: Fred, A., Dietz, J.L.G., Liu, K., Filipe, J. (eds.) IC3 K 2013. CCIS, vol. 454, pp. 370–386. Springer, Heidelberg (2015)

33. Liu, K., Sun, L., Jambari, D., Michell, V., Chong, S.: A design of business-technology alignment consulting framework. In: Mouratidis, H., Rolland, C. (eds.) CAiSE 2011. LNCS, vol. 6741, pp. 422–435. Springer, Heidelberg (2011)

34. Liu, K.: Semiotics in Information Systems Engineering. Cambridge University Press, Cambridge (2000)

35. Liu, S., Li, W., Liu, K., Liu, S., Li, W., Liu, K.: Assessing pragmatic interoperability for process alignment in collaborative working environment. In: Liu, K., Nakata, K., Li, W., Galarreta, D. (eds.) ICISO 2015. IFIP AICT, vol. 449, pp. 60–69. Springer, Heidelberg (2015)

36. Liu, S., Li, W., Liu, K.: Assessing pragmatic interoperability of information systems from a semiotic perspective. In: Liu, K., Gulliver, S.R., Li, W., Yu, C. (eds.) ICISO 2014. IFIP AICT, vol. 426, pp. 32–41. Springer, Heidelberg (2014)

37. Liu, S., et al.: Evaluation frameworks for information systems integration: from a semiotic lens. In: Zhang, R., Zhang, Z., Liu, K., Zhang, J. (eds.) LISS 2013, pp. 1333–1340. Springer, Heidelberg (2015)

38. Maike, V.R., Buchdid, S.B., Baranauskas, M.C.: Designing natural user interfaces scenarios for all and for some: an analysis informed by organizational semiotics artifacts. In: Liu, K., Nakata, K., Li, W., Galarreta, D. (eds.) ICISO 2015. IFIP AICT, vol. 449, pp. 92–101. Springer, Heidelberg (2015)

39. Mendes, G.: Prototipação de interfaces tangíveis de produtos interativos: estado da arte e desafios da plataforma arduino. In: Procecddings of IHC, vol. 5138, pp. 249–258 (2012)

40. Moawad, N., et al.: Knowledge elicitation and representation in a normative approach-a case study in diagnosis of plant diseases in Egypt. In: Proceddings of IS, pp. 28–34 (2012)

41. Moreira, W., Bonacin, R.: A semiotic based method for evaluating automated cockpit interfaces. In: Yamamoto, S. (ed.) HCI 2013, Part II. LNCS, vol. 8017, pp. 530–539. Springer, Heidelberg (2013)

42. de Almeida Neris, V.P., Baranauskas, M.C.C.: Designing tailorable software systems with the users' participation. J. Braz. Comput. Soc. 18(3), 213–227 (2012)

43. Pereira, R., et al.: Considering values and cultural aspects in the evaluation of interactive systems prototypes. In: Proceddings of i-Society, pp. 380–385 (2012)
44. Pereira, R., et al.: Interaction design of social software: clarifying requirements through a culturally aware artifact. In: Proceddings of i-Society, pp. 293–298 (2011)
45. Pereira, R., Baranauskas, M.C., Liu, K.: On the relationships between norms, values and culture: preliminary thoughts in HCI. In: Liu, K., Nakata, K., Li, W., Galarreta, D. (eds.) ICISO 2015. IFIP AICT, vol. 449, pp. 30–40. Springer, Heidelberg (2015)
46. Pereira, R., Buchdid, S.B., Baranauskas, M.C.: Values and cultural aspects in design: artifacts for making them explicit in design activities. In: Cordeiro, J., Maciaszek, L.A., Filipe, J. (eds.) ICEIS 2012. LNBIP, vol. 141, pp. 358–375. Springer, Heidelberg (2013)
47. Pereira, R., Baranauskas, M.C.C.: A value-oriented and culturally informed approach to the design of interactive systems. Int. J. Hum. Comput. Stud. **80**, 66–82 (2015)
48. Pereira, R., Baranauskas, M.C.: Seeing social software analysis and evaluation through the lenses of culture. In: Zhang, R., Zhang, J., Zhang, Z., Filipe, J., Cordeiro, J. (eds.) ICEIS 2011. LNBIP, vol. 102, pp. 374–387. Springer, Heidelberg (2012)
49. Pereira, R., Baranauskas, M.C.C.: Value pie: a culturally informed conceptual scheme for understanding values in design. In: Kurosu, M. (ed.) HCI 2014, Part I. LNCS, vol. 8510, pp. 122–133. Springer, Heidelberg (2014)
50. Piccolo, L.S., Hornung, H., Baranauskas, C., Pereira, R.: Designing to promote a new social affordance for energy consumption. In: Douligeris, C., Polemi, N., Karantjias, A., Lamersdorf, W. (eds.) Collaborative, Trusted and Privacy-Aware e/m-Services. IFIP AICT, vol. 399, pp. 213–225. Springer, Heidelberg (2013)
51. Prado, A.B., Baranauskas, M.C.C.: Capturing semiotic and social factors of organizational evolution. In: Hammoudi, S., Cordeiro, J., Maciaszek, L.A., Filipe, J. (eds.) ICEIS 2013. LNBIP, vol. 190, pp. 264–279. Springer, Heidelberg (2014)
52. Reis, J.C., et al.: Addressing universal access in social networks: an inclusive search mechanism. Univ. Access Inf. Soc. **13**(2), 125–145 (2013)
53. dos Reis, J.C., Bonacin, R., Baranauskas, M.C.: Beyond the social search: personalizing the semantic search in social networks. In: Ozok, A., Zaphiris, P. (eds.) OCSC 2011. LNCS, vol. 6778, pp. 345–354. Springer, Heidelberg (2011)
54. dos Reis, J.C., Bonacin, R., Baranauskas, M.C.C.: Prospecting an inclusive search mechanism for social network services. In: Filipe, J., Cordeiro, J. (eds.) ICEIS 2010. LNBIP, vol. 73, pp. 555–570. Springer, Heidelberg (2011)
55. Stamper, R.: Information in Business and Administrative Systems. Wiley, New York (1973)
56. Suurmond, C.: Information systems and sign systems. In: Liu, K., Nakata, K., Li, W., Galarreta, D. (eds.) ICISO 2015. IFIP AICT, vol. 449, pp. 20–29. Springer, Heidelberg (2015)
57. Suurmond, C.: Sign systems, information systems, and engineering. In: Shishkov, B. (ed.) BMSD 2012. LNBIP, vol. 142, pp. 82–101. Springer, Heidelberg (2013)
58. Suurmond, C.: The business of business modeling. In: Shishkov, B. (ed.) BMSD 2013. LNBIP, vol. 173, pp. 64–83. Springer, Heidelberg (2014)
59. Tan, C., et al.: An evaluation framework for migrating application to the cloud: software as a service. In: Zhang, Z., Zhang, R., Zhang, J. (eds.) LISS 2012, pp. 967–972. Springer, Heidelberg (2013)
60. Tehrani, J., et al.: Semiotics-oriented method for generation of clinical pathways. In: Zhang, Z., Zhang, R., Zhang, J. (eds.) LISS 2012, pp. 477–482. Springer, Heidelberg (2013)

61. Xu, S., Liu, K., Tang, L.C.: Applying organizational semiotics for developing knowledge-based cost estimation of construction project. In: Liu, K., Nakata, K., Li, W., Galarreta, D. (eds.) ICISO 2015. IFIP AICT, vol. 449, pp. 80–91. Springer, Heidelberg (2015)
62. Yao, X., Lin, Y.: Emerging manufacturing paradigm shifts for the incoming industrial revolution. Adv. Manuf. Technol. 1–12 (2015)

Vitalizing Semiotics

Janos J. Sarbo[1](✉) and Jessica H. Yang[2]

[1] ICIS, Radboud University, Nijmegen, The Netherlands
janos@cs.ru.nl
[2] Henley Business School, Reading, UK
j.h.yang@henley.ac.uk

Abstract. The goal of organizational semiotics is to enable a better understanding of organizations by means of an analysis of documents, texts and communications as signs. Its theory is based on Peirce's sign concept, the relation of the sign with itself, with its object, and interpretant. In our view, this restricted use of semiotics may explain some of the limitations of organizational semiotics in practice. A shift of focus from signs as a relation to sign aspects involved in signs may enable a more practical model of interpretation, including organizations as interpreting systems. This is illustrated with an application of semiotics to accounting narratives.

Keywords: Semiotics · Sign aspects · Process model · Accounting narratives

1 Introduction

An oft-cited example of a paradigmatic shift is the planetary system by Copernicus and Kepler. If we ask which one of the two views, Earth- or Sun-centered is more practical, our answer must be that does not matter. In current technology both can be computed efficiently. Why, then, that we may find Kepler's elliptic system more attractive? It is because his model enables a 'natural' representation of the properties of planetary motion such as revolution time and distance. Tycho Brache's system of cycloids does not have that potential.

Organization phenomena ask for natural modeling, analogously. As organizations are human and are subject to our perception, their models must be understandable. An approach complying with this condition is introduced by organizational semiotics [1], which considers organizations to be (sign) interpreting systems. In sign interpretation, the (potential) sign,[1] e.g., a text document, is establishing a relation with itself, with its object, and interpretant. We call this a *sign-relation*. Although this relational view may enable to reveal the constituents of an interpreted sign,[2] the practical use of this approach is limited, as it may not be able to explain how sign-relations arise, what *process* is involved.

According to [2], organizational semiotics can also make use of the more refined concept of a sign type, e.g., for the analysis of media. Although we were not able to

---

[1] As the used concept of a sign involves interpretation, the terms, sign, interpreted, or meaningful sign, are synonymous.
[2] Signs, offered for interpretation, are called a potential sign.

© IFIP International Federation for Information Processing 2016
Published by Springer International Publishing Switzerland 2016. All Rights Reserved
M.C.C. Baranauskas et al. (Eds.): ICISO 2016, IFIP AICT 477, pp. 25–34, 2016.
DOI: 10.1007/978-3-319-42102-5_3

find publications of this kind of an analysis, we suggest that a sign-typical interpretation of phenomena, including organizations, may not be beneficial in practice either. It too is unable to give an account of the process involved in interpretation.

Through analyzing his concept of a sign, Peirce introduced sign aspects [3]. Accordingly, signs can be defined by a relation of sign aspects involved in the relations of the (potential) sign with itself, with its object, and interpretant. Peirce called this a *sign type*. Bense [4] has shown that the Peircean sign aspects can be arranged in a hierarchy. Unfortunately, although all processes involve a partial ordering hence a hierarchy, a hierarchy is not a process.

Information processing is a process, trivially. However, contrary to signs, that are meaningful, information processing is computational (and meaningful from that perspective only). We suggest that this apparent contradiction between meaningful interpretation on the one hand, and computational information processing on the other, can be resolved by introducing a cognitively based model of human processing. Through mapping the events of this model to sign aspects, the involved computational process can be embedded in Peircean semiotics.

In business modeling there is little research which provides insight into how corporate narratives are actually interpreted apart from which signs are used. Corporate narratives in annual reports, press releases, and conference calls offer organizations the opportunity to communicate business messages with shareholders, analysts and media and to engage them in corporate narratives in a persuasive and compelling way. Top management collects stories from their everyday organizational life, and restructure and incorporate them into corporate reports. Stakeholders read these reports to decipher a deeper understanding of organizational life.

Top management views narratives as a powerful managerial tool to make sense of their decisions [5] whilst stakeholders convince themselves of organizational decisions through narratives [6]. From the perspective of organizations, corporate report is an effective management process, which transfers organizational ideology to society [7, 8]. If their stories are logically sound, stakeholders will be more easily persuaded and convinced. Everything established through reasons is in the realm of *logos* and it covers not just deductive reasoning but also inductive and abductive reasoning.

The persuasion process reflects whether audiences are able to read, comprehend and make judgment based on their understanding and interpretation of the narratives. The validity and plausibility of argumentation is key to appeal to audience's logos, which can be analyzed through the aspects of three types of reasoning: deductive being always plausible; inductive being probably plausible; and abductive being hypothetically plausible. As a result, the plausibility of arguments in the text can be identified, which influences the decision-making and sense-making process.

2   Process Model

A cognitively based model of human processing has been introduced in [9], amongst others. Below we restrict ourselves to an overview of the basic ideas (see also Fig. 1). The condition for human interpretation is an interaction between a stimulus or *effect* (q1), on the one hand, and the brain or interpreting system occurring in some *state* (q2), on the other. Interpretation makes use of memory or *context* information (C). The

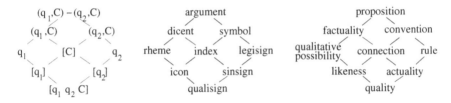

Fig. 1. Process model (left), Peircean sign aspects (middle) and their mundane terms (right). There is an isomorphic relation between the process model and the hierarchy of sign aspects. For instance, [q1] can be mapped to the sign aspect icon, and in turn, the term likeness.

collection of uninterpreted qualities, [q1 q2 C], is the *input* for information processing. The goal of interpretation, as a process, is to establish a relation between q1 and q2, in the context of C. To this end, the qualities are sorted (cf. *sorting;* [q1], [q2], [C]), represented independently from one another (cf. *abstraction:* q1, q2), completed with qualities from the context (cf. *complementation:* (q1,C), (q2,C)), and merged in a single relation (cf. *predication:* (q1,C)–(q2,C)).

The above input representations can be assigned a Peircean sign aspect: [q1], representing the state as a constituent, the sign aspect *icon*; [q2], expressing the effect as a single occurrence, the sign aspect *sinsign*; [C], pointing to background information corresponding to q1 and q2, the sign aspect *index*. The abstract concept q1, standing for the state, as a possible for any effect, can be assigned the sign aspect *rheme*; q2, representing the habitual rule involved in the input effect, the sign aspect *legisign*. Finally, (q1,C), the possible state in context, or the subject of the interaction can be assigned the sign aspect *dicent*; (q2,C), the rule-like effect in context, or the predicate of the interaction, the sign aspect *symbol*; and the relation between subject and predicate, representing the input by a proposition which is a premise, the sign aspect *argument*.

The events of the process model can be assigned an aspect of 'naive' reasoning.[3] An example is the interaction event between q1 and [C]. The state, interpreted as a qualitative possibility (for an effect) is completed by an effect. As information about the effect is fetched from C, this interaction event has the aspect of *deduction*. Analogously, the event, in which, q2, expressing the input as a habitual effect, is tested for a state represented by C, has the aspect of *induction*. The interaction between q1, as an actual event or existent (cf. subject), and q2, as a conventional effect (cf. predicate), represented by a proposition which is hypothesis, has the aspect of *abduction*. The existence of the aspects of the three types of reasoning is an expression of the completeness of the process model, from the perspective of 'naive' reasoning.

3   Semiotic Analysis: A Case Study

In this section we offer a semiotic analysis to a sample text in three ways: from a sign-relational, a sign-typical and a sign-aspectual perspective, and compare the results. The text in question is a paragraph extracted from [10]. See Fig. 2.

---

[3] The term 'naive' is used as a synonym for 'inborn'.

(**s₁**) Over the next three years we (S) will be making significant investment (P) in the infra-structure we need to make the customer experience fair, responsible, easy and personal for all our customers - whether face-to-face, by telephone or online. (**s₂**) The opportunities (S), both for our customers and our business, are outstanding (P); but (**s₃**) our growth strategy (S) will always be driven by (P) the desire to put the customer first in all things. (**s₄**) We (S) intend to grow (P) at a pace and in a way that guarantees our customers an uninterrupted, seamless service.

Fig. 2. A sample paragraph. Sentences are labelled by bold face symbols. For later analysis, syntactic subjects and predicates are marked by an (S) and (P) symbol, respectively.

3.1   Sign-Relational Analysis

For our text (sign), in Fig. 2, we are in search for an object and interpretant. By definition, the object of the sign is what it is standing for and replacing. Arguably, this is "the chairman's intention to provide increasingly better customer services in the coming three years". The interpretant of the sign is the meaning mediated by the sign, in the agent's interpretation. There may be different interpretants (and interpretations), depending on the agent's knowledge (cf. context), his/her mood, emotions, etc. By assuming an optimistic agent, the interpretant could be: "The hypothesis that through significant investment the customers will be more satisfied in the future, can be true".

The concepts, (potential) sign, object, and interpretant, follow from a categorical analysis of Peirce's notion of a sign. As part of the interpretation process, the (po-tential) sign determines an interpretant, and eventually, an object. Determination is always in this order, by virtue of the condition that interpretation is by an agent, as an interpreting system.

We conclude that a sign-relational analysis may enable a systematic approach to phenomena, including organizations. Inevitably, this is an important result by orga-nizational semiotics, as opposed to the traditional approach by Artificial Intelligence, for example, enabling ad-hoc representations, typically. However, the potential to reveal the nature of the constituents involved in a sign-relation and the conditions of their process of determination is beyond the possibilities of this paradigm. Practical models of (meaningful) interpretation ask for a more refined concept of a sign, which is the subject of the next section.

3.2   Sign-Typical Analysis

The Peircean sign aspects can be arranged in three up-right diagonals (cf. Fig. 1). In a right-to-left order, these diagonals are an expression of the sign aspects involved in the sign's relation with itself, with its object, and interpretant. (Interpreted) signs can be characterized by a relation of sign aspects taken from each one of the three diagonals. Such a relation is called a *sign type*.[4] An example is a *dicentic indexical legisign*. The relation of the sign with itself, or simply the sign in itself, has the sign aspect *legisign*.

---

[4] Not all combinations of sign aspects may define a sign type [3]. A treatment of this part of Peircean theory lies outside of this paper.

This is when the sign is perceived is as a rule. For instance, the perception of (the quality of) falling, during walking. The quality of falling is not perceived simply as a quality (cf. qualisign sign aspect), nor only as a quality occurring now (cf. sinsign sign aspect). We habitually know what we have to do and 'generate' motor reactions necessary for the next step in a rule-like fashion. The relation of the sign with its object is *indexical*. This is when the sign is not directly representing the object, except by telling where we may find information about it. The sign functions as a pointer. Finally, the relation of the sign with its interpretant is *dicentical*. This is when the agent is interpreting the sign as a statement, like an expression of an interaction as a (f)actual existence.

We suggest that the text, in Fig. 2, is an instance of the sign type explained above. Let us begin with the sign aspect of the text in itself. The phrases, such as making significant investment and outstanding opportunities, are an expression of an abstract, habitual activity or event (cf. *legisign* sign aspect). These phrases are more than an expression of temporal information characterizing single events (cf. sinsign sign aspect), or that of an appearing, yet uninterpreted quality (cf. qualisign sign aspect).

The relation of the text (sign) with its object is *indexical*. This is witnessed by the phrases such as opportunities and growth strategy, pointing at a set of possibilities without explicitly listing them (over the next three years is an indexical expression of temporal information). The readers – if interested – are invited to look into the list by themselves.

The relation of the text (sign) with its interpretant is *dicentical*. The phrases, desire to … and intend to …, amongst others, are statements of a future act, including its modality. There is no intention for these expressions to be used as an argument, e.g., a premise in a subsequent logical reasoning.

From a categorical stance, sign aspects amount to sub-classes of the constituents involved in a sign-relation. This way of sub-classification can be done recursively, which may explain why sign-types are 'maximal' from an informational stance. A sign-typical analysis of a sign can be complex, it may need proficiency. We are not aware of the existence of a systematic approach. Sign types themselves do not answer the question: how from (formal) relations between text-phrases, meaningful interpretation may arise. From this, we conclude that sign-typical analysis may not be practical for the goals of organizational semiotics either.

3.3 Sign-Aspectual Analysis

Sign-relations are more than a collection of relations involved in the sign. According to Peirce, the sign is in an irreducible relation with its object, and interpretant, or in mundane terms, there is a qualitative change involved in the sign. As we are interested in a semiotically inspired model of signs which suits a computational interpretation as well (cf. a process), we must realize that sign-relations and sign-types are beyond our reach. This holds for sign aspects too. They can be interpreted as signs that are in-the-making, which understanding complies with Peirce's theory of interpretants.[5]

---

[5] This important result is an achievement by A.J.J. van Breemen [9].

We assume that, by virtue of their dependency, more complex sign aspects can be perceived through sign aspects that are simpler. For instance, an interpretation of a dicentic relation of the sign with its interpretant may arise 'bottom-up', from a rhematic interpretation of the same relation, and an indexical interpretation of the relation of the sign with its object.

Although sign aspects are unfinished signs hence qualitatively more complex than mathematical relations, through focusing on the process involved in their interpretation we may get insight in its events, as *dyadic* relations. It is like making a cake using its receipt, but not having the possibility to taste the ingredients nor the cake itself. This restricted view on signs may not be useless nevertheless. Through formally analyzing their receipt we may be able to derive (formal) properties of meaningful interpretation and check their (formal) correctness. An example, in syntactic language processing, checking meaningfulness from a syntactic perspective, is testing whether a text complies with the SV(O) rule, in English.

Below we offer a sign-aspectual analysis to our running text. We assume that a syntactic analysis of the input sentences into subjects and predicates is already available. See Fig. 2. Modifiers are marked as context information (this is not indicated in this diagram). Our analysis is restricted to a 'naive' reasoning interpretation of the sample text. To this end, a pair of subsequent sentences are interpreted as a state and an effect that are in an interaction. Sentences, represented as a proposition, A 'IS' B (where A is short for (q1,C), B for (q2,C), and 'IS' is used as a linking term) are stored in memory as relations, (A,B). Information processing is sentence-wise. We assume that, in 'naive' reasoning processing, constituents of a relation are fetched from memory and represented as a state (A) or an effect (B) which is in focus, or as a state ($\sim$A) and an effect ($\sim$B) which is complementary.[6]

For completeness' sake we mention that our model enables three kinds of an analysis. The first one, 'summarization', merges a pair of sentences into a single sentence. Arising sentences are interpreted as a sign. As for a 'naive' reasoning analysis, summarization enables information involved in a conclusion to be represented explicitly. The second one, sequential processing, is a 'degenerate' version of the first one. Arising expressions, including conclusions, are represented by a sign aspect, e.g., a qualisign. Language processing is an example of this way of interpretation. The third one, considers input sentences to be qualities of a single phenomenon. Conclusions are not explicitly represented.

An analysis of our text, following the second approach above, is depicted in the diagrams Figs. 4, 5 and 6. Interactions between sentences are referred to by their labels, e.g., $(s_{1,2})$–(s_2) designates an interaction between $(s_{1,2})$, the result of an analysis of (s_1)–(s_2), and (s_3). That the conclusions of 'naive' inferences are not represented as a sign complies with actual language use, according to which, the reader is assumed to be able to draw conclusions by himself.

How in sentence processing, memory relations, (A,B), are represented by our model can be derived from a syllogistic interpretation of the sentence interactions. This

---

[6] This enables a proposition to be reversed. In language, this is known as passivization.

is illustrated by Fig. 3. In this and later diagrams we can make use of the free order of premises enabled by Aristotelian syllogistic.

$(s_1)-(s_2)$			**figure–1**
we	IS	*invest*	C IS B
opportunities	IS	outstanding	A IS C
$\Rightarrow$ we	IS	(have) outstanding (opportunities)	A IS B

$(s_{1,2})-(s_3)$			**figure–3**
we	IS	(have) outstanding (opportunities)	C IS B
our growth ...	IS	put customers first	C IS A
$\Rightarrow$ opportunities	IS	(growth in) put customers first	A IS B

$(s_{1,2,3})-(s_4)$			**figure–2**
opportunities	IS	*(growth in) put customers first*	B IS C
we	IS	*intend to grow (at a pace ...)*	A IS C
$\Rightarrow$ we	IS	opportunities (intend to make growing investment, at a pace ...)	A IS B

Fig. 3. A syllogistic interpretation of sentence interactions (left) and corresponding Aristotelian figures (right). In this diagram, quantification is omitted. We assume that in an inference (left) the two expressions of the common term (in italics) can be unified.

Fig. 4. A 'naive' reasoning analysis of $(s_1)-(s_2)$. The final representation can be paraphrased as 'we have outstanding investment opportunities'.

Fig. 5. A 'naive' reasoning analysis of $(s_{1,2})-(s_3)$. The final representation can be paraphrased as 'through our investment (opportunities) customers will increasingly be put first'.

The analysis, depicted in Fig. 4, reveals that $(s_1)-(s_2)$ has the aspect of deduction. There is an increase of information in the relation between q1 and C only. We learn that

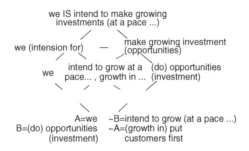

Fig. 6. A 'naive' reasoning analysis of $(s_{1,2,3})$–(s_4).

investment is also known as opportunity. All other events (relations) represent information already available in the premises. The process, displayed in Fig. 5, shows that $(s_{1,2})$–(s_3) has the aspect of induction. There is an increase of information in the relation between C and q2 only. We inductively learn that the growth can be a measure of the effect put customers first. The analysis, in Fig. 6, illustrates that $(s_{1,2,3})$–$s(_4)$ has the aspect of abduction. There is an increase of information in the relation between (q1,C) and (q2,C) only. We learn that we can be the subject, and intend to invest ... the predicate of a hypothetical proposition of the input interaction.

In Figs. 4, 5 and 6, because of their less important meaning, the positions [q1] and [q2] are left unspecified. The position [C] is used for a representation of 'common terms', separated by a comma symbol. Temporal information involved in predicates, and the aspect of negation involved in the coordinator symbol 'but', are omitted. Events involving an increase of information are designated by a horizontal line.

We selected our running text in a random fashion, although under the condition that its content is clear and meaningful to us as a reader. Our analysis shows that meaningfulness of our text (from a naive reasoning perspective) can be a consequence of the aspects of deduction, induction and abduction that are involved. This illustrates what we may learn by making use our process model and sign-aspectual approach.

The processes depicted in Figs. 4, 5 and 6 can be combined into a single process, through considering the text to be a single phenomenon (cf. sentence), and the constituent sentences to be qualities (cf. words). The result of this, third type of an analysis, is displayed in Fig. 7.

Fig. 7. Analysis of the entire text, in Fig. 2, as a single phenomenon. The position [C] is used for an expression of complementary information. We assume the existence of lexical information: desire ~ intention, investment ~ opportunity.

4   Towards a Measure of Plausibility

Interpretation may terminate hence exist as a process, only if a propositional representation of the input is obtained. From this it follows that interpretation processes must
involve all three types of 'naive' reasoning aspects. Note that representation of a
reasoning aspect can be omitted, e.g., in the case of an incomplete sentence. More
interesting is the case in which a reasoning aspect is represented repeatedly. This is
when a text, consisting in a number of sentences, can be analyzed in a single instance of
the process model. How is this related to plausibility?

Figure 3 illustrates the three figures of syllogistic. According to Aristotle, inferences of the form of figure-1 are naturally truthful; those of figure-3 and figure-2 (in this
order) are increasingly less plausible. This feature of syllogistic is respected by our
theory as well. We assume that our model is capable of processing inputs (cf. premises)
that conform to figure-1. Inputs corresponding to the other two figures need to be
transformed into figure-1, through a conversion of the minor premise, in the case of
figure-3, and that of the major premise in the case of figure-2.

According to Peirce, in a syllogism, the major premise stands for information that
we already know, the minor premise must be an account of an observation. The
representation of known information, such as habitual or rule-like knowledge, can be
extensive. This means that conversion of the major premise can be difficult (it boils
down to the definition of an inverse relation). This is opposed to conversion of the
minor premise, which can be simple (e.g., a paraphrasing of a relation from active to
passive). We assume that the complexity of the transformation required is negatively
proportional to the truth perception or plausibility of an inference (cf. sentence interaction). Roughly, the more it takes to interpret, the less its plausibility will be.
A consequence of the different transformations is an increase of information in different
events of the process and a difference in the degree of plausibility of those events.

The relation between the truth of the syllogistic figures and the reasoning aspect of
the events of our process model, depicted in Fig. 1, allows the definition of a measure
of plausibility. Events expressive of the aspect of deduction can be assigned a high
value of plausibility, those of the aspect of induction and abduction an increasingly
lower value. Plausibility can be represented by a sum of those values. In a simpler
approach, the input text is analyzed into relations that correspond to the structure of the
three syllogistic figures. An experimental validation of the proposed measure of
plausibility is on our current agenda.

5   Conclusion

Organizational semiotics recognizes the importance of sign theory and applies semiotics to real problems (this is an important element behind the successful research, e.g.,
at the University of Reading (UK)). However its reach is limited by virtue of the
restricted use of semiotic theory. We suggest that a process interpretation of the
Peircean hierarchy of sign aspects may open new perspectives. We reinforce our
hypothesis with an analysis of an extended example.

The potential of the proposed model for organizational semiotics, in particular, for an analysis of business documents, is discussed. This model is oriented toward the processes involved in the texts interpreted as signs. We conclude that organizational semiotics could benefit from a shift of focus from signs as a relation to the sign aspects involved in signs.

In future research, there would be value in designing an experiment to investigate whether sign aspects affect plausibility and understandability. It contributes to business research by introducing a formal textual analysis approach and bringing corporate narrative research to pragmatic level.

References

1. Stamper, R.K.: Information in Business and Administrative Systems. Wiley, New York (1973)
2. Gazendam, H.W.M.: Organizational semiotics: a state of the art report. Semiotics **1**(1) (2004). http://www.semioticon.com/semiotics
3. Peirce, C.S.: Collected Papers by Charles Sanders Peirce. Harvard University Press, Cambridge (1931–1958)
4. Bense, M.: Das System der Theoretischen Semiotik. Semiosis (1), 24–28 (1976)
5. Weick, K.E.: Sensemaking in Organizations. Sage Publications, London (1995)
6. Gabriel, Y.: Storytelling in Organizations: Facts, Fictions, and Fantasies. Oxford University Press, Oxford (2000)
7. Boje, D.M.: The storytelling organization: a study of story performance in an office-supply firm. Adm. Sci. Q. **36**, 21 (1991)
8. Boyce, M.E.: Organizational story and storytelling: a critical review. J. Organ. Change Manag. **9**, 5–26 (1996)
9. Sarbo, J.J., Farkas, J.I., Van Breemen, A.J.J.: Knowledge in Formation: A Computational Theory of Interpretation. Springer, Berlin (2011)
10. Annual Report and Account of the Co-operative Bank plc (2009). www.co-operativebank.co.uk

Semiotics of Interactions and Socially Aware User Interface Design

The Roles and Challenges of Semiotics Unraveling Big Data in the Glocal Contemporaneity Ruled by Dromocracy

Janaina Antunes[✉]

Pontifícia Universidade Católica de São Paulo, PUC-SP, Sao Paulo, Brazil
tcheina@hotmail.com

Abstract. Big data is capable of hugely impacting the decision-making process, regarding that we are able to correctly interpret it. The challenge of analysing big data lies exactly on the balance between two things: its rapid-pace nature and our lack of a humanly possible capacity of following such speed. It is exactly Digital Semiotics that gives meaningful organization to big data, transforming it from data trash into a sea of useful information. Semiotics can tell us the nature of big data and it can also show us how to experience, manipulate and control it within the cultural conditions of global interactivity and of the velocity of production so typical of our era. Dromocracy, the life governed by a fast speed, is the name of the phenomenon which articulates the process of the so-called glocalization, which is a cultural development that staggers to the planetary territory and empowers to the infinite the hybridization of realms of existence, through such velocity. The role and the importance of Semiotics grow in Dromocracy, especially considering big data; and what sets Semiotics apart from any other science and makes it stand out is exactly that it could be the answer to understanding such world for all areas of knowledge, if, and only if, Semiotics is able to look inside itself for a deep, introspective adaptation to the ways of Dromocracy.

Keywords: Big data · Digital semiotics · Cybercultural Dromocracy · Glocality

1 Introduction

Big data is capable of hugely impacting the decision-making, regarding that we are able to correctly interpret it. Nonetheless, the challenge of analysing big data lies exactly on the balance between its rapid-pace nature and our lack of a humanly possible capacity of following such speed.

The greatest role of Semiotics in this scenario is to make big data "smaller". Through Semiotics we are able to divide it, restructure it and understand what is beneath and beyond it. Semiotics is the tool through which we can "translate", decode big data.

We will walk through this task analysing how the Unclassifiable, the Glocality and the Dromocracy are spread and how they work, being this way able to find a solution to their challenges through Semiotics strategies, and being able to define the new roles of

© IFIP International Federation for Information Processing 2016
Published by Springer International Publishing Switzerland 2016. All Rights Reserved
M.C.C. Baranauskas et al. (Eds.): ICISO 2016, IFIP AICT 477, pp. 37–42, 2016.
DOI: 10.1007/978-3-319-42102-5_4

Semiotics in our contemporaneity. We shall start with the most challenging part of the process: classifying things. A contemporary problem not only regarding big data.

2 Cyberculture and the Unclassifiable

The clear time lineage of culture, of the evolution of culture is gone in the advent of cyberculture (which is precisely characterized as a real-time interactive digital culture), because the latter makes it possible for a person to be influenced by cultures originally completely unlinked, completely out of a given time order, or geographical order. We may be jointly influenced by a Neolithic Asian art and by African Expressionism.

> *The fact nowadays is that the cyberspace brought us an enormous number of possibilities of influences from many different cultures, from different times and localizations. We are ravished with infinite influences, many times not being able to personally tell what they were or where they came from, consequently creating a great difficulty to name ourselves, because nowadays we are atemporal and nongeographical.* [1, p. 5]

The matter takes greater proportions regarding big data. Even if all its contents were very easily definable, we would still have much difficulty separating them into categories. With the introduction of contents that by themselves are already unclassifiable, our task as semioticians became herculean, especially since we do not know yet how to proceed in such scenario.

We are accustomed to work with a large taxonomization and with very concrete concepts, opening up just for their hybrids. But while hybrids have characteristics of different trends all mixed into one place, and while they may or may completely not be linked to the cyberculture, the unclassifiable is unique: origins and influences may be many, but they are impossible to be recognized or to be traced, making it impossible to be named and taxomizated.

As semioticians we have to be able to analyse whether such taxonomies could be implemented, if they are applicable to, i.e., social media analytics; and run more widely into, i.e., free text or unscripted data analysis. This could be done through a combination of mechanical coding and automated coding systems.

There is such a hunger, a supposed necessity to give those systems taxonomies, when actually, due to the velocity so characteristic of our contemporary digital world, the moment they are named, they no longer have the same purpose once had when they originated. There are so many semioticians in charge of these nominations; when, in reality, what we really need is semioticians knowing how to use tools, and developing such tools to decode big data, no matter what are their taxonomies.

On the other hand, there is such a big extent to which assumptions and biases get in the way of the Semiotics work, much more than the unnamed items, because they have to be identified and corrected before being decoded, whereas the first ones can be directly decoded disregarding the fact that they do not have a specified name. We have to wonder if taxonomies are more helpful or unhelpful: did the current pressure to name everything cause the rise of the aforementioned assumptions and biases as a result of mislabelling, or was the lack of definitions responsible for them?

That is where the true value of Digital Semiotics comes in: the contemporary processes that create big data are happening and will continue to happen independently of our ability to name them. Howsoever, Semiotics is the tool through which we can follow the process, predict the next steps, even considering how challenging it can be due to the velocity of our cyberculture.

3   Glocality and Velocity

The unclassifiability is emerging as the main cultural characteristic of the twenty-first century, born under the technological and cultural conditions of the contemporary world, a consequence of global interactivity and of the velocity of production.

This is a phenomenon simultaneously local and international, situated in the cyberspace era, which utilizes cyberspace as a means for the internationalization of culture. It is deeply embedded in the typically cibercultural concept of glocality.

> *The process of glocalization staggers to the planetary territory and empowers to the infinite the phenomenon of this hybridization of realms of existence, transforming the world into a kaleidoscope of intersecting glocal strongholds for the circulation of information and data.* [4]·

Glocal is where we are when not localized in the local nor global. For instance, when we visit a virtual museum, we are not literally in the city of this museum, in its geographical localization; on the other hand, we are not at the place where our physical body is, because we are not experiencing those surroundings. We are experiencing the glocality of the museum that welcomes us through the virtual.

Glocality is the a worldwide phenomenon that affects all people through cyberspace and reaches even those without Internet access, which are influenced indirectly, because they suffer this influence on contact, however sporadic, with an individual who has a direct influence of cyberspace. The cyberculture undergoes a universal dissemination provided by all individuals who have contact with the cyberspace.

> *The glocal equates to a socio-technical homeostatic entanglement, obliterated and irreversible (...) at the regional, national or international level.* [4, p. 13]

In glocality we are always isolated, both in the so named Glocal Lato Sensu as in the Glocal Stricto Sensu. The first is the situation in which we are isolated by lack of access to internet, and the second is the one in which we are isolated from the territorial world around us protected by a Glocal Bunker, that is, our infinite gadgets that separate us from the physical environment in which our body is. Even though we are isolated geographically, we are also always united to everyone by cyberspace. An individual may be isolated from technology, but s/he can never escape the irreversible process of glocality.

> *The logic of relationships is not direct and dependent upon defined elements, but it is associated with a complex process of factors and trace elements, apparent and non-apparent, establishing transversal paths of relationship and causing countless reciprocal connection developments, conflicting and/or excludent that are beyond the reach of an accurate perception, yet thorough and experienced.* [2, p. 87]

This union between global that circulates and the "where" the body is (or "where" it acts), which is the communication basis of this current civilizing process, occurs by several garments (which for now are smartphones, tablets, computers), but these garments are of no importance because the glocal lies not in them. The glocal quality of communication is given more in the functional sense than in the structural sense of experience. This is what sustains the inextricable link between the global network and what circulates instantly through the interactive or hybrid mass communication.

> *Communication is every day less and less confined to fixed locations, and the new telecommunication modes have produced transmutations in the structure of our daily conceptions.* [3, p. 25]

The new status of glocality produces such transmutations, imposing a restriction: one that it is no longer possible to separate the content that is circulating internationally, nationally, or locally; or even in terms of the place that you occupy and the place where your body is. This new feature introduced by digital communication modifies the dynamics and the consistency of global communication that happens in the physical realm in which we operate. The process of glocalization also means cultural development to the extent that it permits miscegenation in the culture field, a content hybridization in the web without borders. The direct result of glocality on big data is this transmutation: glocality makes big data placeless, more than it ever was; because even though we could not specifically point out a location for any piece of data before, now we cannot trace its origins as well. Big data is not virtual anymore, it is glocal.

> *From this perspective without horizon in which the city access ceases to be a door or a triumphal arch to transform itself into an electronic hearing system (...), the break of the continuity does not occur either in space or in a limited urban sector, but mainly in duration (...) and successive or simultaneous occultations that organize and disorganize the urban environment to the point of causing irreversible decline of local. (...) Since then no one can be considered separately by physical obstacle or large "distances of time."* [6, pp. 8–10]

The cyberspace and digital culture have eroded our ability to identify the cultural lineage of artefacts and even people. We are being ravished by so much data at such a rapid flow of information that at one moment or other people get fed up, because we are not yet adapted to this velocity, we did not have time to develop the skills to learn, to do so many things at once. Some people have developed more aptitudes to deal with the fast pace of the world, although no one has reached such a level of geniality to be able to run after this pace.

4   Dromocracy

This velocity aforementioned is the factor that moves and controls our lives and our society. This "era of velocity" is called Dromocracy. The expression was coined by Virilio [5] based on the greek prefix *dromos*, which means the social articulation towards racing, velocity, speed; and thusly making Dromocracy a world view and/or a life governed by velocity. Dromocracy is a phenomenon that articulates the glocal through velocity. It is a system, a process. It rose in the twentieth century, when it was still a social process happening more isolatedly. Nowadays, Dromocracy is still a social process, but it has also become a regime that rules our lives, it has become this era. It is the congruency among the media, the state, the market, the companies and most importantly, the individuals that live under this regime willingly and that feed such system with their collaboration: the regime of Dromocracy is not imposed or forced on anyone.

Nobody (...) supervenes the "world" except by acting on it from the glocal context; no one can appear or speak to each other, as well as act in reality in a fast and effective mode except in and through the instant world of media signs, so the effect of glocalization; and even with severity, no one can predict about oneself or about any object or mark that has been or is being(...) Thus, everything becomes or tends to pass through the semiotic network in real time (...), socially structured as a kind of media-operating system (...) of contemporary culture in its interactive phase, established as Cybercultural Dromocracy. [4, pp. 25–26]

What every single person on the planet is already doing is a new kind of decision-making. We are overwhelmed with information not only from cyberspace but also from every other kind of media, and despite the fact that we are not able to process all that, we are already considering it, no matter how unconsciously, when we make a decision. In this new reality, such tools as surveys (among others) to find out why people buy what they buy, are no longer reliable. It is not the answers that the people give that matter anymore; it is the signifiers within the answers – exactly because, as previously mentioned, we are not able to pinpoint our flow of influences and interests. Consequently, in that scenario, the only tool for such a task is Semiotics, only it can show us how that is actually working. The role and the importance of Semiotics grow in Dromocracy, especially considering big data.

5   The New Roles and Challenges of Semiotics: Strategies

The challenge, once again, lies on velocity. The moment something catches our eye is because it is already big enough to be seen (no matter how insignificant it may be considered), and at this moment, in our rapid pace contemporary world, it is generally already about to die.

Nonetheless, we have to change our semiotic reading. It is not only about the changes in language, in media, etc. It is also about new archetypes – they changed – we are still practicing Semiotics based on archetypes that do not represent reality anymore.

However, things are changing in a pace that we cannot establish which are the new archetypes, so we come back to velocity: since archetypes and models change faster than we are able to identify and name them, we also have to be able to read these things not based on these old models, but we have to develop a new innovative method to do these readings without models. It is a new paradigm for Semiotics.

Big Data is endless and we will never be able to decode it entirely no matter how much time we spend on it, no matter how fast we do it, because it will always be changing, with new data appearing and disappearing at a faster pace than the human one. Acknowledging that fact is the first step to a new and urgently necessary Digital Semiotics based on ever-changing signifiers.

Semiotics' taxonomy will nevermore be as stable as chemistry's or biology's taxonomies are, if it ever was. Semiotics has to learn to deal with fluid structures, because the old fixedness of structures is already not enough to decode big data, and very soon it will be completely useless. There is still this fixedness, but we have to stop trying to make it last longer – the duration it is going to last does not matter anymore – what is crucial to be done is to adapt our methods or to create new ones that are as flexible and that flow as much as data and the contemporary culture do. It may seem counterintuitive, unnatural or even completely "unsemiotical", but the survival of Semiotics depends on learning how to analyse the data on our hands without standards and/or with fluid, ever-changing standards.

What sets Semiotics apart from any other area and makes it stand out is exactly that it could be the answer to understanding such world for all areas of knowledge, if, and only if, Semiotics is able to look inside itself for a deep, introspective adaptation to the ways of Dromocracy. There is no magic solution, and that is exactly why there is no research, no literature about this in the field of semiotics (even though very few academics, all cited here, have done so in other fields): we just have to learn how to deal with such challenges, not lose time developing theories that will not be accurate by the time they are developed, that is the simplest and most demanding solution.

For all that, the Semiotics field needs not only to develop new tools, but also adapt old ones. We can have a tool deeply based on structure, i.e. the square, but we can use it for completely unstructured objects of study, we simply have to make adjustments. We can indeed decode the unstructurable through structuring Semiotics tools without changing the unclassifiable nature of the object. We simply have to let go of the old habits that tell us that we need names and taxonomies to have something analysed. We have to look for a new framework of understanding, more flexible and supported by the dynamic comprehension of human phenomena beyond the visible and sortable; not at all less valid and representative, but quite the contrary: much more representative of our world even without the possibility of being represented by a specific name.

References

1. Antunes, J.Q.: História da Cultura Contemporânea: Cibercultura e Cultura Nobrow. In: Proceedings of Simpósio Nacional de História Cultural, Edição, vol. 1, issue 5, São Paulo (2014)
2. Sakamoto, C.K.: Criatividade e Construção da Realidade Contemporânea. Trama Interdisciplinar, vol. 3, issue 1, pp. 86–96, São Paulo (2012)
3. Santaella, L.: Linguagens Líquidas na Era da Mobilidade. São Paulo, Paulus (2007)
4. Trivinho, E.: Glocal: Visibilidade Mediática, Imaginário Bunker e Existência em Tempo Real. AnnaBlume, São Paulo (2013)
5. Virilio, P.: Velocidade e política. Estação Liberdade, São Paulo (1996)
6. Virilio, P.: O Espaço Crítico. Editora 34, São Paulo (2014)

Preliminary Reflections on Affective Affordance in HCI: A Semiotic-Informed Perspective

Elaine C.S. Hayashi[✉], Alessandro Arpetti,
and M. Cecília C. Baranauskas

Institute of Computing, University of Campinas (UNICAMP),
Campinas, SP, Brazil
{hayashi,cecilia}@ic.unicamp.br, arpetti@gmail.com

Abstract. In spite of some divergence on interpretations of the concept of "affordance", the term is fundamental in HCI and interaction design. More recently, the recognition of the affective quality of systems is becoming increasingly important as well. As an emerging subject, there is a lack of discussion on related concepts and, ultimately, on their practical implications. The objective of this paper is to bring into discussion the concept of affect under the perspective of affordance. From a socio-cultural view, this paper articulates affective affordances within the theoretical references of Organizational Semiotics and the Socially Aware Design; and concludes with prospections on potential applications for the design of technology.

Keywords: Affectability · Emotional design · Affordance · Affective affordances · Semiotic onion · Organizational Semiotics · Socially Aware Design · Human-computer interaction

1 Introduction

Ubiquitous computing devices, wearable, tangible or natural user interface tools, social software: these are some of the ways in which Information and Communication Technology (ICT) has become a pervasive part of our personal and social lives. As an intrinsic part of our daily interactions and socially constructed reality, technology must be aligned with our intentions, values, beliefs and social practices. The design process focused only on the technical system itself is no longer enough [21]. This new reality demands new theories and methods in HCI [8, 17], which now have to consider and reflect other elements that used to be left aside, such as: social values, emotions, intentions of use, and the device's, the users' and the environment's conditions and characteristics [14, 17].

The concept of affordance, analyzed under an Organizational Semiotic (OS) perspective, has provided basis to inform the design of an inclusive social network [14]. Similarly, the present article builds upon the original definition of affordance from Gibson [6] to discuss design for Affectability [9]. At a higher level of abstraction, this article investigates the concept of affordance, proposing a discussion on Affective

M.C.C. Baranauskas et al. (Eds.): ICISO 2016, IFIP AICT 477, pp. 43–52, 2016.
DOI: 10.1007/978-3-319-42102-5_5

affordance framed by an artifact from OS: the Semiotic Onion [13, 21]. Although the term Affective affordance had been used before, e.g., in [12, 23, 25], the field of HCI could benefit from further discussion and informed formalization from a socio-technical perspective.

We revisit concepts of affordance and we use the perspective of the Semiotic Onion [13, 21, 22] and the Socially Aware Design [1, 2] to articulate the concept of Affective affordance with possible design practices. This paper is organized as follows: Sect. 2 summarizes the concepts that form the theoretical bases of the analysis presented in Sect. 3, which articulates affect and affordances. Section 4 draws on Sect. 3 to discuss the application of these concepts in interaction design. Section 5 concludes this paper.

2   Theoretical References

Organizational Semiotics (OS). [13, 21, 22] provides artifacts and methods to understand, model and design information systems. Information systems, from the OS perspective, are a result of social interactions. Starting from an informal level, a community (organization) is seen as a collection of members and the values, beliefs and habits of each member are relevant to form the group. In a formal level, the patterns of behavior from the informal level are modeled into norms that compose requirements in the direction of the technical layer, in which the system per se is derived. These informal, formal and technical layers form the Semiotic onion [13, 21]. The analogy with an onion illustrates how each level is embedded into the other to compose meaningful information systems, in which computer systems (or digital artifacts) are embedded in the formal and informal organization. As Stamper [21] argue, usually traditional design methods tend to focus on the formal and technical levels – or layers – without meeting the requirements of the informal level of the organization.

The layers of the Semiotic Onion are rooted in the definition from Hall [7], who proposes that cultural conventions (the way humans operate) can be classified in informal, formal and technical levels.

The **Socially Aware Design** [1, 2], in its turn, was based on the Semiotic Onion to propose a design flow that starts in the society (with its needs and abilities), enters the onion, goes throughout the layers until reaching the technical one; and goes back to impact society, as technology changes the norms and informal practices of a social group.

The Semiotic Onion and the Socially Aware Design were the starting point for our research on affect in design processes, and they also form the basis for the discussion we present in Sects. 3 and 4.

Affective Computing. [18] is a relatively new field that concerns the development of digital technology that can automatically recognize, interpret and respond (or adapt behavior) according to affective expressions of users. In order to grant computation systems with this ability to recognize affect, affective responses need to be categorized and treated as pieces of information. It is, therefore, assumed that emotions are internally created and then put out to the world, existing independently of context and interaction. Boehner et al. [3] call "Informational approaches" those approaches that are in line with Affective Computing, in which emotions are seen as fixed information. On a different direction, the authors call "Interactional approach" the point of view that considers affect as dynamic results of social interactions, loaded with cultural influences and rich in interpretation possibilities.

In line with interactional approaches, however not totally denying informational ones, the concept of Affectability [9] delineates an endeavor to understand the characteristics that have the capacity of evoking varying (which can depend on cultures or contexts) affective responses from users interacting with a digital artifact in a given context (or environment). The objective is to bring awareness to designers on the creation of products with improved affective quality.

Affective quality can be defined as the characteristics of an object (or place, events, systems) that can influence the affective state of a person [26], as he/she perceives those characteristics in the object. This perception can be based on how easy/hard to use, how pleasant/not pleasant, boring/exciting, etc., the object is.

Affordance is a concept created by Gibson [6], who defines it as the action possibilities that an animal perceives from an environment. With the word "affordance", Gibson wants to refer to both: the environment and the animal, in a way that one is complementary to the other. In Kaptelinin and Nardi's [11] interpretation of the Gibsonian theory of affordances, "*animals directly perceive affordances as possibilities for action in the environment, which are determined, on the one hand, by the objective properties of the environment, and, on the other hand, by the action capabilities of the animal*" [11, p. 968]. Moreover, as Gibson [6] explains, "*The perceiving of an affordance is not a process of perceiving a value-free physical object to which meaning is somehow added in a way that no one has been able to agree upon; it is a process of perceiving a value-rich ecological object*" [6, p. 60].

To Gibson, affordances exist independently of whether or not they are perceived or desired by the actor. The classic example is that of a chair. A chair affords sitting, even when the actor does not will to sit. Even when one cannot see the chair, it is still sit-able [24]. This constitutes a point of divergence between Gibson's and Norman's understanding of the concept. Norman [15] is more interested in processing mechanisms and how the mind processes the information perceived. There are authors who argue for separating affordances from perception, as it was originally proposed by Gibson [11, 24]. The claim is that there is an advantage of considering the existence of affordance independently of it being perceived by the actor or not. This separation of affordances from perception helps to differentiate between two aspects of design elements: its affordance and its usability [11, 24]. For Norman, "affordances can be not only real but also just perceived" [11, p. 969] that is only affordance itself, without being perceived, plays a relatively minor role as designers should be more concerned with what users can **perceive** [15].

The contrast between the various theoretical positions and the different interpretations of the concept of affordance can be analysed by going back to the work of Gibson in its roots, namely the theory of ecological perception. As we reported in reference to the concept of affordance by Gibson, the ecological term is understood in the sense of adaptation of an animal to its environment, or in the relations between individuals of a species, the organized activities of this species and the environment of these activities. In this sense, the environment is not the "external world", but is intended as 'ecological niche', that is, the behaviour of a species living under specific environmental conditions.

This definition of affordance establishes a mutual connection between the animal and the environment, and the indivisibility between perception and action. Gibson himself [5] characterizes the perceptual system as a connection between the action and its perception. For the author, the perception is an emerging process of animal-environment system. This implies that the perception does not reside in the brain, but is a process of extracting information from the environment, by means of exploration. In fact, if the primitive affordances linked to survival instincts are innate, all the others are the result of exploration of the environment through which the animal with its characteristics and capacity for action relates to an environment with specific characteristics. The information derived from this exploration is already meaningful information, since it is an element of the animal-environment system and is not compatible with the internalist interpretation proposed by cognitivism, according to which this information is a description of the environment that will be processed by the mind to give it a meaning.

Stoffregen [20] who provides a formal definition of affordances says that the emergent properties of the system are not present individually in the actors that are part of the system. For example, if we consider the climbability (affordance) of stairs, we should consider a system composed by a person (animal), the action of climbing (action) and the stairs (environment). The person and the stairs have individual properties (length of the leg, height of the step), but the system has a unique feature that is not present individually in any of the two actors, and is the scalability of the step, namely the relationship between the height of the step and the length of the person's leg.

The affordances therefore suggest possible behaviours that a system allows, but Stroffregen [20] states that it is the "psychological choice" of the actor that will bring the effective implementation of the action. In this choice, the emotions and the affective states can participate and produce a relationship with either a particular property of the environment to create an affordance or as part of a behaviour, by means of the consequences that an action produces in a person.

3   Affective Affordance

Extending the formalization of the concept of affordances proposed by Stroffregen [19], we can define an affective affordance by introducing an affective response of the user:

Let W_{pq} (e.g., a user-interaction-artifact system) = (X_p, Z_q) be composed of different things X (e.g., user) and Z (e.g., artifact).
Let p be a property of X and q be a property of Z.

The relation between p and q, p/q, defines a higher order property (i.e., a property of the user–artifact system), h.
Then h is said to be an affective affordance of W_{pq} if and only if:

(i) $W_{pq} = (X_p, Z_q)$ possesses h
(ii) Neither Z nor X possesses h
(iii) h produces an affective response A(X).

The main difference between a general affordance and an affective affordance lies in the fact that a general affordance is directly linked to a behavior, while an affective affordance produces an emotional state that can or cannot precede the eventual psychological choice of implementing a behavior.

Considering the environment as ecological niche and the user as participant of a group, we can argue that affective responses are influenced by culture and society and depend on varied factors. As Boehner et al. [3] argue, the sense people make out of feelings and other affective states are intertwined with the way such emotional episodes are experienced and to the way they are translated into words. These processes happen both in the individual and collectively. While emotions come from inside an individual (as a result of either internal or external stimuli), it is in the collectivity that the meanings and translations into words (or gestures – especially in the case of sign languages or other cultural gestures, images, sounds, etc.) are formed and shared.

Affect, emotions and the words that attempt to define them have a social and cultural nature. Boehner et al. [3] give as an example the concept of "song", from the Ifaluk Atoll. "Song" could be directly translated to "anger". However, while in a Western context, "anger" has a rather negative connotation, the Ifalukan "song" is considered a justifiable anger, as it is provoked by someone's lack of responsibility or failure to properly respond to social norms.

Similarly, affective responses also have cultural background. The Sensual Evaluation Instrument (SEI) [10], a self-assessment tool for affect, was created based on the premise that emotions can be explored from a non-verbal perspective as well as they can be evoked by different stimuli, like colors and shapes. The authors created and experimented objects with different shapes. In their experiments they observed that objects with sharp edges tended to be related to negative valence. On the other hand, objects with smooth surface and few protrusions were often associated to positive valence. The authors believe that SEI could be used across cultures and indeed one can easily recall personal experiences that validate those examples (that sharp edged objects are often related to negative affective responses; and smooth surfaces, to positive affective responses). While it is true and interesting for that self-assessment instrument, other objects with similar shapes can evoke opposite responses, which roots might be considered cultural or dependent on specific contexts. Figure 1 illustrates this idea: it can be said that a baby hedgehog tends to have positive affective affordance, even

Fig. 1. In spite of its prickly appearance, a hedgehog baby[1] might have positive affective affordance, whereas maggots[2], with its soft appearance, would evoke negative affective affordance – contrary to the notions of what spiky and smooth objects usually evoke. [Sources: [1]Hedgehog baby https://pixabay.com/en/hedgehog-animal-baby-cute-small-468228/; [2]Maggots: https://commons.wikimedia.org/wiki/File:Maggots.jpg]

though it has a prickly appearance. Other similar shaped objects would probably evoke not-touching. On the opposite way, maggots have soft looking surfaces but they tend to have negative affective affordance, usually evoking disgust or aversion. These responses are culturally learned. Babies inspire care; worms and larvae, disgust. Take other animals for examples. Guinea pigs are adorable pets in some countries. In other countries, they are a traditional dish, usually grilled as a whole. Cows are sacred in some cultures, tortured to death for meat in others. These contrasting ways to treat animals are socially accepted in their own cultures and cause people with different background to present different affective responses.

From an ecological perspective, this scenario becomes even more complex since user-system interactions are contaminated not only by socio-cultural elements but also by the individual's life experience. In the light of the formal definition of affective affordance in which $W_{pq} = (X_p, Z_q)$. It is arguable that the image Z (the artifact, in this case a baby hedgehog (cf. Fig. 1)) has some characteristics $_q$ (colors, size, lights, position, background, etc.). The user X has some characteristics $_p$ (physical characteristics, social values, beliefs, affective state, etc.). The system W_{pq} (user-relationship-image) affords an affective response A(X) which may or may not be expressed in behavior. This affective response is strongly linked to the system to all the meanings contained in it. For example, the image can afford a sentiment of sweetness in a young parent that can smile and eventually share the image in social media; or it can afford a feeling of disgust in a user who has just had a bad experience with a small rodent and, viewing the image, grimaces and shuts down the computer.

Affective responses are therefore the result of combinations of numerous elements in a complex system. To overcome the fragmentation of these responses and provide useful guidelines for interaction designers it is necessary to analyze, in a systemic way, the influences of the different actors in the formation of affective affordances.

4 Affective Affordance and the Design of Digital Artifacts

Affective responses could be analyzed within the Semiotic Onion and the flow of the Socially Aware Design. Take the example of Internet memes, i.e., media that are spread in the Internet, usually for fun. The "success kid" (Fig. 2a) is an example of Internet meme.

Fig. 2. From left to right: (a) original picture taken by the child's mother; (b) internet meme example; (c) meme used by the USA White House in a Tweet [Sources: (a) and (b) http://globalnews.ca/news/1939419/success-kid-needs-your-help-getting-his-dad-a-new-kidney/; (c) http://www.nydailynews.com/news/politics/success-kid-meme-pass-immigration-reform-article-1.1376952, Accessed: April 2016]

It started as a common social action of taking pictures and a spontaneous affective expression that starts at the outmost layer of the semiotic onion: the informal layer. In order to reach a digital format and gain space online (technical layer), the picture was once treated and meanings were formalized with texts (formal layer). Going back the path towards the society, the online use of the Success kid meme gained a specific format (formal layers) as shown in Fig. 2b. As it became viral and worldwide known (informal layer), it even became theme for advertisement, in a billboard add. Also the White House in the United Stated used the meme, in a Tweet in their campaign to urge Congress to pass the immigration reform (Fig. 2c) representing the impact in society.

While it is hard to determine whether a product will be successfully accepted by users, one can investigate elements that can be of influence in the process. Tang et al. [23] have shown the relevance of consumers' perceived affordances (namely physical, cognitive, affective and control affordances) in the success of some specific ads in China. We argue that affective affordances have the potential to influence the design of ICT in general. The design for Affectability [9] is the design that is concerned with affective affordances throughout the entire design process. We had presented the concept of Affectibility and the Framework for Affectibility based on the same theoretical roots explained in Sect. 2. Next we present the creation and development of an application, which illustrates the design towards improved Affectibility – that is, the design that is concerned with the possible affective affordances that could be collectively constructed and perceived by users.

4.1 Designing AmigoDaHora

We had been immersed in an underprivileged community of a public school in Brazil, taking active part in the school's daily activities as participant observers. From this endeavor we identified many characteristics of that group of children; one of them was the very noticeable tendency to negative thoughts and behavior. Not only children but also teachers and other employees from the school were often prone to see defects and points of complaint in almost any subject. Seeing positive aspects was difficult for them. Following the flow of the Socially Aware Design [1], this predominance of rather negative affective affordances in schools interactions can be seen as a characteristic from the school as a group (society). From this need (of practicing more positive views and attitudes) we proposed the creation of an application based on a social activity (informal layer) known as "Secret Santa" ("Amigo secreto" or "Amigo oculto" in Brazil). In this practice, each participant raffles the name of another and he/she has to buy the other a present. In our proposed version, each participant should gift the other a compliment, creating a gift representing that compliment.

Children played the role of our design partners in the development of the application. In participatory practices they helped us to better understand and formalize the rules of this new activity of gifting compliments (formal layer). By enacting the activity we tried to understand what elements the interface should represent as to provide the necessary characteristics to help achieve the desired affective responses. Children informed us not only about what they needed the application to have in order to create

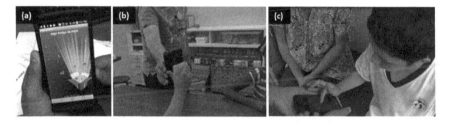

Fig. 3. (a) Main screen of AmigoDaHora (b) enrolling a child in the game (c) child drawing a smile face to illustrate his gift/compliment

the gifts as they wanted, but they also named the application: AmigoDaHora - slang meaning something similar to "cool friend" (cf. Fig. 3a).

The technical layer is the application itself. We developed a mobile application that made use of RFID cards for tangible interaction. Only one mobile was needed and it was based on Android platform. Each child would have their own card. We asked children to personalize the cards by hand drawing something to represent them on the card. The application would read the card and identify each child as participant of AmigoDaHora. After registering all participants for a round (cf. Fig. 3b), the application would secretly assign the participants to each other. Each child would then take turns to privately interact with the application in order to find out who his/her friend was and create a gift/compliment for that friend (cf. Fig. 3c). The application let children speak the compliment out loud and it transcribed what they said. Children could also take pictures and/or make drawings as to compose the gift/compliment. After all children had created their gifts, they could take turns again to use the application and receive their gifts/compliments.

Going back from the technical layer (the development and evaluation of Amigo-DaHora application) to society, we observed the use made of the application. Right on the first round playing with AmigoDaHora, children organized themselves and set rules to determine how they would take turns to interact with the application (formal layer). Sharing the single mobile device and making use of the application in the group (informal layer) should potentially direct children to the desired outcome of practicing seeing positive aspects in others and develop positive attitudes (impact back on society).

The factors (e.g., aesthetical, motivational, etc.) that might contribute to the establishment of positive affective affordances were listed in the form of design principles for Affectability (PAff), which were followed in the creation of AmigoDaHora. Among the six principles presented [9], for example, the PAff 1, Free interpretation and communication of affect, suggests to (i) make available features to allow communication and expression; (ii) avoid predetermining meanings (of signs, words, images, etc.) and let affect be freely expressed and interpreted; and (iii) avoid automatic identification of affect. One affective affordance of the AmigoDaHora mobile application (A(X)) could be: affective expression by drawing smile faces with the finger. This possibility exists from X_{p1} = children fingers, Z_{q1} = touch screen, and $^{p1}/_{q1}$ = children application on a mobile device for the creation and exchange of compliments.

5   Conclusion

Digital artifacts have to make sense to users. The Socially Aware Design argues for design processes that start in the society, with the understanding of the main stakeholders and the comprehension of the target users' main abilities and needs. In OS it is by understanding the informal practices of a social group that practices can be translated into the designed artifact.

Being affective responses a result of cultural and social interactions, in order to aim for improved Affectibility in the resulting solutions, designers could start their analysis from the society as well, following the path of the design throughout the Semiotic Onion. This approach can not only contribute to the creation of more meaningful systems, but also help designers having in mind the possible affective outcomes that the designed system might have when it, in its turn, influence back social practices. This article discussed the concept of Affective affordances, presenting a definition from an ecological perspective in which the environment and users are mutually connected, although perception and action are not always necessarily directly linked. Future work could explore the norms that help inform the design for improved Affectibility.

Acknowledgments. We would like to thank our colleagues from InterHAD for insightful discussions; CAPES and CNPq (Process # 308618/2014-9) for financial support.

References

1. Baranauskas, M.C.C.: Social awareness in HCI. Interactions **21**(4), 66–69 (2014)
2. Baranauskas, M.C.C.: Socially aware computing. In: The 6th International Conference on Engineering and Computer Education, Buenos Aires, pp. 1–5 (2009)
3. Boehner, K., DePaula, R., Dourish, P., Sengers, P.: How emotion is made and measured. Int. J. Hum. Comput. Stud. **65**(4), 275–291 (2007)
4. Bødker, S.: Third-wave HCI, 10 years later-participation and sharing. Interactions **22**(5), 24–31 (2015)
5. Gibson, J.J.: The Senses Considered as Perceptual Systems. Houghton Mifflin, Boston (1966)
6. Gibson, J.J.: The theory of affordances. In: The People, Place, and Space Reader, p. 56 (1979)
7. Hall, E.: The Silent Language. Doubleday, New York (1959)
8. Harrison, S., Tatar D., Sengers, P.: The three paradigms of HCI. In: Proceedings of ACM AltCHI 2007, pp. 1–21 (2007)
9. Hayashi, E.C.S., Baranasukas, M.C.C.: 'Affectability' and design workshops: taking actions towards more sensible design. In: The 12th Brazilian Symposium on Human Factors in Computing Systems, pp. 3–12. Brazilian Computer Society (2013)
10. Isbister, K., Höök, K., Sharp, M., Laaksolahti, J.: The sensual evaluation instrument: developing an affective evaluation tool. In: The SIGCHI Conference on Human Factors in Computing Systems, pp. 1163–1172. ACM (2006)
11. Kaptelinin, V., Nardi, B.: Affordances in HCI: toward a mediated action perspective. In: The SIGCHI Conference on Human Factors in Computing Systems, pp. 967–976. ACM (2012)

12. Krampen, M.: Semiotics in architecture and industrial/product design. Des. Issues **5**(2), 124–140 (1989)
13. Liu, K.: Semiotics in Information Systems and Engineering. Cambridge University Press, Cambridge (2000)
14. Neris, V.P.A, Baranauskas, M.C.C.: User interface design informed by affordances and norms concepts. In: The 12th IFIP WG 8.1 International Conference on Informatics and Semiotics in Organizations, ICISO, pp. 133–140 (2010)
15. Norman, D.A.: Affordance, conventions, and design. Interactions **6**(3), 38–43 (1999)
16. Norman, D.: Emotional Design: Why We Love (or Hate) Everyday Things. Basic Books, New York (2004)
17. Pereira, R., Baranauskas, M.C., Liu, K.: On the relationships between norms, values and culture: preliminary thoughts in HCI. In: Liu, K., Nakata, K., Li, W., Galarreta, D. (eds.) ICISO 2015. IFIP AICT, vol. 449, pp. 30–40. Springer, Heidelberg (2015)
18. Picard, R.: Affective Computing. MIT Press, Cambridge (1995)
19. Stoffregen, T.A.: Affordances as properties of the animal-environment system. Ecol. Psychol. **15**, 115–134 (2003)
20. Stoffregen, T.A.: Breadth and limits of the affordance concept. Ecol. Psychol. **16**, 79–85 (2004)
21. Stamper, R.: A semiotic theory of information and information systems. Invited paper on Information by the ICL/University of Newcastle (1993)
22. Stamper, R., Liu, K., Hafkamp, M., Ades, Y.: Understanding the roles of signs and norms in organisations: a semiotic approach to information systems design. J. Behav. Inf. Technol. **19**(1), 15–27 (2000)
23. Tang, J., Zhao, X., Zhang, P.: Perceived affordances of web advertisements: implications for information artifacts design. In: Proceedings of the Fifth China Summer Workshop on Information Management, pp. 25–26 (2011)
24. Torenvliet, G.: We can't afford it!: the devaluation of a usability term. Interactions **10**(4), 12–17 (2003)
25. Vugt, H.C., Hoorn, J.F., Konjin, E.A., Dimitriadou, A.B.: Affective affordances: improving interface character engagement through interaction. J. Hum. Comput. Stud. **64**, 874–888 (2006)
26. Zhang, P., Li, N.: The importance of affective quality. Commun. ACM **48**(9), 105–108 (2005)

Robust Social Recommendation Techniques: A Review

Feng Jiang[1,2], Min Gao[1,3(✉)], Qingyu Xiong[1,3], Junhao Wen[1,3], and Yi Zhang[1,3]

[1] Key Laboratory of Dependable Service Computing in Cyber Physical Society, Ministry of Education, Chongqing University, Chongqing 400044, China
{jiangfeng,gaomin,xiong03,jhwen,
cquzhangyi}@cqu.edu.cn
[2] College of Construction Engineering, Chongqing Technology and Business Institute, Chongqing 400052, China
[3] School of Software Engineering, Chongqing University, Chongqing 400044, China

Abstract. Social recommendation plays an important role in solving the cold start problem in recommendation systems and improves the accuracy of recommendation, but still faces serious challenges and problems. Ratings or relationships injected by fake users seriously affect the authenticity of the recommendations as well as users' trustiness on the recommendation systems. Moreover, the simplification of relationship treatment also seriously affects the recommendation accuracy and user satisfaction to the recommendation systems. This paper first analyzes up to date research of social recommendation and the detecting technology of multiple relationships. Furthermore, it proposes a future research framework for robust social recommendations including modeling and feature extraction of multidimensional relationships, social recommendation shilling attack models based on social relationships, the analysis of the relationships in social networks as well as the roles of relationships on recommendation, and robust social recommendation approaches taking multiple relationships into consideration.

Keywords: Social recommendation · Multiple relationships · Shilling attack

1 Introduction

At present, the rapid development of electronic commerce retail and the rise of social network marketing make social recommendation a research hotspot [1]. Social recommendation refers to recommendation technology taking social relationships as additional input [2] to improve the sales of merchandise and users' satisfaction [1–3].

Social recommendations mainly combine users' social relationships and collaborative filtering technologies [4] to make recommendations. The social relationships between users can be combined with memory-based collaborative filtering method to find nearest neighbor or model-based collaborative filtering as an implicit vector constraints to form memory-based or model-based social recommendation. Social

© IFIP International Federation for Information Processing 2016
Published by Springer International Publishing Switzerland 2016. All Rights Reserved
M.C.C. Baranauskas et al. (Eds.): ICISO 2016, IFIP AICT 477, pp. 53–58, 2016.
DOI: 10.1007/978-3-319-42102-5_6

recommendations utilize users' similarities reflected from social relationships [5] to play an important role in solving the cold start problem in the recommendation systems and improve the accuracy of recommendations, but still face serious challenges and problems. First, shilling attacks seriously affect the authenticity of the recommendation in a social recommendation system [6, 7]. Second, the noise relationship will lead to recommendation failure. There are many relationships in social networks. These relationships are usually dealt with as the same, which is an important reason that explains current social recommendations did not play its due role [8].

Comments injected by fake users seriously affect the authenticity of the recommendation list as well as users' trust degree to the recommendation system; while the simplification of relationship treatment also seriously affects the accuracy of the recommendation list and users' satisfaction to the recommendation system. To solve these issues, the social relationship is a key factor. This paper analyzes up to date research of social recommendation and the detecting technology of interference relationships, as well as proposes a research framework to solve these issues.

2 Social Recommendations and Multiple Relationships Detection

In this section, we will analyze up to date memory-based and model-based social recommendation approaches, fake user detection approaches, and multiple relationship detection approaches because these approaches are essential techniques to robust social recommendation.

2.1 Social Recommendations

Social recommendations usually refer to utilizing social relationships to conduct the merchandise recommendation, conducting the recommendation of friends, micro-blogs, or utilizing celebrities' social influences to conduct the recommendations. The social recommendations in this paper belong to a narrowly-defined social recommendation [9]: a kind of item recommendation technique combining the social relationships. Social recommendation can be divided into memory-based one and model-based one. Memory-based social recommendations directly use ratings and directly linked users as neighbors. Rokach et al. [10] propose a social relationships' weighed average method to find the neighbors. According to the shortest path length from the target user to all users, Golbeck [11] gradually calculate the trust degree and chose those users whose trust values were greater than a threshold value as the neighbor. Jithin and Beegom [12] use the theory of thermal diffusion for reference to conduct trust transfer in the social relationship networks, meanwhile combined it with traditional rating similarities. Model-based social recommendation takes the model-based collaborative filtering as its foundation, such as the probability matrix decomposition models [15] making relationships between users reflected to preference relationships and achieved the method of social trust integration, the random walk model [13] on social relationships to deal with both positive and negative relationships under the condition of ensuring the convergence and then realize the recommendations, the Social Bayes Personalized Rank (SBPR) model [14] used in combination with friends' preference to predict ratings, the tensor decomposition model [16] and the multidimensional trust relationship model [17].

These social recommendation approaches utilize users' social relationships and generate effective recommendation as rating matrices are sparse or recommending cold start items. Therefore, the approach can solve the sparsity problem and the cold start problem to some extents; meanwhile improve the accuracy of recommendation. Social recommendation widely drew academia and the industry's attention, but due to a lower cost of establishing social relationships in social networks, social recommendation suffers from the problems related with interference relationships: (1) fake users who improve or lower items' recommendation probabilities by injecting fake users and relationships, which is called the social recommendation shilling attack [6]; and (2) The problem of noise relationship leading to recommendation failure. There are multiple noise relationships that have side-effects on the recommendation, such as temporary friendships or random friendships [18]. If these relationships are treated equally with friendships and colleague relationships, it will make the recommendation results be questioned to a certain extent.

2.2 Social Relationships Detection

Fake User Detection. At present, the studies on fake users' interference mainly concentrate on shilling attacks detection in the traditional recommendation systems as well as the methods of detecting fake users in social networks.

In the recommendation systems, Mobasher et al. [19] propose a supervised learning method that used the rating degree mean agreement (RDMA), Degsim, and other features training classifiers to detect fake users. Other researchers [22, 23] put forward a non-supervised learning method based on feature clustering to detect fake users. Cao et al. [23] raise a semi-supervised learning method which utilized a small amount of labeled data and a large amount of non-labeled data to improve the detection accuracy. Zhang [24] put forward a method to improve recommendation systems' anti-shilling attacks ability by building a users' multi-layered trust model. Wang et al. [25] raise an attack detection algorithm based on target item identification.

In social networks, fake users with the intention of spreading particular contents also can be called "shills" [7] or "water army". The research on fake users in social networks concentrates on that detecting abnormal users based on user features or network structures. Aggarwal et al. [26] extract characteristics from users' registration information, published contents and other information and then built classifiers. Limsaiprom and Tantatsanawong [27] detect fake users by clustering users' source and target addresses.

In social recommendation, Zhang et al. [7] detect fake users based on the cluster of friends' trust relationships. Shrivastava et al. [6] raise that detecting random link attacks by clustering social network diagrams.

Multiple Relationship Detection. Some research on the multiple relationship are focused on raising problems [8]. Liu et al. [4] believe that social recommendation did not distinguish friendships is one of reasons for its recommendation failure in some case at present. Ghosh et al. [28] raise that in social networks, real users might also build up unreal relationships.

In the aspect of solving the problems, Yeung and Iwata [18] introduce the concept of relationship strength, and used the method of matrix decomposition and optimization to solve the relationship strength. Tang et al. [17] analyze multidimensional trust relationships based on themes' multidimensional trust tensors and then conducted the recommendation.

3   Analysis and Discussion

At the time of achieving recommendation accuracy and solving the cold start problem, social recommendation is easy to receive fake users' shilling attacks and noise relationships' interference. The detection on fake users in the traditional recommendation system [19–21], the recommendation based on the calculation of trust degree or target items' abnormality [24, 25] and the detection on fake users in social networks [26, 27] all involved less in the problem of shilling attacks produced when social networks are combined with the e-commerce to conduct product recommendations. In current study on fake users of social recommendation [6, 7], it is assumed that attackers use random link attacks to establish links randomly between fake users and normal users, and if attackers use other strategies to conduct attacks, then it would be difficult to deal with.

The future research should focus on robust social recommendation, four research points are shown in Fig. 1: (1) The modeling of users' social relationships is the foundation of robust social recommendation. It focuses on the study of using complex network modeling to build fake user injection strategies and shilling attacks models of social recommendation; (2) Utilize the multi-view collaborative training, probabilistic graphical model, tensor decomposition, and other technologies to form the method of probability estimation of multidimensional social relationships; (3) Aim at the cold start, hot and general item exploration to explore function mechanisms of multiple

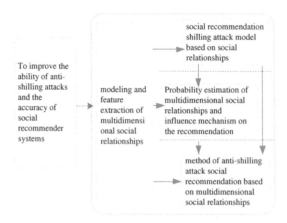

Fig. 1. The further research of robust social recommendation

social relationships on the recommendation. The influence of relationships on different types of items can be analyzed by comparing the baseline recommendation algorithms with that by the social recommendation algorithms; and (4) Combine the multidimensional social relationship probability matrix, and finally build up the algorithm of anti-interference social recommendation to achieve a robust social recommendation system.

4 Conclusion

This paper started from the analysis of the study of social recommendation and existing problems. It explained the characteristic that social recommendation is easy to be attacked by bogus social relationships and be interfered by multiple social relationships. It analyzed the future research point of robust social recommendation, and proposed four aspects: (1) the users' relationship modeling and characteristic extraction faced anti-shilling attack social recommendation; (2) strategies of fake relationship injection and social recommendation shilling attack models; (3) probability estimation of users' multidimensional social relationships and function mechanism of relationship types on social recommendation; and (4) robust social recommendation approaches combined multidimensional social relationships with traditional social recommendation algorithms.

Acknowledgments. This research is supported by the Basic and Advanced Research Projects in Chongqing (cstc2015jcyjA40049), Chongqing University Young Scholar Program, the Scientific and Technological Research Program of Chongqing Municipal Education Commission (KJ121607 and KJ131603) and the Chongqing Social Science Planning Project (2010QNRW54).

References

1. Li, S.S., Karahanna, E.: Online recommendation systems in a B2C e-commerce context: a review and future directions. J. Assoc. Inf. Syst. **16**(2), 72–107 (2015)
2. Tang, J., Hu, X., Liu, H.: Social recommendation: a review. Soc. Netw. Anal. Min. **3**(4), 1113–1133 (2013)
3. Levandoski, J.J., Sarwat, M., Eldawy, A., Mokbel, M.F.: LARS: a location-aware recommender system. In: IEEE, pp. 450–461 (2012)
4. Liu, J., Zhou, T., Wang, B.: Progress in personalized recommender systems. Prog. Nat. Sci. **19**(1), 1–15 (2009)
5. Gao, H., Tang, J., Liu, H.: Exploring social-historical ties on location-based social network. In: ICWSM (2012)
6. Shrivastava, N., Majumder, A., Rastogi, R.: Mining (social) network graphs to detect random link attacks. In: Proceedings of IEEE 24th International Conference on Data Engineering, pp. 486–495 (2008)
7. Zhang, X.L., Lee, T.M.D., Pitsilis, G.: Securing recommender systems against shilling attacks using social-based clustering. J. Comput. Sci. Technol. **28**(4), 616–624 (2013)
8. IBM: IBM's Black Friday report (2012). https://strme.wordpress.com/2012/11/27/ibmsblack-friday-report-says-twitter-delivered-0-percent-of-referral-traffic-and-facebooksentjust-0-68percent/

9. Ester, M.: Recommendation in social networks. In: ACM RecSys, pp. 491–492 (2013)

10. Rokach, L., Shapira, B., Kantor, P.B.: Recommender Systems Handbook. Springer, New York (2011)

11. Golbeck, J.: Generating Predictive Movie Recommendations from Trust in Social Networks. Springer, Heidelberg (2006)

12. Justin, J., Beegom, A.S.: Nearest neighbour based social recommendation using heat diffusion. In: Proceedings of the 6th ACM India Computing Convention, p. 10 (2013)

13. Chen, Y.C., Lin, Y.S., Shen, Y.C., Lin, S.D.: A modified random walk framework for handling negative ratings and generating explanations. ACM Trans. Intell. Syst. Technol. **4**(1), 12 (2013)

14. Zhao, T., McAuley, J., King, I.: Leveraging social connections to improve personalized ranking for collaborative filtering. In: Proceedings of the 23rd ACM International Conference on Information and Knowledge Management, pp. 261–270 (2014)

15. Jiang, M., Cui, P., Wang, F., Zhu, W., Yang, S.: Scalable recommendation with social contextual information. IEEE Trans. Knowl. Data Eng. **26**(11), 2789–2802 (2014)

16. Zou, B., Li, C., Tan, L., Chen, H., Wang, S.: Social recommendation based on user trust and tensor decomposition. J. Softw. **12**(10), 2852–2864 (2014)

17. Tang, J., Gao, H., Liu, H.: mTrust: discerning multi-faceted trust in a connected world. In: Proceedings of the 5th ACM International Conference on Web Search and Data Mining, pp. 93–102 (2012)

18. Yeung, A.C.M., Iwata, T.: Strength of social influence in trust networks in product review sites. In: Proceedings of the 4th ACM International Conference on Web Search and Data Mining, pp. 495–504 (2011)

19. Mobasher, B., Burke, R., Bhaumik, R., Williams, C.: Toward trustworthy recommender systems: an analysis of attack models and algorithm robustness. ACM Trans. Internet Technol. **7**(4), 23 (2007)

20. Wu, Z., Zhuang, Y., Wang, Y., Cao, J.: Shilling attack detection based on feature selection for recommendation systems. Acta Electron. Sinica **40**(8), 1687–1693 (2012)

21. Li, C., Luo, Z.: A metadata-enhanced variational bayesian matrix factorization model for robust collaborative recommendation. Acta Autom. Sinica **9**, 1067–1076 (2011)

22. Lee, J.S., Zhu, D.: Shilling attack detection-a new approach for a trustworthy recommender system. Informs J. Comput. **24**(1), 117–131 (2012)

23. Cao, J., Wu, Z., Mao, B., Zhang, Y.: Shilling attack detection utilizing semi-supervised learning method for collaborative recommender system. World Wide Web **16**(5–6), 729–748 (2013)

24. Zhang, F.G.: Preventing recommendation attack in trust-based recommender systems. J. Comput. Sci. Technol. **26**(5), 823–828 (2011)

25. Wang, H., Yang, W., Wang, S., Li, S.: A service recommendation method based on trustworthy community. J. Comput. **37**(2), 301–311 (2014)

26. Aggarwal, A., Almeida, J., Kumaraguru, P.: Detection of spam tipping behaviour on foursquare. In: Proceedings of the 22nd International Conference on World Wide Web Companion, pp. 641–648 (2013)

27. Limsaiprom, P., Tantatsanawong, P.: Social network anomaly and attack patterns analysis. In: Proceedings of the 6th International Conference on Networked Computing, pp. 1–6. IEEE (2010)

28. Ghosh, S., Viswanath, B., Kooti, F., et al.: Understanding and combating link farming in the Twitter social network. In: Proceedings of the 21st International Conference on World Wide Web, pp. 61–70. ACM (2012)

SAwD - Socially Aware Design: An Organizational Semiotics-Based CASE Tool to Support Early Design Activities

José Valderlei da Silva[1]([⊠]), Roberto Pereira[2],
Samuel Bastos Buchdid[1], Emanuel Felipe Duarte[1],
and Maria Cecília Calani Baranauskas[1]

[1] Institute of Computing, University of Campinas – UNICAMP,
Av. Albert Einstein, 1251, Cidade Universitária Zeferino Vaz, Campinas
SP 13083-852, Brazil
{vander.silva,buchdid,emanuel.duarte,
cecilia}@ic.unicamp.br
[2] Federal University of Paraná– UFPR - R. Cel. Francisco H. dos Santos, 100,
Centro Politécnico, Jardim das Américas, Curitiba, PR 81531-980, Brazil
rpereira@inf.ufpr.br

Abstract. Developing technology to attend to social demands is an increasing challenge for the Information and Communication Technology (ICT) area. Ubiquitous Computing, Wearable Computing, Social Software, and the Internet of Things are examples of how ICT has permeated personal and collective life. Technology affects people, even the ones who do not use it. Therefore, designing technology now requires higher social awareness and responsibility, as well as ethical commitment from all stakeholders. Naturally, such a process demands for artifacts and methods grounded on different theories and practices, capable of facilitating the understanding of the social world and its complexity, in an effective way. In this paper, we introduce a Socially Aware Design (SAwD) system which is a CASE tool designed to support early design activities when a problem is understood and a solution is proposed. This tool aids to articulate ideas from Organizational Semiotics and Participatory Design. We present the theoretical and methodological grounds of our work about the design rationale for SAwD and how it disseminates both the practice of a socially aware design and an adoption of theories.

Keywords: Socially Aware Computing · Organizational Semiotics · Participatory Design · Collaborative design tool

1 Introduction

In Software Engineering, Sommerville [20] and Chung et al. [8] draw attention to "early requirements" or "organizational requirements", arguing that knowing the problem and envisaging solutions before creating a technical solution tend to avoid large future expenditures regarding human, time and financial resources. If the problem context is not well understood, a "bad" or neglected requirement can trigger additional

M.C.C. Baranauskas et al. (Eds.): ICISO 2016, IFIP AICT 477, pp. 59–69, 2016.
DOI: 10.1007/978-3-319-42102-5_7

problems. These additional problems may raise maintenance costs, restrict or affect the technology necessary to solve the problem, affect the project's scope and lead to changes in other requirements. Changes in other requirements, for instance, may impact later on stages of the project, sometimes causing a product rejection by some stakeholders or even rendering unfeasible the whole project.

Traditional software development models (e.g., cascade, iterative and incremental) tend to focus problem understanding on the identification of functional and non-functional requirements [20]. This vision focuses on the solution of technical aspects and prevents a more comprehensive understanding of the problem being addressed, preventing those involved from having a wider sense-making of the problem and the proposed solution. A broader design view should include the point of view from different stakeholders, and pay attention to informal (e.g., culture, values, behavior patterns, preferences, etc.) and formal (e.g., laws, regulations, rules and policies) aspects related to these parties. However, IT professionals are rarely trained to deal with social, ethical and normative issues, and the mainstream methods, techniques and devices used do not favor the consideration of these aspects [4].

There is a relevant amount of works and initiatives that either recognizes the need for a sociotechnical approach for Information and Communication Technology (ICT) design, or that favors the focus and attention to non-technical issues, especially in the Human-Computer Interaction (HCI) field. However, there is still a demand for a design process that meets the needs of a diverse audience to make design socially responsible. One initiative is Baranauskas' Semio-Participatory model, which we refer here as a Socially Aware Computing approach to design [1, 5]. In such approach, Baranauskas articulates and extends ideas inspired by Organizational Semiotics (OS) [11] and Participatory Design (PD) [12], proposing a framework that considers a dialogue with design materials and, mainly, among individuals in their different roles (e.g., designer, developer, end-user, sponsor, other stakeholders) in order to conduct participatory work towards interactive system design. In Baranauskas' view, technical aspects of a system design depend on and affect the formal and informal aspects of organizations and society. As opposed to a technically centered perspective, the Socially Aware Computing support stakeholders in forming a wider sense-making of the problem and the proposed solution.

Baranauskas' approach has been applied in design contexts of high diversity in terms of users (e.g., skills, knowledge, age, gender, special needs, literacy, intentions, values, beliefs) and for creating different design products. For example: inclusive social networks [1], applications; physical devices [13]; interactive digital television [7, 14]; systems for supporting problem solving and decision making in a manufacturing organization [3]; and accessible technologies [18]. It has also been used as a theoretical and methodological ground for other design approaches and frameworks, such as [17]. However, although practical results have demonstrated the contributions of her approach for a social responsible design in both academic and industrial settings, there is a demand for tools that support it and allow inexperienced designers to treat informal and formal aspects in their projects in a guided and practical manner. Such tools may support the dissemination of the approach, its usage by other professionals in different design contexts, as well as the dissemination of its background theories, such as Organizational Semiotics and its artifacts.

In this paper, we draw on the Socially Aware Computing approach as a theoretical and methodological background for the creation of an online system that supports the approach itself. The CASE tool, named Socially Aware Design (SAwD), is developed by experts in the approach and IT developers. Its current version offers a subset of artifacts used, created or adapted by Baranauskas' research group in its different projects, and was experimented in a case study by members of the InterHAD[1] research group, from the Computing Institute of the State University of Campinas, to understand and organize the 17th International Conference on Informatics and Semiotics in Organizations (ICISO'16). The results suggest there were benefits of using an online and collaborative CASE tool to support Baranauskas' approach for organizing the ICISO'16 conference. The current version of the CASE tool is available for free use on the Web.

The paper is organized as follows: Sect. 2 introduces the SAwD approach and its background. Section 3 describes the methods and practices applied to design the SAwD system. Section 4 presents the case study, and Sect. 5 discusses some findings from the CASE tool design and the case study. Finally, Sect. 6 presents our final considerations and directions for future work.

2 Background Theories

Hall [9] introduces the notions of informal, formal, and technical levels in which humans operate and understand the world. The Organizational Semiotics (OS) theory proposes a structure nicknamed "Semiotic Onion" [21] to explain how these levels coexist in the context of organizations and information systems, explaining that any technical artifact is embedded in a formal system that, in turn, is embedded in an informal one. The informal system represents organizational culture, customs, and values that are reflected as beliefs, habits, and individual behavior patterns of its members. The formal corresponds to aspects that are well established and accepted, becoming social conventions, norms, or laws. Finally, the technical, situated at the core of the onion, represents aspects that are so formalized that they can be technically approached and supported. The Socially Aware Computing [2] understands the design process as a movement that begins at society, crossing the informal and formal layers of signs to result in a technical system considering relevant aspects of the informal and formal layers of knowledge of the social group. Baranauskas [4] argues that when a technical system is designed, it will impact on formal and informal layers alike, including the society and target audience.

The Socially Aware Computing approach makes use of other artifacts and methods created and inspired by OS to bring to participatory discussions a structured and systemic view of the problem. This view involves knowledge layers (informal, formal and technical) and their interdependence, brought to discussion in order to propose a solution for a complex social system in which people and their behavior patterns are organized. For instance, the Problem Articulation Methods (PAM) from OS [10]

---

[1] http://www.nied.unicamp.br/interhad.

provide practical artifacts (e.g., structures, guides, templates) that support the problem understanding from different perspectives. In Baranauskas' approach, the method attempts to bring out the complexity of the addressed problem and the solutions proposed among and for different stakeholders in a participatory way. Because problem clarification should be the first step in a project, the PAM can be used regardless of the design process, the technologies that will be used, and even the nature of the design.

The Stakeholders Identification Diagram (SID) and the Semiotic Framework (SF) are examples of PAM's artifacts. The SID [11] facilitates the identification of the ones direct or indirectly involved in a particular design process, allowing the identification of stakeholders according to five different categories (Operation, Contribution, Source, Market and Community) that represent different levels of involvement, interests, and expectations. The SF [21], in turn, favors the identification and organization of requirements according to six different levels that represent different aspects of signs. The first three levels can be related to technological issues (the physical, empirical, and syntactic), and the other three levels can be related to aspects of human information functions (semantic, pragmatic and social world).

Baranauskas and colleagues have also proposed and adapted other artifacts to support problem clarification and prospection of design solutions. For instance, the Evaluation Frame (EF) [1] is an artifact to favor anticipation and discussion of problems and solutions related to each stakeholder identified through the SID, contributing to the identification of requirements and issues that might impact the solution to be designed. Other examples are the Culturally Aware Requirements Framework, Value Identification Frame [15] and Value Pie [16]. The SAwD CASE tool is intended to support the use of such artifacts in a collaborative and practical way.

3   SAwD: A CASE Tool to Support the Socially Aware Computing

The SAwD[2] CASE tool is a result of a design process inspired by Baranauskas' Socially Aware Computing [1]. The activities were structured in three main steps: (i) understanding the problem domain to identify general requirements; (ii) proposing and developing the CASE tool; and (iii) technical evaluations and improvements.

Problem Understanding: Activities begun early 2010 with only three people (researchers), one of them an **expert** in Organizational Semiotics and Socially Aware Computing. Weekly meetings were held to discuss and brainstorm about the possibility of a set of tools to support the use of PAM artifacts. It was then decided to use PAM artifacts to understand PAM artifacts themselves, and how they could be useful as an online CASE tool that supports the process of problem understanding. The Stakeholder Identification Diagram, Evaluation Frame and Semiotic Framework were the 3 artifacts used to support this activity; they were available in a plug-in for the Sakai environment used in closed distance learning courses. The project was initially named WebPAM.

---

[2] www.nied.unicamp.br/dsc.

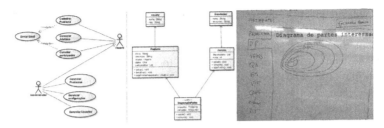

Fig. 1. UML diagrams and design proposals for the CASE tool.

Solution Proposal and Development: Iteratively, the team evolved the problem understanding, specifying and prototyping a solution to support the collaborative and open use of PAM artifacts on the Web as part of design projects. The Brain Drawing participatory technique was used to generate proposals for the tool user interface. After several iterations, a first formal specification of the CASE tool was developed, and four new members (undergraduate students) were added to the project to work in software engineering and development activities. Figure 1 illustrates the UML use case and class diagrams, as well as one prototype developed in 2012 to achieve a usable digital version of the artifacts.

Evaluation: The tool's first version, see Fig. 2, was evaluated by 24 Information Technology undergraduate students of the University Center of Maringá[3] in Brazil (UNICESUMAR). The evaluation was conducted using the System Usability Scale (SUS) [6]. The students discussed a hypothetical problem by means of the CASE tool, and then evaluated it by answering a SUS questionnaire.

Fig. 2. The CASE tool's first version named WebPAM.

Considering that the SUS questionnaire scale ranges from 0 (worst possible score) to 4 (best possible score) mapped for Usability Goals [19], the 2012 version of the CASE tool had a score between 2 and 3 for Effective (effective to use), Efficient (efficient to use), Utility (have good utility) and Learnable (easy to learn). Memorable (easy to remember how to use), in turn, had a score lower than 2. Even though the

---

[3] http://www.unicesumar.edu.br.

overall results are positive, the results indicated that the CASE tool could be improved in several aspects, including usability and accessibility ones.

Based on the results from the first evaluation and on the artifacts used to clarify the problem, the team started improvement tasks focusing both usability and technical improvements. From a back-end perspective, the nature of the data processed (mostly unstructured data, such as texts and images) led to the adoption of the non-relational (noSQL) database MongoDB[4]. Also from a back-end perspective, the need for efficiency when dealing with a relatively large number of concurrent connections led to the adoption of the Node.js[5] runtime, due to its event-driven, non-blocking I/O model. To improve the usability, it was decided to adopt the well-established and documented Material Design language from Google[6]. Therefore, from a front-end perspective, it was decided to adopt Angular Material[7], which is a reference implementation of Google's Material Design Specification for the Angular.js[8] framework, and that provides reusable, well tested and accessible UI components. Finally, to improve the data communication between back-end and front-end, it was decided to adopt the Socket.io[9] library, which allows real-time bidirectional event-based communication, making possible for users to collaborate remotely in real time during the use of OS artifacts. Figure 3 shows an abstraction for the SAwD Software Architecture: the front-end (chat, people, description, artifacts) are linked to the back-end (messages, artifacts data sharing) and communication between back-end and database.

The results from the problem clarification and the tool evaluation led to a change in the project's purpose. From a web tool that would support the open use of PAM's artifacts it was transformed in a tool for supporting problem understanding from a systemic and socially responsible perspective, i.e., Baranauskas' view for design, in an open and collaborative way, regardless the nature of the problem and solution to be designed. The CASE tool was, then, renamed to Socially Aware Design (SAwD). During the following years, technologies were experienced and the first version of the

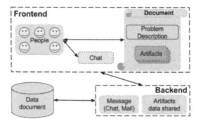

Fig. 3. System components for SAwD tools.

---

[4] https://www.mongodb.org/.

[5] https://nodejs.org/.

[6] https://www.google.com/design/spec/material-design/.

[7] https://material.angularjs.org/.

[8] https://angularjs.org/.

[9] http://socket.io/.

SAwD CASE tool was developed. In August 2015, the CASE tool first version was made available online and is being experienced by the InterHAD research group since then.

4   Tool Experimentation

The International Conference on Informatics and Semiotics in Organisations (ICISO), promoted by the International Federation for Information Processing (IFIP), is held annually to discuss new research outcomes, applications, challenges and trends in OS. The first edition was held in 1995 in Twente, The Netherlands, and since then it has taken place in different countries (e.g., Brazil, Canada, China, France, United Kingdom). Over the years, the conferences covered research themes such as people and information systems; web of things; information and knowledge management in complex systems, and socially aware organisations and technologies: impact and challenges. In 2016, ICISO will be held for second time in Campinas, Brazil.

This activity involved a group of 10 people with experience in using OS artifacts and in organizing conferences. Because the participants were experienced in both OS and the problem domain, this was considered an ideal scenario to evaluate the current version of the CASE tool in terms of possible conceptual problems, technical issues and overall usability. This scenario also highlights how the CASE tool can be used for a wide range of problem understanding contexts, not only the development of a technological product. Figure 4 illustrates the beginning of the planning activities, in which the group uses the SID to list and map every stakeholder that is involved and may somehow affect/be affected by the conference. Participants identified and mapped stakeholders from different layers, for instance, while technical stakeholders (e.g., EasyChair) are placed in the onion's core, social ones (e.g., Audience) are placed in the outermost layer of the onion.

Following, the participants used the EF to discuss how the conference might influence/affect or be influenced/affected by the different stakeholders identified

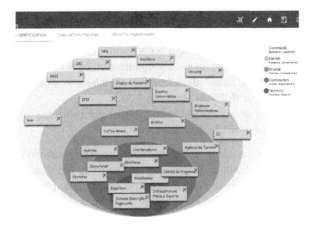

Fig. 4. SID for ICISO'16

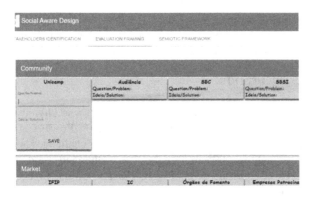

Fig. 5. Evaluation frame for ICISO'16

through the SID. Figure 5 illustrates the design choice for the digital version of the EF artifact developed for the CASE tool. Every stakeholder identified in the SID is automatically displayed in the EF to assure they will not be forgot when switching between the artifacts. In the EF, the participants discussed every stakeholder identified previously in the SID, raising possible problems regarding them, and then discussing ideas and solutions for these problems.

5 Discussion

The SAwD CASE tool goes beyond a set of digital version of OS-based artifacts, being a solution for bringing social awareness to development processes. The CASE tool favors joint problem understanding and provides a practical way for a group of people to perceive and discuss how problems and design solutions may affect society. The following points reinforce how the CASE tool supports social awareness in design:

1. It is a project-oriented tool that allows the collaborative, free and open participation;
2. It is based on the PAM, providing a solid base for problem understanding;
3. Allows the inclusion of new artifacts, which, if needed, can share or access data with or from other used artifacts;
4. It has an internal communication tool (chat) with messages persistence, allowing both synchronous and asynchronous communication between project members;
5. Real time data synchronization allows project members to work collaboratively in real time in the same or different artifacts;
6. It allows the creation of a consolidated report of the project, providing a holistic view of the project in a single document.

The online CASE tool enables new possibilities to reach stakeholders and involve them in the process of problem understanding and solution proposal. Because the tool allows people to remotely join the discussion and collaborate, physical distance is no longer an issue when it comes to stakeholders being included in the process. In this sense, a broader stakeholder engagement contributes to a more comprehensive and socially aware design process.

In the CASE tool current version, the included artifacts allow the discussion of relevant questions related to culture and human values during problem understanding. These artifacts were evaluated through practical research projects and learning activities, and the real case study about the ICISO'16 organization, providing positive results regarding a socially aware design. Additionally, the use of the CASE tool can also increase awareness about the importance of the socially aware design approach, especially among designers, developers and researchers without experience with OS. Because some of the artifacts were used to clarify the design problem for the SAwD, it was also possible to see technical issues (e.g., the used database system and interface framework) and abstract requirements (e.g., collaboration, flexibility) that were identified since the early stages of design, and that could have been neglected/ forgotten if stakeholders, their problems, ideas and needs have not been considered in an explicit way.

Finally, the use of the CASE tool allowed an understanding about how this new set of tools would affect its stakeholders and society, with focus on how each stakeholder can benefit from this tool.

6 Conclusion

Technology influences people's daily activities, which, in turn, are formally defined. Thus, the design of a solution goes through informal, formal and technical layers of signs. By using artifacts from OS it is possible to understand and discuss the social impacts of a proposed solution; therefore, the development team may be able to make informed decisions regarding stakeholders' culture and values. There was a need for tools to support this process of problem understanding and ideally, these tools should be available to every stakeholder, so that they could contribute to the understanding of the problem and be part of the development of a solution that affects positively everyone involved.

The SAwD implements some PAM artifacts and allows a collective work for discussion and understanding of the problem, leading the group to build a solution that makes sense to all the involved ones. The Tool is available online, favoring participatory work, enabling designers to propose creative solutions and promoting a decision-making space with stakeholders. The tool is in its first increment with six artifacts, and some minor programming and usability problems have been reported during the case study. These problems are addressed and the tool is being gradually improved. For future work, new artifacts will be incorporated into the tool to support the SAwD approach, such as Pereira's [16] Value Pie. These artifacts are relevant in the process of socially aware design and will be part of the SAwD CASE tool in a new deliverable.

Finally, the tool is experienced in Computer Science graduate and undergraduate disciplines, such as Software Engineering and HCI (Human Computer Interaction), at University of Campinas, Federal University of Technology – Paraná (UTFR) and Federal University of Paraná UFPR in 2016 first semester. Its usage will contribute to both the evaluation of the tool itself, and the dissemination of the OS artifacts and the Socially Aware Computing approach to design.

Acknowledgments. We thank the Brazilian Research Foundations CNPq (Grant #308618/2014-9) and CAPES and States Secretary of Education of Parana (SEED). The authors thank the SAwD design and case study participants for their collaboration. The opinions expressed in this work do not necessarily reflect those of the funding agencies.

References

1. Baranauskas, M.C.C., Schimiguel, J., Simoni, C.A.C., Medeiros, C.M.B.: Guiding the process of requirements elicitation with a semiotic approach. In: The 11th International Conference on Human-Computer Interaction, pp. 100–111. Lawrence Erlbaum (2005)
2. Baranauskas, M.C.C., de Almeida Neris, V.P.: Using patterns to support the design of flexible user interaction. In: Jacko, J.A. (ed.) HCI 2007. LNCS, vol. 4550, pp. 1033–1042. Springer, Heidelberg (2007)
3. Baranauskas, M.C.C., Bonacin, R.: Design – indicating through signs. Des. Issues **24**, 30–45 (2008). MIT Press
4. Baranauskas, M.C.C.: Socially aware computing. In: Proceedings of VI International Conference on Engineering and Computer Education, pp. 1–5 (2009)
5. Baranauskas, M.C.C.: Social awareness in HCI. Interactions **21**(4), 66–69 (2014)
6. Brooke, J.: SUS: a 'quick and dirty' usability scale. In: Jordan, P.W., Thomas, B., Weerdmeester, B.A., McClelland, I.L. (eds.) Usability Evaluation in Industry, pp. 189–194. Taylor and Francis, London (1997)
7. Buchdid, S.B., Pereira, R., Baranauskas, M.C.C.: Designing an IDTV application in a situated scenario: a participatory approach based on patterns. In: Cordeiro, J., Hammoudi, S., Maciaszek, L., Camp, O., Filipe, J. (eds.) ICEIS 2014. LNBIP, vol. 227, pp. 341–360. Springer, Heidelberg (2015). doi:10.1007/978-3-319-22348-3
8. Chung, L.K., Nixon, B.A., Yu, E., Mylopoulos, J.: Non-functional Requirements in Software Engineering. Kluwer Publishing, Dordrecht (2000)
9. Hall, E.T.: The Silent Language. Anchoor Books, New York (1959)
10. Kolkman, M.: Problem articulation methodology. Ph.D. thesis, University of Twente, Enschede (1993)
11. Liu, K.: Semiotics in Information Systems Engineering. Cambridge University Press, Cambridge (2000)
12. Schuler, D., Namioka, A.: Participatory Design: Principles and Practices. Lawrence Erlbaum Associates, Hillsdale (1993)
13. Miranda, L.C., Hornung, H., Baranauskas, M.C.C.: Adjustable interactive rings for iDTV. IEEE Trans. Consum. Electron. **56**, 1988–1996 (2010)
14. Piccolo, L.S.G., Melo, A.M., Baranauskas, M.C.C.: Accessibility and interactive TV: design recommendations for the Brazilian scenario. In: Baranauskas, C., Abascal, J., Barbosa, S.D. J. (eds.) INTERACT 2007. LNCS, vol. 4662, pp. 361–374. Springer, Heidelberg (2007)
15. Pereira, R., Buchdid, S.B., Baranauskas, M.C.C.: Keeping values in mind-artifacts for a value-oriented and culturally informed design. In: Proceedings of the 14th International Conference on Enterprise Information Systems (ICEIS), pp. 25–34 (2012)
16. Pereira, R., Baranauskas, M.C.C.: Value pie: a culturally informed conceptual scheme for understanding values in design. In: Kurosu, M. (ed.) HCI 2014, Part I. LNCS, vol. 8510, pp. 122–133. Springer, Heidelberg (2014)
17. Pereira, R., Baranauskas, M.C.C.: A value-oriented and culturally informed approach to the design of interactive systems. Int. J. Hum. Comput. Stud. **80**, 66–82 (2015)

18. Santana, V.F., Almeida, L.D.A., Baranauskas, M.C.C.: Aprendendo sobre Acessibilidade e Construção de Websites para Todos. Revista Brasileira de Informática na Educação **16**, 71–83 (2008)
19. Sharp, H., Rogers, Y., Preece, J.J.: Interaction Design: Beyond Human-Computer Interaction, 3rd edn. Wiley, London (2010)
20. Sommerville, I.: Software Engineering, 9th edn. Pearson, London (2012)
21. Stamper, R.: Information in Business and Administrative Systems. Wiley Inc., New York (1973)
22. Stamper, R., Liu, K., Hafkamp, M., Ades, Y.: Understanding the role of signs and norms in organisations – a semiotic approach to information systems design. J. Behav. Inf. Technol. **19**(1), 15–27 (2000)

Digital Business Ecosystems

Service Innovation in Business Ecosystem: The Role of Enablers and Formation Cycle

Buddhi Pathak[(⊠)]

Business Informatics, Systems and Accounting, Henley Business School,
University of Reading, Reading RG6 6UD, UK
b.n.pathak@pgr.reading.ac.uk

Abstract. Service innovation in business ecosystem is attracting more research interest; however, there is less insight into how the formation of ecosystem enables service innovation. The limited prior research on the formation of an ecosystem is characterized by different phases and activities associated with lifecycle of an ecosystem, however it is not connected to the service innovation processes. This work addresses this gap by proposing formation cycle of an ecosystem for service innovation.

Keywords: Service innovation · Business ecosystem · S-D logic

1 Introduction

Service innovation in business ecosystem (SIBE) refers to the process of innovating services through combining ecosystem partners (business partner, customer and other stakeholder) and their resources (e.g., knowledge and capabilities) that not only collaborate relationship amongst ecosystem but also appropriately configures value proposition for ecosystem partners.

Various studies in service innovation (SI) and ecosystem research stress the role of resources for successful innovation [1–3]. These studies show that resources are key element of successful ecosystem. Integration of resources is seen as key component of service innovation [4]. Regardless of acknowledgement of the significance of resource in the formation of ecosystem for service innovation, existing research has little to say about how firms can essentially develop ecosystem with regards to service innovation.

Therefore, research opportunity arises since little knowledge is known about formation of business ecosystem for service innovation [5], their resources configuration, actor interaction, network facilitation and its management [2, 6]. To address this research gap, this work aims to examine how firms can use resources in the formation of business ecosystem and linked that with service innovation. More precisely the paper;

- identifies the service innovation enablers; factors that support service innovation in ecosystem
- suggests the formation cycle of ecosystem consisting the role of resources that is used for crating ecosystem for service innovation purpose

© IFIP International Federation for Information Processing 2016
Published by Springer International Publishing Switzerland 2016. All Rights Reserved
M.C.C. Baranauskas et al. (Eds.): ICISO 2016, IFIP AICT 477, pp. 73–78, 2016.
DOI: 10.1007/978-3-319-42102-5_8

This aim is achieved by drawing on an extensive literature on service innovation, ecosystem and resources from mainly resource based view (RBV) and Service-dominant logic (SDL) and Service Science theoretical lenses. The first Section presents literature on service innovation in business ecosystem. Service innovation enablers in ecosystem are identified in Sect. 3. Having suggested ecosystem formation cycle, the final Section presents further research agenda on the topic.

2 Service Innovation in Business Ecosystem

The service industry makes more than three quarters of major economies of the world and is seen as a key for growth and competitiveness [7, 8]. The functions and significance of SI is defined as "it introduces something new into the way of life, organization, timing and placement of what can generally be described as the individual and collective processes that relate to consumers" [9]. Additionally, specifying the types of SI, IFM and IBM [10] defines service innovation as the combination of technology innovation, business model innovation, socio-organizational innovation, and demand innovation to improve existing or create new service value propositions (offerings or experiences) and service systems.

Service Science and SDL define innovation differently than traditional approach of manufacturing. It considers the role of customer as co-creator of value, where they use resources to co-create value [11]. It also defines innovation as a continuous and interactive process that involves the interaction among groups of actors who are interrelated in a dense network [4]. Therefore, service perspective conceptualizes innovation as a process of joint value creation with customer and other partners based on a wide integrated network approach [12].

As these definitions propose the previously ignored field e.g., network approach [12] or service systems [10] to maximize the value of innovation, it imagines the concept of ecosystem, where the value is co-created with its partners. This idea of business ecosystem was initially proposed by Moore [13], which is defined as "an economic community supported by a foundation of interacting organizations and individuals - the organisms of the business world" [13]. According to European Commission (EC), *business ecosystem* is the network of buyers, suppliers and makers of related products or services as well as the socio-economic environment [14].

This concept of SIBE denotes the process of innovating services e.g., types [10] through combining ecosystem partners. This concept of business ecosystem has been used widely. For example, European Commission (EC) has promoted the concept of ecosystem and service innovation under Euro 2020 to boost growth and jobs [15].

The concept of ecosystem flourishes from establishing relationships between business networks to the level of co-creation of value with business partners and their customers. In this process of co-creation of value in business ecosystem various factors play key role, which are termed as enablers. The following section discusses SIBE enablers.

3 Identification of Service Innovation Enablers in Ecosystem

The study of Tax and Stuart [16], Fyrberg and Juriado [17], and Vargo et al. [18] supports the active involvement of actor in service innovation. Similarly, RBV approach to service innovation [1, 2, 19] supports the view that service innovation process requires bundle of resources. The study of Vargo and Lusch, [19], Vargo et al. [11] argue that value proposition or benefit that any innovation brings must be considered for any tie ups. Similarly, work of Edvardsson and Tronvoll [6] demonstrates the significance of schemas in service innovation process. Thus, it is proposed that SIBE is enabled and simplified by four fundamental factors as;

- Resource capabilities: this includes all the operant i.e., skills and knowledge and operand i.e., physical resources [11] required for service innovation
- Actor involvement: this involve actor willingness, relationship, trust amongst innovation actors, their leadership skills and vision
- Changes in schemas: these are norms and rules that guide the actor and institutionalised forces that supports innovation [6]
- Value proposition: this includes for example, benefits that new offerings bring, equal distribution of value amongst service provider and customer

Capabilities are competence of resources mobilization and resources are as taken from the S-D logic both operant and operand resources that are required for service innovation [11, 19]. Actors are considered as resource integrators [19] who guide service innovation process. Changes in schemas such as to challenge status quo, norms and rules e.g., from inward R&D focus to open innovation orientation also enable service innovation [6]. Appropriate distribution of value amongst actors, and the benefits that new innovation brings to the ecosystem is defined as value propositions, which play key role to enable service innovation [11, 19].

These enabling factors bring S-D logic to the center of service innovation concept as it introduces service-dominant thinking [18, 19] to elaborate these factors e.g., operant resources i.e., application of skills and knowledge of actors to propose value. Proposed model also highlights the significance of social norms for service innovation, which was previously ignored [6].

These four factors set the foundation for firm to instigate their ecosystem. Ecosystem formation cycle is presented in the following section.

4 Towards Ecosystem Formation Cycle for Service Innovation

Moore [13], Thomas and Autio [5] presented various phases of ecosystem emergence. Service science and S-D logic have extended the boundary of firm for value creation. The significance of ecosystem is that no single firm could have created alone [20]. Based on the earlier discussion, as well as considering the theory of RBV and S-D logic this work offers six phases of ecosystem formation for service innovation. Figure 1 provides the six different steps that are required for the firm to initiate service innovation activities within their ecosystem.

Fig. 1. Formation cycle of an ecosystem for service innovation

The formation of ecosystem for the purpose of service innovation starts right from the instigation of ecosystem [13] by identifying purpose of new initiative, partner, supplier, market, customer or other stakeholder who may be interested in the development of new service [5]. Ecosystem instigator needs to clarify the purpose of ecosystem that they want to build. The first step may involve the ecosystem activities identified by Thomas and Autio [5].

Having identified purpose, partners and market for the new development, the next step requires assessing and identifying resources which are needed for the new development. The work of Rusanen et al. [2] provides guidelines for identifying resource need for the new service offerings.

As value is created through integration of resources that is brought forwards by actors [21], it is essential for firms to establish system/procedure that simplifies resources integration between different stakeholders. However, this step is challenging as there is less academic insight as well as danger of disrupting existing service system of a firm. It also involves cost, time and effort [16].

Choosing types of resources is also reliant on types of service innovation [10]. Type of service innovation can be divided into several dimensions such as business model innovation and process innovation [10]. Choosing one dimension over other options vary in terms of available resources and objective of ecosystem formation. Business model innovation, for example, may need more customer operant resources in comparison to organization's internal process innovation. Similarly, nature of business also affects this choice, e.g., a mining company may need more operand resource in comparison to a consulting firm. Thus, choosing resource is dependent on the nature of business and types of SI.

Similarly, resources implementation stage brings various challenge, e.g., firm needs to carefully design processes that fulfil the resources for new development. Only the right resource implementation strategy brings assurance of finishing the new development at the right time. Therefore, proper planning is required, which involves various managerial works. Last but not least, the overall process may end up producing something unique that can be achieved as a result e.g., product or services. Customer can experience the service, or they may use product. How they experience the service/use product, their feedback is valuable to improve the overall function of ecosystem. It can be improved based on market feedback, and it is continuous process, thus, it is called formation cycle.

From the ecosystem instigation to the resource implementation phase, the success of process is more dependent on the initiator of the service innovation project, as initiator is the one who wants to create new space or modified service system. The rest of the phases of formation cycle rely on the customer as they are the ones who can define new space for new offerings.

5 Conclusion and Future Research

This work has drawn literature on service innovation in ecosystem. It has identified service innovation enablers as well as proposed ecosystem formation cycle. By proposing such enablers and cycle, we have responded the call of Thomas and Autio [5] among others [2, 6] The work contributed to the Service Science and SDL literature by identifying service innovation enablers and ecosystem formation cycle. The paper also attempts to discuss the concept of ecosystem from the perspectives of Service Science and SDL. In our knowledge the concept of SDL is not applied to the ecosystem literature, and previous researches have ignored the application of SDL in ecosystem [5, 13]. This study reveals that there are many factors that enable service innovation in ecosystems and firm has to go through various stages of ecosystem formation cycle. Initiating firm's own business ecosystem needs wider attention from the management so as to better manage enabling factors and formation cycle. Proposed model could serve as a basis for studying ecosystem formation cycle.

There are various limitations of this work; the overall work needs to be empirically validated as it only offers conceptual progressions requiring practical application of the model to validate the ecosystem formation cycle. Similarly, there are various challenges associated with every step of ecosystem formation. How an ecosystem initiator overcomes these challenges that makes a difference in the success of an overall project. Therefore, resources integration as well as their implementation for the new development remain research opportunity.

References

1. Mention, A.L.: Co-operation and co-opetition as open innovation practices in the service sector: which influence on innovation novelty? Technovation **31**(1), 44–53 (2011)
2. Rusanen, H., Halinen, A., Jaakkola, E.: Accessing resources for service innovation-the critical role of network relationships. J. Serv. Manag. **25**(1), 2–29 (2013)
3. Akaka, M.A., Vargo, S.L., Lusch, R.F.: An exploration of networks in value co-creation: a service-ecosystems view. Rev. Mark. Res. **9**, 13–50 (2012)
4. Gummesson, E., Mele, C.: Marketing as value co-creation through network interaction and resource integration. J. Bus. Mark. Manag. **4**, 181–198 (2010)
5. Thomas, L., Autio, E.: Emergent equifinality: an empirical analysis of ecosystem creation processes. In: Proceedings of the 35th DRUID Celebration Conference, Barcelona, Spain (2013)
6. Edvardsson, B., Tronvoll, B.: A new conceptualisation of service innovation grounded in S-D logic and service systems. Int. J. Qual. Serv. Sci. **5**(1), 19–31 (2013)

7. OECD: Growth in Services – Fostering Employment, Productivity and Innovation. Meeting of the OECD Council at Ministerial Level, Paris, France (2005)
8. Ostrom, A.L., Bitner, M.J., Brown, S.W., Burkhard, K.A., Goul, M., Smith-Daniels, V., Demirkan, H., Rabinovich, E.: Moving forward and making a difference: research priorities for the science of service. J. Serv. Res. **13**(1), 4–36 (2010)
9. Barcet, A.: Innovation in services: a new paradigm and innovation model. In: Gallouj, F., Djellal, F. (eds.) The Handbook of Innovation and Services: A Multidisciplinary Perspective, pp. 49–67. Edward Elgar, Cheltenham (2010)
10. IFM and IBM, Succeeding Through Service Innovation: A Service Perspective for Education, Research, Business and Government. University of Cambridge Institute for Manufacturing (2008). www.ifm.eng.cam.ac.uk/ssme/documents/080428ssi_us_letter.pdf. Accessed 10 Feb 2014
11. Vargo, S.L., Lusch, R.F., Akaka, M.A.: Advancing service science with service-dominant logic; clarifications and conceptual development. In: Maglio, P.P., et al. (eds.) Handbook of Service Science: Research and Innovation in the Service Economy, pp. 133–156. Springer, New York (2010)
12. Russo-Spena, T., Mele, C.: "Five Co-s" in innovating: a practice-based view. J. Serv. Manag. **23**(4), 527–553 (2012)
13. Moore, J.F.: The Death of Competition: Leadership & Strategy in the Age of Business Ecosystems. Harper Business, New York (1996)
14. European Commission: Digital Ecosystems. http://www.digital-ecosystems.org/. Accessed 15 June 2014
15. European Commission: Europe 2020 (2012). http://ec.europa.eu/europe2020/europe-2020-in-a-nutshell/flagship-initiatives/index_en.htm. Accessed 10 July 2014
16. Tax, S.S., Stuart, I.: Designing and implementing new services: the challenges of integrating service systems. J. Retail. **73**, 105–134 (1997)
17. Fyrberg, A., Juriado, R.: What about interaction? Networks and brands as integrators within service-dominant logic. J. Serv. Manag. **20**(3–4), 420–432 (2009)
18. Vargo, S.L., Maglio, P.P., Akaka, M.A.: On value and value co-creation: a service system and service logic perspective. Eur. Manag. J. **26**(3), 145–152 (2008)
19. Vargo, S.L., Lusch, R.F.: From goods to service(s): divergences and convergences of logics. Ind. Mark. Manage. **37**(3), 254–259 (2008)
20. Adner, R.: Match your innovation strategy to your innovation ecosystem. Harvard Business Review (2006). https://hbr.org/2006/04/match-your-innovation-strategy-to-your-innovation-ecosystem/ar/1. Accessed 16 June 2014
21. Vargo, S.L., Lusch, R.F., Morgan, F.W.: Historical perspectives on service-dominant logic. In: Lusch, R.F., Vargo, S.L. (eds.) The Service Dominant Logic of Marketing: Dialog, Debate and Directions, pp. 29–42. M.E. Sharpe, Armonk (2006)

Evolution of Norms in the Emergence of Digital Business Ecosystems

Prince Kwame Senyo[1,2(✉)], Kecheng Liu[2,4], Lily Sun[3],
and John Effah[1]

[1] Department of Operations and Management Information Systems,
University of Ghana, Accra, Ghana
{pksenyo, jeffah}@ug.edu.gh
[2] Henley Business School, Informatics Research Centre,
University of Reading, Reading, UK
k.liu@henley.ac.uk
[3] School of Systems Engineering, University of Reading, Reading, UK
lily.sun@reading.ac.uk
[4] School of Information Management and Engineering,
Shanghai University of Finance and Economics, Shanghai, China

Abstract. As digital business ecosystems emerge from traditional business ecosystems, norms evolve or remain. However, less is known about evolution of norms in relation to digital business ecosystems. Norms are rules that govern behaviour; as such they drive activities in business ecosystems. Therefore, this paper uses Ghana's import-export ecosystem to trace the evolution of norms when traditional business ecosystems transition to digital business ecosystem in order to understand which norms change or remain and the reasons that account for the changes.

Keywords: Digital business ecosystem · Business Ecosystem · Norms · Organisational semiotics · Import-export ecosystem

1 Introduction

Business Ecosystem (BE) is a network of interdependent organisations with shared goals to co-create [1] value. BE can be traditional or digital. While interactions in traditional BEs (TBEs) rely on direct business to business communication, that of digital business ecosystems (DBEs) is based on an integrated dynamic organisational network supported by the Internet [2]. As DBEs emerge from TBEs, norms may evolve or remain. Norms are rules or standards that guide activities [3]. Hence, their evolution when TBEs transition to DBEs is an important phenomenon for information systems and organisational research.

Even though BE have witnessed some studies (e.g., [2, 4–6]) in information systems research, less attention has been paid to evolution of norms. Therefore, this study contributes to BE research by investigating how norms evolve when DBEs emerge

© IFIP International Federation for Information Processing 2016
Published by Springer International Publishing Switzerland 2016. All Rights Reserved
M.C.C. Baranauskas et al. (Eds.): ICISO 2016, IFIP AICT 477, pp. 79–84, 2016.
DOI: 10.1007/978-3-319-42102-5_9

from TBEs. The rest of this paper is organised as follows. Section 2 discusses related works on TBE and DBE. Section 3 presents organisational semiotics models, namely organisational onion and morphology as theoretical lenses for this study. Section 4 presents a case study of Ghana's import-export ecosystem to demonstrate emergence of a DBE from a TBE and how norms evolve or remain after the transition. Section 5 concludes the paper and presents directions for future research.

2   Related Works

2.1   Traditional Business Ecosystem

The traditional use of the term BE [7] describes interdependency among organisations in a network. BE is analogous to biological ecosystem [1]. However, one feature that distinguishes BE from its biological counterpart is the shared goal of value co-creation, which is beyond the scope and capabilities of individual partners. As a network of organisations, TBEs need to be guided by norms that regulate the behaviour of partners. The interactions among partners in TBEs are mostly direct organisation to organisation communication without centrality of the Internet [8]. However, with the emergence of the Internet, some TBEs have evolved into DBEs [2].

2.2   Digital Business Ecosystem

DBE is an organisational network that enables digital collaboration [2]. However, the main distinguishing feature of DBE from TBE is the centrality of digital network infrastructure in the interaction of its partners. Following the transition of some TBEs to DBEs, much focus of related research has been on architecture redesign [2, 8], new areas of practical application [4] and regulatory issues [9]. For example, Razavi et al. [8] investigate the evolution of TBEs to DBEs and focused on how static TBE hubs are converted to dynamic DBE hubs. However, evolution of norms in the emergence of DBE from TBE is yet to receive the necessary attention in information systems and organisational research. This study therefore focuses on evolution of norms when DBEs emerge from TBEs.

3   Organisational Semiotics

Organisational semiotics is a branch of semiotics that studies organisations as information systems made up of collection of signs. A sign itself is anything that stands for something to someone [3, 10]. Creation and use of signs are subject to norms as rules or standards that shape organisational activities. This study draws on two organisational semiotics models; the organisational onion and the organisational morphology, to analyse the evolution of norms when TBEs transition to DBEs.

3.1 Organisational Onion

The organisational onion categorises norms into informal, formal and technical [10] as shown in Fig. 1. Informal norms represent unstructured and undocumented rules or standards. On the other hand, formal norms are documented bureaucratic rule or standards. Technical norms represent formal norms that have been digitized [3]. Both the informal and formal norms are carried out in the physical domain while technical norms are carried out within the digital domain [11]. This study draws on the organisational onion to analyse evolution of informal, formal and technical norms as TBEs transition to DBEs.

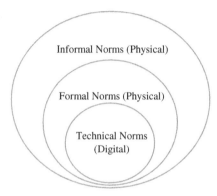

Fig. 1. Organisational onion [11]

3.2 Organisational Morphology

Organisational morphology (Fig. 2) classifies behavioural norms into substantive, communication and control norms [3]. First, substantive norms define core activities of organisations. Second, communication norms concern exchange of information among organisational actors. Third, control norms monitor and regulate substantive as well as communication norms. This study draws on the organisational morphology to analyse norm evolution from physical to digital domains in terms of substantive, communication and control norms.

Fig. 2. Organisational morphology [3]

4   Evolution of Ghana's Import-Export Digital Ecosystem

This section presents the case of the transition of Ghana's import-export ecosystem to DBE. Given the complexity of the whole import-export system, the current focus of this paper is on the import ecosystem, which is used to illustrate norm evolution from TBE to DBE.

4.1   The Import Traditional Business Ecosystem

Until 2000, the import ecosystem was traditional. The members included importers, shipping lines, Customs, banks, logistics companies, Ministry of Trade and Industry (MOTI), Destination Inspection Companies (DICs) and the Ghana Port and Harbour Authority. The norms that guided activities in the TBE were physical. Table 1 shows the behavioural norms and their types.

Table 1. Norms under the import traditional business ecosystem

Norm #	Norm definition	Norm type
T1	An importer was required to purchase import declaration form (IDF) from MOTI	Substantive
T2	An importer was required to submit completed IDF to a DIC for valuation	Communication
T3	A DIC was required to send Final Classification and Valuation Report (FCVR) to the importer	Communication
T4	An importer was required to purchase Customs import declaration form	Substantive
T5	An importer was required to complete and submit Customs import declaration form and FCVR, shipping manifest as well as bill of lading to Customs	Communication
T6	Customs was required to review, verify and validate documents submitted by an importer	Control
T7	Customs was required to send review and verification report to the importer	Communication
T8	An import was required to pay import duties at the bank	Substantive
T9	The bank was required to notify Customs of payment	Communication
T10	A Customs official was required to physically examine consignment	Control
T11	Consignment was required to be released after physical examination	Substantive

4.2   The Import Digital Business Ecosystem

In 2000, the import ecosystem transitioned from TBE to DBE. As a result, an electronic integrated digital platform was deployed. Table 2 shows the behavioural norms, types and domain under the emerged DBE.

Table 2. Norms under the import digital business ecosystem

Norm #	Norm definition	Norm type	Domain
D1	An importer is required to purchase IDF from MOTI	Substantive	Physical
D2	An importer is required to submit the IDF to a DIC	Communication	Physical
D3	A DIC is required to send FCVR to the importer	Communication	Physical
D4	An importer must complete Customs import declaration form on the digital platform	Communication	Digital
D5	An importer must submit FCVR, shipping manifest and bill of lading to Customs through the digital platform	Communication	Digital
D6	Customs must review, verification and validation documents submitted by importer	Control	Digital
D7	Customs must send review and verification report to importer through the digital platform	Communication	Digital
D8	An import must pay import duties at the bank	Substantive	Physical
D9	The bank must notify Customs through the digital platform	Communication	Digital
D10	Customs officials must physically examine consignment	Control	Physical
D11	Consignment must be released electronically after examination	Control	Digital

4.3 Evolution of Norms from TBE to DBE

To address the research purpose, this section presents the evolution of norms when a DBE emerge from a TBE. Norms T1, T2, and T3 in Table 1 on physical purchase, submission and notification of import valuation under the TBE continued as D1, D2, and D3 in Table 2 under the emerged DBE. The reason for the continuance is that the law that required submission of physical forms has not yet been revised to enable submission of electronic documents. Norms T8 and D8 on payment of import duties in Tables 1 and 2 respectively also did not evolve. The reason for their continuance is the unavailability of a national electronic payment system in Ghana. Under both the TBE and the emerged DBE, norms T10 and D10 in Tables 1 and 2 respectively on physical examination of consignment also did not evolve. The reason for their continuance is to check the deliberate act of importers to under-declare value of goods in order to pay less import duties.

However, norms T4 and T5 in Table 1 on physical purchase and submission of Customs import declaration forms under the TBE evolved into D4 and D5 in Table 2 where importers were now required to log into the digital platform, complete and submit Customs import declaration forms as well as other supporting documents. In the same vein, norms T6 and T7 in Table 1 on physical review and verification of import documents under the TBE as well as sending review report to the importer also evolved into D6 and D7 in Table 2 respectively where these norms are now carried out on the digital platform. As such, Customs officials use the digital platform to electronically review, verify and validate import related documents and also send review reports to the importers digitally. Norm T9 in Table 1 on physical notification of Customs of duty payments under the TBE evolved to D9 in Table 2 under the emerged DBE. As such, banks were now required to send digital payment notifications to Customs. Under the TBE, norm T11 in Table 1 on physical release of consignment evolved into norm D11 in Table 2 under the emerged DBE where after physical examination, the consignment is released digitally to end the import process.

Comparing the evolving of the behavioural norms following the emergence of the DBE from the TBE, it was evident that most communication norms have easily evolved from informal and formal to technical norms. On the other hand, substantive and control norms required more restructuring such as change in legislation as well as development of national information and communication technology infrastructure to enable transition from the physical to the digital domain.

5 Conclusion and Future Works

The aim of the study was to analyse which norms evolved and which ones remained as well as the reasons for the changes. This study points out that as TBEs evolve to DBEs so will their norms. This study reemphasizes that all norm types may evolve during the transition. However, communication norms are the easiest to digitize during the transition from TBE to DBE. This study also acknowledges the importance of a nation electronic payment systems and technology infrastructure as well as appropriate legislation in developing country context to facilitate the transition of norms. These knowledge facilitate better understanding and reconfiguration of norms when DBEs emerge from TBEs. Again, this knowledge provides practitioners with understanding of norms that can or cannot be migrated to digital domains and the factors that can constrain the transition to DBE. However, one key consequence of the evolving of norms from TBE to DBE is the issue of availability of the digital platform. Future research call is made to consider the conceptualization and actuality of norms in DBEs. We also call for further studies from the developed world perspective and other digital ecosystems to understand how contextual factors shape norm evolution in TBE to DBE transition.

References

1. Iansiti, M., Levien, R.: Strategy as ecology. Harvard Bus. Rev. **82**(3), 1–14 (2004)
2. Nachira, F., et al.: A network of digital business ecosystems for Europe: roots, processes and perspectives. In: Proceedings of Digital Business Ecosystem. European Commission Information Society and Media (2007)
3. Stamper, R., et al.: Understanding the roles of signs and norms in organizations - a semiotic approach to information systems design. J. Behav. Inf. Technol. **19**(1), 15–27 (2000)
4. Adner, R.: Match your innovation strategy to your innovation ecosystem. Harvard Bus. Rev. **84**(4), 98–107 (2006)
5. Ceccagnoli, M., et al.: Cocreation of value in a platform ecosystem: the case of enterprise software. MIS Q. **36**(1), 263–290 (2012)
6. Li, Y.: The technological roadmap of Cisco's business ecosystem. Technovation **29**, 379–386 (2009)
7. Moore, J.F.: Predators and prey: a new ecology of competition. Harvard Bus. Rev. **71**(3), 75–83 (1993)
8. Razavi, A.R., et al.: From business ecosystems towards digital business ecosystems. In: Proceedings of the 4th IEEE International Conference on Digital Ecosystems and Technologies, pp. 290–295 (2010)
9. Tsatsou, P., et al.: Towards a taxonomy for regulatory issues in a digital business ecosystem in the EU. J. Inf. Technol. **25**, 288–307 (2010)
10. Liu, K.: Semiotics in Information Systems Engineering. Cambridge University Press, Cambridge (2000)
11. Effah, J.: Virtual process control modelling in organisational semiotics: a case of higher education admission. In: Liu, K., Nakata, K., Li, W., Galarreta, D. (eds.) ICISO 2015. IFIP AICT, vol. 449, pp. 51–59. Springer, Heidelberg (2015)

Open Digital Business Ecosystems: A Pathway for Value Co-creation

Lily Sun[1], Chekfoung Tan[2,3(✉)], Simon Robertson[3], Kecheng Liu[2,4],
Mark Cook[3], and Claire Collins[2]

[1] School of System Engineering, University of Reading, Reading, UK
lily.sun@reading.ac.uk
[2] Henley Business School, University of Reading, Reading, UK
{chekfoung.tan,k.liu,claire.collins}@henley.ac.uk
[3] United Bible Societies, Swindon, UK
{ctan,srobertson,mcook}@biblesocieties.org
[4] School of Information Management and Engineering,
Shanghai University of Finance and Economics, Shanghai, China

Abstract. Individual businesses enthuse over participating in the 4 "We Economy" era [1] through a digital business ecosystem (DBE). DBE is seen as a gateway for an individual company to penetrate new markets where new products, services, and highly personalized experiences are delivered to their customers. Despite the benefits of DBE, collaboration uncertainty is the main challenge for a company wanting to participate in a wider ecosystem. This paper presents an open digital business ecosystem model that prepares companies prior to participating in the world of digital business and to secure multi-faceted benefits. This model demonstrates three key functionalities: (1) evaluating a company's current digital and non-digital business capabilities driven by its vision, (2) capturing these capabilities in a value cloud register, and (3) integrating the business capabilities determined by innovative collaborations. A case study of a global non-profit organization is employed to demonstrate how a company connects its partners in an innovation ecosystem.

Keywords: Open digital business ecosystems · Digital business capabilities · Value cloud · Affordance · Open innovation

1 Introduction

Digital business has become a strategic transformation paradigm for a company to redefine its business model in a business network. Such a business network also redefines its environment as digital business ecosystems (DBE) which connect multiple companies to deliver products and customer experience as well as co-create values in a win-win-win fashion, a Business win, a Customer win, and an Innovation win [modified from 1]. However, new business environments impose collaboration uncertainties between the focal company and its lead partners, such as ineffective collaboration that affects the co-development of products or services and ill-aligned business capabilities that impact on achieving win-win-win innovation values. Hence, it is vital for the stakeholders to recognize these uncertainties prior to participation in the DBE.

M.C.C. Baranauskas et al. (Eds.): ICISO 2016, IFIP AICT 477, pp. 85–94, 2016.
DOI: 10.1007/978-3-319-42102-5_10

There is active research on evolving from a traditional business model to a networked digital business. This kind of business transformation reveals that the ecosystem approach has been incorporated for sharing vision and integrating other partners in the ecosystem from the business and IT perspective such as incorporating open data and the cloud computing approach [adapted from 2]. There are new challenges in the business and IT alignment research for a modern digital society that incorporates the ecosystem approach and innovation elements [3, 4]. However there is a lack of mechanism for assessing a company's readiness prior to joining a DBE.

This paper hence presents a conceptual model of open digital business ecosystems (ODBE) that comprises a methodology for assisting a company prior to joining the ODBE. The paper is structured as follows: Sect. 2 reviews the related literature, Sect. 3 illustrates the conceptual model of ODBE, Sect. 4 demonstrates the application of ODBE in a global non-profit organization, Sect. 5 discusses and contributions, limitations and concludes the research with future work.

2 Theoretical Background

2.1 Digital Business and Ecosystems

Digital business research concerns what and how technologies create business value and build a digital economy [5, 6]. Such research discovered that digital businesses compete and collaborate among diverse entities in a self-organized and self-evolved ecosystem which is formally defined as Digital Business Ecosystems (DBE) [4, 7, 8]. This concept enables organizations within the ecosystem to create new connections for offering new services or products, sharing experiences and all these ultimately drive open innovation. A digital business strategy is imperative for forming DBE that maximizes co-created values by leveraging the digital resources [9].

The study of enterprise architecture (EA) is instrumental for modeling a digital business ecosystem [10]. The future of EA research predominantly lies in developing the digital business strategy and capturing the co-created value through an innovation ecosystem [3]. The innovation ecosystem encourages the organizations within the ecosystem to strategically collaborate and develop new digital business capabilities for competitive advantages [11].

2.2 Value Co-creation Through Affordances in Innovation Contexts

Business participants in a DBE collaborate among each other to achieve mutual business goals and this mechanism promotes innovation that fosters value co-creation. The innovation context of a DBE is described as an affordance that realizes business transformation. The concept of affordance is used to describe the behavior of an organism made available by some combined structure of entity and its environment [12] This concept studies all organized behavior being affected by communications and interpretation of signs by people [13]. Affordance and norms are often employed for identifying semantic units of a domain of study and hence establishing relationships among these semantic units [14].

The study of affordances and norms clearly contributes to identifying value co-creation in a DBE. The typical values co-created in a DBE are: (1) customer value, which helps to increase customers' satisfaction towards the product or service; (2) information value, where information is shared across the ecosystem and the partners within the DBE; (3) operational value, where a certain level of process interoperability is established; (4) business value, where partners within the ecosystem share their best capability in driving the best product or service; and (5) talent value, where people knowledge or human capital are shared across the DBE [modified from 15].

3   Open Digital Business Ecosystem (ODBE)

DBE is seen as a disruptive business infrastructure at the business strategy and policy level but still it is a lack of a methodology in facilitating the participation of multiple companies. Therefore, the ODBE model introduced in this paper aims to facilitate open innovation that enables an alignment between open innovation and value co-creation in a manner of self-evolving and self-managing towards co-development of products [16]. Figure 1 depicts a conceptual architecture of ODBE that consists of four key functional components: (1) the business participants and their digital business capabilities, (2) the Digital business competency valuation, (3) DBE value cloud, and (4) an Innovation ecosystem.

Fig. 1. A conceptual model of ODBE

Business Participant Component. A focal company specifies its collaboration requirements which are used to qualify the participation of other partners based on their business capabilities. Such collaboration relationship is defined as a set of firms $F=\{f_1, f_2, ..., f_m\}$.. These firms may serve as a focal company in their own ecosystems. Each firm possesses a set of capabilities $C=\{c_1, c_2, ..., c_n\}$ which could potentially contribute to the ODBE. C is a proper subset of F, denoted by $C \subset F$, $\forall x\{x \in C, x \notin F\}$. $f \in F$ is a candidate firm to enter digital business competency valuation where $c \in C$ will be evaluated.

Digital Business Competency Valuation Component. The digital business competency valuation components provides a set of assessment techniques that examine by the readiness of a company prior to participating to the ODBE adopting the capability-resource analysis [17, 18] (Fig. 2). The capability-resource analysis requires input from the organizational aspects which are represented by digital business strategy, objectives

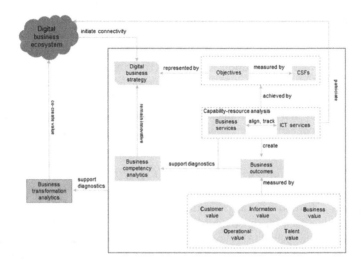

Fig. 2. Assessment of the digital business competencies

and the critical success factors (CSFs). The objectives set the business goals which are part of the digital business strategy and the performance of the core competency is measured by CSFs.

C is represented through a unique pair of {*business service, ICT service*}, at the business operational level [19]. *Business services* provide the business functionality of business roles that serves business needs for the customer. This is achieved through internal behavior, i.e., business processes, which require resources, competencies, knowledge and skills in order to produce products and values [20]. The *business services* profile captures the description about the stakeholders and their roles, operational capabilities, business processes, and business norms. The social perception of the stakeholders while consuming the resource to produce the outcome is also captured in the *business services*. The *ICT services* profile captures the enterprise ICT resources, such as hardware, applications, infrastructure, and contracted ICT components and the cost of each ICT element is associated with its total cost ownership (TOC).

Both profiles are used to determine digital business capabilities which resulted from mapping the specific *business service* and *ICT service* [21]. A group of digital business capabilities form the basis of an assessment by using a cost-benefit analysis model in conjunction with a SWOT model. The insights can be generated from large volumes of corporate datasets and external social media repositories. The assessment produces *Business outcomes* which can be used to identify the candidate digital business capabilities for DBE value cloud. *Business outcomes* are specified by a set of measures based on {C, I, B, O, T} [adapted from 15], where C is consumer experience value; I is relevant and quality information value [22]; B is B-B market share value, O is internal process and productivity value, and T is level of employees' knowledge, skill, and experience value [23]. These measures reveal the quality of business performance and how the firm engages with customers, employees and partners. For those business capabilities with {C, I, B, O, T} that are scored High or a high end of Medium, they are likely able to enable co-creation of value when they are connected through *Innovation ecosystem*.

The business competency analytics technique diagnoses a current internal stage of a firm f in moving towards a sustainability-led innovation. This diagnostic analysis adopts the prescriptive and predictive analytical methods, e.g., business performance and margin predictive analytics [24], customer relationship analytics [25], marketing analytics [26], cost-benefit analysis, and talent analytics [27]. A key purpose of this analysis is for f to predict its business by recognizing its SWOT dynamics, being aware of influential issues, and evaluating the implementation of the Digital business strategy. $F=\{f_1, f_2, ..., f_m\}$ can internally carry out such diagnostic analysis when appropriate so that each f remains innovative.

Business transformation analytics diagnoses the current stage of f in its external environment and it puts the emphasis on how f should respond to the pressures from the marketplace as well as the impact for change required by the Innovation ecosystem. Any changes for optimizing the business performance may be revolutionary or evolutionary and require strategic decisions from the stakeholders. The decision making process is then influenced by the SWOT analysis [28], competitor analysis [29], risk analysis [30] and change impact analysis [31]. The result may reform the existing Digital business strategy where each f can maintain its co-created value in an Innovation ecosystem and stay competitive.

DBE Value Cloud Component. The *DBE value cloud* is a repository of sharable digital capabilities owned by the *business participants*. A digital business capability is seen as-a-service [8] that is featured as automated business processes, IT-enabled capabilities, data analytics models, technology infrastructures and data host services. Figure 3 depicts an information model that registers business capabilities in the value cloud. The value cloud interfaces with the *Innovation ecosystem (IE)* via a connector. The connector: (1) registers and publishes the capability, (2) discovers the capability based on a query (i.e., a set of criteria) from the *IE*, (3) selects the appropriate capabilities, and (4) transfers the resultant capabilities (e.g., URIs) to the connector at the *IE* end.

Innovation Ecosystem Component. An *Innovation ecosystem (IE)* is an affordance of the business transformation from the connected individual companies where these companies co-create values. A connection is driven by the qualitative requirements of an *IE* based upon which the "fit for purpose" digital business capabilities contained in the *DBE value cloud*. An affordance function of discovering and deploying digital capabilities is executed through connectors and it deploys the participating digital business capabilities (e.g., API-led connectivity), manages the service level agreement (SLA), and communicates the feedback of impact for change with the concerned firm (f). The SLA related function deals with the shared responsibilities for the collaboration quality and outcomes of the F and the C, and relevant cost and profit models.

Co-creation of value is the strategic goal of *IE*. All the alliance of C must aim at this common goal. The performance of each c is monitored and their joint business

Firm	Capability	Value Cloud Register Scale ={High, Medium, Low, Not Applicable}									
		Customer		Information		Operational		Business		Talent	
		Scale	Description	Scale	Description	Scale	Description	Scale	Description	Scale	Description

Fig. 3. Information model of the *DBE value cloud*

outcomes are assessed. As a result, the impact of change is fed back to those concerned F. The feedback suggest changes to (1) the existing $c \in C$ for improving its quality of offering due to the evolutional change in the *IE*, (2) the existing F for investing further in their own C or developing new c to meeting the revolutionary change in the *IE*, and (3) the *IE* affordance to deploy different alliances with more appropriate quality and performance to satisfy customers' new needs.

4 ODBE Application in a Global Non-profit Organization

ODBE is employed in the United Bible Societies (UBS) which is a case study of a global non-profit organization (NPO). UBS is one of the largest Christian fellowships in the world and it consists of approximately 146 Bible Societies (BS) operating in more than 200 countries and territories [32]. The key ministry services provided by UBS are bible translation, publication and distribution, literacy training, bible engagement and advocacy. These services often involve collaboration with other bible societies within the fellowship, partners such as the local churches and other faith-based NPOs. In this case study, BS5, a focal bible society, intends to run a mission project teaching *women's literacy* on a large scale. BS5 is then seeking collaboration with other fellowship partners who have registered business services in the *value cloud* (Fig. 4). BS5 looks for service providers who could offer the capabilities in *women's literacy*: (1) producing literary training materials, (2) providing funding opportunities, (3) experience in training the tutors. These services in the *DBE value cloud* were selected by conducting *capability-resource analysis*. Figure 5 shows the *business outcomes* of various literacy services available in the *DBE value cloud*.

By following the affordance of business transformation process, BS5 decided to collaborate with BS4 and BS2 as: (1) BS4 has delivered high customer value in the

| | | Value Cloud Register | | | | Scale =(High, Medium, Low) | | | | | |
| | | Customer (e.g. scale of benefiting the audience) | | Information (e.g. what sort of information the firm can offer) | | Operational (B-B from the process perspective) | | Business (B-B from the market share perspective) | | Talent (e.g. knowledge sharing, sharing skills and expertise) | |
Bible Societies	Capability in the Literacy	Scale	Description	Scale	Description	Scale	Description	Scale	Description	Scale	Description
BS1	Women's Literacy	L	Engage with church and local partners, service delivered to 100 women	L	Produce literacy brochures and materials	L	Establish literacy centres	L	Establish relationship with the funding BS	L	Recruit and train literacy tutors
BS1	Distribution of Holy Scriptures	M	Engage with church and local partners, service delivered to 1500 target audiences in rural areas	L	Basic literacy brochures	M	Organise trauma healing workshop	L	Weak relationship with funding BS	M	Recruit and train distributors
						M	Organise distribution campaign				
BS2	Women's Literacy	M	Engage with church and local partners, service delivered to 1000 women	M	Produce literacy brochures and materials	M	Start literacy classes in church	H	Establish relationship with the funding BS	M	Recruit and train literacy tutors
						H	Equip with printing facilities				
BS2	Community based literacy	H	Engage with local government	H	Produce literacy brochures and materials	H	Establish literacy centres	L	No partnership	H	Recruit and train literacy tutors
		H	Engage with partners, service delivered to 3000 target audiences			H	Distribute bibles				
BS2	Prison related literacy	H	Engage with partners, service delivered to 3500 prisoners	H	Produce literacy brochures and materials	H	Conduct theological education	L	No partnership	H	Recruit and train literacy tutors
BS2	Listening based literacy (Faith Comes by Hearing)	H	Engage with partners, service delivered to 6500 people in the local community	L	Basic literacy brochures	H	Identify the existing listening groups	H	Extend the listening related literacy to other rural areas	H	Recruit and train listening-literacy tutors
						H	Distribute Proclaimers (the listening device)				
BS3	Women's Literacy	L	Engage with church and local partners, service delivered to 50 young women in church	L	Basic literacy brochures	L	Establish literacy classes in schools	L	Extend the literacy classes to other regions	L	Recruit and train literacy tutors
BS4	Women's Literacy	H	Engage with church and local partners, service delivered to 5000 women	L	Basic literacy brochures	H	Establish literacy centre	L	Rely on limited local funding	H	Recruit and train literacy tutors
						H	Test the learners			H	Set up training workshops

Fig. 4. Value cloud register of C owned by F

Business Service Description		
Bible Seciety ID:	BS4	
Business service name: *Women's literacy*	Date: *21-December-2015*	Version no:
Business service goal: *Help illiterate women attain basic literacy (read, write, count), scripture engagement and transformation of individuals and society*	Business process: *Standard literacy framework*	
	Business norms: *Standard literacy framework*	
Business capability	Business service strategic value (0-5):	*4*	
	Perceived business service performance		
		Actor	Responsibility
	Stakeholder	*GMT Literacy Facilitator*	*Support the operational activities*
		GMT Grant Manager	*Manage the grant funded by the resourcing bible societies and ensure sufficient resource is supplied to the member bible societies that are running projects*
		Resourcing Bible Society Facilitator	*Oversee the progress of the mission project*
		Church Facilitator	*Support the implementation of the project*
Business outcomes:	{H, L, H, L, H}		

Fig. 5. Business service description for the *women's literacy* provided by BS4

experience of engaging with local churches to reach 5000 women, and possesses high operational and talent value in the experience of setting up a literacy center and talent pool of trainers, and (2) BS2 possess medium *information* value in terms of producing literacy materials, high *operational* value as they have own printing facilities, and high *business* value as they have good relationships with the funding bible societies. BS2 and BS4 also perceive certain mutual benefits yielded from this collaboration.

BS2 and BS4 adopted the UBS standard literacy framework for project execution and management. Hence, there are no conflicts in terms of the *business process* and *business norms*. As a result of the affordance process, $F_{BS5}=\{f_{BS2}, f_{BS4}\}$, the *innovation ecosystem* of *women's literacy* is formed. This collaboration has co-created five values which are qualitatively defined based on the actual outcomes achieved (Fig. 6). These values are beneficial to the partnership $F_{BS5}=\{f_{BS2}, f_{BS4}\}$ as whole. However, these values also impacted f_{BS2} and f_{BS4} so that they improved their c_{BS2} and c_{BS4} (Fig. 7). For example, the information value of BS2 has changed from M to H, impacted by VC_3 and VC_5, where they are now capable of conducting *women's literacy* in different demographic. Similarly, the business value of BS4 has changed from L to M, impacted by VC_4, as they have grown in reputation by helping other BS.

Fig. 6. The *innovation ecosystem* of *women's literacy*

BS5, who originally did not possess any capability in *women's literacy*, now is specialized in the *women's literacy* service provision with connected strengths from BS2 and BS4. BS5 can expend its *women's literacy* service to other areas by utilizing its local resources of $\{f_{BS2}, f_{BS4}\}$. Furthermore, F_{BS5} can become a fellow partner in other innovation ecosystems.

Increased from M to H | Increased to L | Increased from L to M | Increased from L to M | Impacted by the value co-created (VC)

Bible Societies	Capability in the Literacy	Impact for Change Scale = { High, Medium, Low} Customer (e.g. scale of benefiting the audience)			Information (e.g. what sort of information the firm can offer)			Operational (B-B from the process perspective)			Business (B-B from the market share perspective)			Talent (e.g. knowledge sharing, sharing skills and expertise)		
		Scale	VC	Description	Scale	VC	Description	Scale	VC	Description	Scale	VC	Description	Scale	VC	Description
BS2	Women's Literacy	H		Engage with church and local partners, service delivered to 1000 women	H		Produce literacy brochures and materials	H	VC3	Start literacy classes in church (enhance the learning experience of the audience)	H	VC4	Establish relationship with the funding BS (the gained reputation helps attracting more funding BS)	H	VC3	Recruit and train literacy tutors (better knowledge in recruiting the trainers)
			VC4	Gained good reputation from helping an inexperienced BS		VC3	Learned new knowledge of how to conduct women's literacy in different demographics	H		Equip with printing facilities						
						VC5	Gained the new workbook produced	L	VC5	Learned how the new workshop is produced and capable in producing the same in						
BS4	Women's Literacy	H		Engage with church and local partners, service delivered to 5000 women	M	VC3	Learned new knowledge of how to conduct women's literacy in different demographics	H	VC3	Establish literacy centre (enhance the learning experience of the audience)	M	VC4	The reputation gained from helping other BS helps attracting more funding	H	VC3	Recruit and train literacy tutors (better knowledge in recruiting the trainers)
			VC4	Gained good reputation from helping an inexperienced BS				H		Test the learners				H		Set up training workshops
								L	VC5	Learned how the new workshop is produced and capable in producing the same in						
BS5	Women's Literacy	L	VC1	Delivered a literacy project that reaches 5000 women	L	VC3	Shared knowledge on women's literacy of a particular demographics	L	VC3	Learned how to establish literacy centre	L	VC2	Learned how to efficiently use the project funds	L	VC3	Gained knowledge of how to recruit and train the tutors
								M	VC5	Gained the new workbook produced in shared language hence capable in providing similar consultation in future						

Fig. 7. The *innovation ecosystem* of *women's literacy* impacted on the fellowship partners (Color figure online)

5 Discussions and Conclusion

The ODBE model has implications for the modern business environment in areas such as the digital oriented business network, business-ICT alignment, innovation and management. From the theoretical perspective, ODBE brings new ideas to the field of business and IT alignment by applying its principles to the existing digital business landscape and by introducing the ODBE, which enables companies to respond to the market changes driven by business and disruptive technologies. From the methodological perspective, ODBE enables companies to identify their digital business capabilities and assess their readiness for value co-creation in collaboration with multiple organizations. The assessment techniques are robust and can be iteratively carried out whenever appropriate. From the practical perspective, ODBE addresses the uncertainty inherent in new collaborations by indicating the values that could be gained by individual companies in a partnership through the *DBE value cloud.*

There are a few limitations in the ODBE. Each *business participant* has to be formally profiled. This profile provides useful inputs (structured and unstructured data) for the *digital business competency valuation* to instantiate the business analytics. External data sources need to be appropriately discovered and integrated to support the valuation analysis. The *DBE value cloud* requires technical mechanisms to register, store, manage, and discover business capabilities. An affordance query can then configure the innovation alliance collaboratively. The innovation ecosystem needs to be robust in co-creating values and can also generate feedback to aid the participants to maintain their service sustainability.

As for the future work, a number of structural methods will be developed for the ODBE such as the formal representations for *DBE value cloud* and *innovation ecosystem* and the interfaces for information exchange between the components. The technique of *digital business competency valuation* needs an integration of those analytical methods and executes the various analyses in a robust methodology. Furthermore, the technical functions of two types of *connectors* should be developed so that the ODBE model can be simulated scientifically. In addition, ODBE will be applied to multiple case studies in order to prove that it works in the real world.

Acknowledgments. This project is partially sponsored by Innovate UK (No. H4014200). We gratefully thank our industry partner who provided their substantial financial support and knowledge to the experiment of this study. This work is also partially supported by National Natural Science Foundation of China under grant No. 71532002 (key project), 71371125 and 61374177.

References

1. Accenture: Accenture Technology Vision 2015 Digital Business Era: Stretch your Boundaries. Accenture, Chicago (2015)
2. Rong, K., Wu, J., Shi, Y., Guo, L.: Nurturing business ecosystems for growth in a foreign market: incubating, identifying and integrating stakeholders. J. Int. Manag. **21**(4), 293–308 (2015)
3. Coltman, T.R., Tallon, P.P., Sharma, R., Queiroz, M.: Strategic IT alignment: twenty-five years on. J. Inf. Technol. **30**(2), 91–100 (2015). doi:10.1057/jit.2014.35
4. Nachira, F., Nicolai, A., Dini, P., Louarn, M.L., Leon, L.R.: Digital business ecosystems. Eur. Comm. Inf. Soc. Media (2007)
5. Barua, A., Kriebel, C.H., Mukhopadhyay, T.: Information technologies and business value: an analytic and empirical investigation. Inf. Syst. Res. **6**(1), 3–23 (1995)
6. Melville, N., Kraemer, K., Gurbaxani, V.: Review: information technology and organizational performance: an integrative model of IT business value. MIS Q. **28**(2), 283–322 (2004)
7. Nachira, F.: Towards a Network of Digital Business Ecoystems Fostering the Local Development. European Commission, Bruxelles (2002)
8. Dini, P., Darking, M., Rathbone, N., Vidal, M., Hernandez, P., Ferronato, P., Briscoe, G., Hendryx, S.: The Digital Ecosystems Research Vision: 2010 and Beyond. European Commission, Bruxelles (2005). Position Paper
9. Bharadwaj, A., El Sawy, O.A., Pavlou, P.A., Venkatraman, N.: Digital business strategy: toward a next generation of insights. MIS Q. **37**(2), 471–482 (2013)
10. Blosch, M., Burton, B.: Future of EA 2025: Evolving From Enterprise to Ecosystem. Gartner, Inc., Stamford (2014). G00269850
11. Grover, V., Kohli, R.: Cocreating IT value: new capabilities and metrics for multifirm environments. MIS Q. **36**(1), 225–232 (2012)
12. Gibson, J.J.: The Ecological Approach to Visual Perception. Lawrence Erlbaum Associates, Hillsdale (1968)
13. Stamper, R.: Information in Business and Administrative Systems. Wiley, New York (1973)
14. Liu, K.: Semiotics in Information Systems Engineering. Cambridge University Press, Cambridge (2000)
15. Korpela, K., Kuusiholma, U., Taipale, O., Hallikas, J.: A framework for exploring digital business ecosystems. In: The 46th Hawaii International Conference on System Sciences, Maui, USA (2013)

16. Han, K., Oh, W., Im, K.S., Chang, R.M., Oh, H., Pinsonneault, A.: Value cocreation and wealth spillover in open innovation alliances. MIS Q. **36**(1), 291–325 (2012)
17. Amit, R., Schoemaker, P.J.H.: Strategic assets and organizational rent. Strateg. Manag. J. **14**(1), 33–46 (1993). doi:10.1002/smj.4250140105
18. Day, G.S.: The capabilities of market-driven organizations. J. Mark. **58**, 37–52 (1994)
19. Ray, G., Muhanna, W.A., Barney, J.B.: Information technology and the performance of the customer service process: a resource-based analysis. MIS Q. **29**, 625–652 (2005)
20. Jonkers, H., Lankhorst, M., Van Buuren, R., Hoppenbrouwers, S., Bonsangue, M., Leendert, V.: Concepts for modeling enterprise architectures. Int. J. Coop. Inf. Syst. **13**(03), 257–287 (2004)
21. Sun, L., Liu, K., Jambari, D.I., Michell, V.: Evaluating business value of IT towards optimisation of the application portfolio. Enterp. Inf. Syst. **10**, 1–22 (2014)
22. Izquierdo, S.S., Izquierdo, L.R.: The impact of quality uncertainty without asymmetric information on market efficiency. J. Bus. Res. **60**(8), 858–867 (2007)
23. Duncan, A.D., Buytendijk, F.: How to Establish a Data-Driven Culture in the Digital Workplace. Gartner, Inc., Stamford (2015)
24. Chandler, N., Hostmann, B., Rayner, N., Herschel, G.: Gartner's Business Analytics Framework. Gartner, Inc., Stamford (2011)
25. Gartner: Customer Relationship Management (CRM) Analytics (2015). http://www.gartner.com/it-glossary/crm-analytics. Accessed 10 July 2015
26. Hauser, W.J.: Marketing analytics: the evolution of marketing research in the twenty-first century. Direct Mark. Int. J. **1**(1), 38–54 (2007)
27. Davenport, T.H., Harris, J., Shapiro, J.: Competing on talent analytics. Harv. Bus. Rev. **88**(10), 52–58 (2010)
28. Pickton, D.W., Wright, S.: What's swot in strategic analysis? Strateg. Change **7**, 101–109 (1998)
29. Collis, D.J., Rukstad, M.G.: Can you say what your strategy is? Harv. Bus. Rev. **86**(4), 82–90 (2008)
30. Peltier, T.R.: Risk analysis and risk management. EDPACS **32**(3), 1–17 (2004)
31. Malek, R., Yazdanifard, R.: Overview of change management and its implementation. In: Zhu, M. (ed.) Business, Economics, and Financial Sci., Manag. AISC, vol. 143, pp. 149–154. Springer, Heidelberg (2012)
32. UnitedBibleSocieties: About Us (2015). http://www.unitedbiblesocieties.org/about-us/ Accessed 28 Oct 2015

Knowledge Management
and Engineering

Making Sense of Non-compliance: A Semiotic Approach

Kwasi Dankwa[(✉)] and Keiichi Nakata

Henley Business School, Informatics Research Centre,
University of Reading, Reading, UK
k.d.dankwa@pgr.reading.ac.uk, k.nakata@henley.ac.uk

Abstract. Compliance is an important aspect of operational requirements, and is essential to have a system that allows for compliance to be monitored, managed and improved. However, why non-compliance occurs in organisations is not always well understood. This paper proposes that the semiotic approach can aid in making sense of non-compliance behaviour by analysis of the actions of the agents. In particular, the organisational containment analysis highlights the division between informal and formal treatment of compliance. It also indicates that the established norms which are as a result of rules, regulations, beliefs and other patterns can influence behaviour. The paper proposes that these norms and patterns constitute the culture and beliefs of the organisation and determines how the agents embrace rules and regulations. An example of analysing compliance using the semiotic approach is presented using a case study of non-compliance to the quality management system at NHS Blood and Transplant (NHSBT).

Keywords: Compliance · Norms · Semiotics · Non-compliance · Agents · Behaviour

1 Introduction

Compliance is central to the operations of organisations and its relevance cannot be over emphasised. It is an important component that can influence the behaviour of agents [1], and impact on output of the organisation. The need for compliance may be as means of ensuring safety of consumers, quality of products or as a legal requirement. It is seen as the means of ensuring conformance to a rule: such as a specification, policy, standard or law [2]. According to O'Neill [3], compliance is initiated by three main steps. 'First the societal imposition of rules and regulations; second, the organisation's decision to abide by the regulation and defines internal responsibility; and third, the act of implementing and managing the regulatory processes within the organisation to address the societal requirements'. To allow for this, the standards and regulations are well defined and act as means of measurement or audit of deviation within the organisation. Thus compliance describes the efforts organisations go through to ensure that they are aware of and take steps to comply with relevant laws and

Published by Springer International Publishing Switzerland 2016. All Rights Reserved
M.C.C. Baranauskas et al. (Eds.): ICISO 2016, IFIP AICT 477, pp. 97–106, 2016.
DOI: 10.1007/978-3-319-42102-5_11

regulations. According to Governatori [4], regulatory compliance is the set of activities an organisation does to ensure that its core business does not violate relevant regulations which allows the organisation to thrive.

As a result of the increasing number of regulations to allow for operational transparency, organisations are increasingly adopting the use of consolidated and harmonised sets of compliance controls [2]. Furthermore, the culture within many organisations has been changed to essentially promote climate which fosters the attitude to compliance matters [5]. However, although many organisations may have systems in place to control compliance, there are instances where compliance to regulatory standards are not met. This has been shown to be apparent across different sectors; aviation, nuclear industries, banking, processing, health and manufacturing [6, 7]. Evidently, these failures indicate that the current systems to manage compliance are not working and there is the need for further investigation.

2 Background

The motivation for this research derives from cases of non-compliance to the Quality Management Systems (QMS) at NHS (National Health Service) Blood and Transplant (NHSBT). The NHSBT collects blood and organs from voluntary donors to meet the demands of patients. To support these activities, it is essential that work is done within an efficient and effective QMS. Although QMS is in place, there have been reported instances of non-compliances. Examples include: (a) Failure to supply specially matched product with resultant delay in treatment; (b) Failure to correctly label product leading to delay in treatment; and (c) selection of wrong donor leading to delay in stem cell collection. These instances of non-compliance have been shown to occur across different departments and involves different staff grades within the organisation with their effects ranging from impact on treatment and reputational impact on the organisation. The non-compliances have been reported across the NHS.

A 2014 report by the Medicines and Healthcare products Regulatory Agency (MHRA) indicated that the number of Serious Adverse Events (SAEs) reported across NHS shows an increase of 8 % (705/766) from 2013 [8]. The cases of non-compliance indicate that although organisations have systems in place to manage compliance, there are still reported failures. These have led to a number of research across sectors such as the health, manufacturing, banking, aviation, food etc., to improve compliance [3, 6, 7]. Although there have been improvement, there are still some gaps in knowledge when it comes to understanding non-compliance behaviour. In view of this, the research reported in this paper seeks to address the following research problems:

- What are the reasons behind non-compliance within organisations?
- How can compliance to rules, standards and regulations be improved within the organisation in light of understanding the reasons behind non-compliance?

The next section reviews existing researches related to compliance to ascertain the current understanding of (non)compliance behaviour.

3   Compliance Behaviour

The review of literature shows that compliance is an important component required for organisations to thrive. It is therefore not surprising that measuring the level of compliance has emerged as a key performance indicator. As such, organisations have developed compliance performance indicators to facilitate analysis of compliance activities and its enforcement trends [9]. Importantly, compliance culture within organisations have been shown to be vital to meet regulatory requirements to address customer needs in the competitive global market. This led to strategic plans to improve compliance culture and to encourage staff to align their values with the values of the organisation. Understanding compliance culture across organisations is important to understand compliance behaviour.

3.1   Compliance Cultures

The culture within different organisations may differ depending on the sector and how they perceive compliance issues. According to Jenkinson [5], a compliance culture is essentially the climate which fosters the attitude to compliance matters.

Compliance culture within organisations can be grouped into three main types [5] as non-compliance, anti-compliance and pro-compliance cultures. In non-compliance culture, compliance rules are frequently breached by the organisation with no recognition of the need for compliance. This is more accepting to increase profits [10]. With anti-compliance, compliance is generally seen as a threat and is merely tolerated. There is high risk of breach as compliance is seen as a reactive approach to the standards. Finally, in the pro-compliance culture, the organisation is inherently compliant and all the activities are compliantly performed. This view of categorization of different types of compliance culture is also shared by [11] who split organisations between those that view compliance and risk management as an opportunity for continuous improvement and those that simply see it as a tick box exercise to satisfy periodic audit requirements. This shows that the culture within the organisation can relate to the way the agents perceives the rules and regulations. This can be useful when assessing the compliance behaviour as the culture within the organisation may determine how they comply. There may therefore be a link between the compliance cultures of the compliance behaviour of the staff.

3.2   Compliance Culture Across Different Sectors

Many international institutions and conventions share a common aim of establishing and strengthening authorities to deliver effective compliance programs and enforcement [9]. Such institutions try to promote effective ways of ensuring essential compliance culture that strengthens the compliance levels within organisations. This makes understanding compliance across different sectors useful.

In conservation [1], compliance is critical to the success of any conservation project, regardless of the scale of the conservation actions or the means of conservation governance. It is not different in the food supply chain as is critical to ensure safety of the supply chain [10]. It is seen as a critical factor in the safety of products and services. Also, in the education sector, QMS for teaching and learning have been developed for the purpose of quality assurance for example to monitor theses of Ph.D. students to ensure completion on time [12]. The health care sector is no exception as researches have been conducted from drug compliance to information governance of medical information. According to Cramer et al. [13], studies have demonstrated that inadequate compliance and non-persistence with prescribed medication regimens result in increased morbidity and mortality. These are not the only sectors that require compliance as many industries such as nuclear, aviation and chemical, see it as very important for the desired outcome to be achieved [6].

However, although there is enough evidence to demonstrate that organisations strive for compliance, there are still gaps in the literature in respect of systems and frameworks to assist organisations in managing compliance [3]. This is supported by [14] who indicated that there are still gaps between staff compliance behaviour to standards of practice. Moreover, despite many actions and systems, inadequate compliance is frequently observed [9]. These systems and actions; Compliance Action Framework, Analytical Framework and ICT Approach as applied by [3, 4, 13] in dealing with compliance, have mainly focused on addressing the symptoms but fail to understand the reasons behind the non-compliances. There is therefore the need to have a system or approach that allows for the behaviour of the agents to be analysed to understand and make sense of the non-compliance behaviour. The semiotic approach which allows for the analysis of behaviour based on the interpretation of signs within the organisation and the norm analysis of the agents lends itself to the understanding of non-compliance behaviours. The next section analysis the semiotic approach and how it can be used to understand and to make sense of non-compliance behaviour.

4   Semiotic Analysis

4.1   Conceptual Background

Semiotics is 'the study of signs', and is concerned with their creation, representation and interpretation. Peirce (1958) defined a sign 'as something which stands to somebody for something in some respect or capacity'. Peirce's concept of a sign involves three parts: the Representamen (the sign), the Object (which is signified by the Representamen) and the Interpretant (that links the Representamen to the Object).

Within the organisation, every setting and sign presents the potential for training, development and for relaying information between stakeholders. A significant but often overlooked resource is the everyday experience of interacting with the infrastructures (building, equipment, and procedures) and communication structures that are available within the organisation [15]. These structures represent cultural values and the beliefs of the organisation which influences the operations within the organisation. It is therefore useful to understand these elements and to make sense of them. According to [15], a semiotic interpretive approach allows for critique in the ways cultural structures help to understand the ideas and the values that binds the people within the organisation. Essentially, the semiotic approach can be applied in the analysis and understanding of non-compliance behaviour as it embraces culture.

4.2 Application of Organisational Containment Model

To understand non-compliance behaviour, an Organisational Semiotics (OS) perspective [16] is used. This allows for an organisation to be seen as an information system with interdependent links between the organisation, the business process and the IT system [16]. These links can be expressed as an organisational containment model [19] that models organisation as comprising three systems – informal, formal and automated (technical) – whereby the automated system is contained within the formal system which in turn is contained within the informal system. This means that changes in any of the systems may have impact in other systems. Typically the informal system is the organisation itself. Figure 1 illustrates the organisational containment with the three systems and how they interact with each other.

The informal system is a sub-culture where meanings and beliefs are established and intentions confirmed. At this level, the cohesive relationship between individuals are built and commitments are formed. However, at the formal system, there is formation of rules and procedures and individuals are made to follow bureaucratic rules which is in contrast to the informal system. The automated system is part of the formal system which is automated, for example, by a computer-based system [16]. In the problem addressed in this paper, we focus on informal and formal systems as there is no automated system involved.

Because the organisation is seen as a social system in which people behave in a manner that conforms to certain norms, compliance analysis can be assessed using the organisational containment model. The norms may be as a result of rules, regulations, beliefs and other patterns which have been established over a period of time through practical experience [16]. They have been shown as the rules which determine how social organisms interact and controls their ability to perform actions [17]. They have the ability of directing, coordinating and controlling the actions of the agents. Norm has been described as a field of force that coerces the people in the community to think in a certain manner [18]. Essentially, the agents within the organisation may act as a result of existing interactions between the systems and experience established over the years.

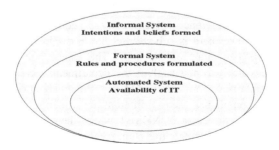

Fig. 1. The organisational containment model [19]

By introducing the formal system, there is move towards automation of the system where the agents in the organisation work without understanding the meaning behind what they do. This is evident in NHSBT where there are rules and procedures as part of the QMS to guide the performance of task within the departments. This formal system replaces the meaning and the intention that existed at the informal system and this can lead to conflict between the two systems. This conflict can lead to staff detachment as they only efficiently perform their task due to the formal system but are not satisfied because of the decline in the meaning and commitment that existed in the informal system.

Shapiro [15] indicates that culture has two aspects: the known meanings and directions which members are trained to and the observed meanings which are offered and tested. In essence, the agent may follow a norm conforming action or norm-breaking action although they have been trained and have knowledge of the rules and regulations. The agents may prefer to act in line with the norms in place to fit in due to the measure of patterns of behaviour set by the norms. This may be done depending on the prevailing situation at the time of the action. Consequently, an individual in a community who has learned the norms will be able to use the knowledge to guide their actions. However, the actions performed is invoked by different norms which may be irrelevant of the outcome. This is because norms selected are subjective and may not have predetermined connection to a particular outcome. In performing their task, agents may not think of the consequence of their actions as they invoke the norms they deem appropriate at the time. This may either be compliant or non-compliant behaviour to the procedures and rules that exist in the organisation. This analysis shows that the understanding of interaction between informal and formal systems is useful in making sense of non-compliance behaviour. The next section will analyse how analysing the norms can contribute to understanding of non-compliance behaviour.

5 Analysing Compliance Through Norms

5.1 Culture of Compliance

For NHSBT to meet customer needs, performance of task in the departments requires a shared understanding of norms and culture among staff within the organisation. In semiotic terms, the interpretation of various signs that are used and exchanged among the staff is influenced by the experience, knowledge and the beliefs of the staff in the various departments. Although the culture within NHSBT is pro-compliance, there appears to be departmental differences when it comes to compliance with the rules and procedures. This is because there is sub-culture that exists in the department which tends to influence the behaviour of the staff. The established norms within the departments influences the way the staff in the departments perceive the rules and procedures. Review and discussion with the QA department about compliance to QMS revealed different non-compliances across different departments.

Let us analyse one of the cases at NHSBT where there was a failure to supply specially matched product. Although the staff received the correct order from the hospital, the wrong product was produced. This is because, in selecting the initial material, the staff failed to check that the correct material had been selected as per the procedure. Moreover, although there was requirement in the procedure to check the order against the selected material in the manufacturing department, this did not happen. There appeared to be an incorrect understanding and belief that existed between the staff which influenced the observed behaviour in this case. Consequently, the established meanings and beliefs in conflict with the formal system resulted in the non-compliant behaviour. The wrong product selected resulted in a conflict between the formal and informal system. The informal system, which tolerated the non-compliance behaviour, was considered as the established norm in the department which influenced the behaviour of the staff as evident in this non-compliant behaviour. The informal system which is the organisation itself contains the intentions, norms and beliefs which influences the behaviour of the agents.

5.2 Norm Analysis in Compliance

Norm analysis aids understanding of the agents' behaviour in the organisation. This helps to capture the details of norms enacted by the agents and authorities who are responsible for the norms and the triggers which cause the norm to come into effect. In the case above, the staff involved in dealing with the orders were aware of the procedures and rules in place but failed to comply due to established beliefs and norms. Five norms, namely, perceptual norms, cognitive norms, evaluative norms, behavioural norms and denotative norms [16], have been considered to control human behaviour and, in turn, organisational behaviour.

The perceptual norms influence how people react to signals from their environment through their senses. Here, the norms and values are embedded in the physical structures which influences the behaviour of the staff in the department. When the order was received, the staff might have been selective in terms of what aspects of the order to be recognised, which may have influenced the behaviour of the staff. The cognitive norms enabled the staff to interpret what they perceived based on the beliefs and knowledge. The staff interpreted the order based on the belief and knowledge that existed which may have led to the non-compliance behaviour. Although there is established rules and procedures, the acquired knowledge and beliefs coerced each staff differently to interpret the procedures. As such compliance in the organisation may be different across departments depending on experience of staff. In the analysis, the Evaluative norms aid in explaining the beliefs, values and objectives in the departments within the organisation. This helped in explaining the behaviour of the staff due to the understanding of the relationship between the formal and informal system. The behavioural norms govern the behaviour of the staff within the departments. These behaviours are as a result of the norms that exist within the department and this influenced the non-compliant behaviour observed. The knowledge, beliefs, values and the objectives that has been established within the departments controlled the behaviour of the staff in performing their actions. Finally, the denotative norms direct the choices of signs for signifying. These are culture dependant and may influence performance of task by staff within the department. This may have influenced the choice of flow of the process between the staff that received the order and the staff that manufactured the product.

Evidently, the behaviour of the staff is impacted by these norms which influenced non-compliance behaviour. In applying this to the case above, the staff involved in the process used one or a combination of the norms to complete the task. The performance of the task was initiated by staff who have the responsibility to select the initial material. The staff may have perceived or analysed the process differently to the required procedure leading to the failure to capture the required information from the order. Subsequently, staff in the chain of process also interpreted the task based on the established knowledge and beliefs culminating in the issue of non-compliant product. This is because, in the organisation the responsibility is determined by the established common agreements or policies. This leads to formation of 'life cycle' of responsibility which determines the role of each staff in the process. Non-compliance at this level was as a result of combination of one or more factors in the 'life cycle' of responsibility between all the stakeholders. This was due to persistent failures on the part of all the stakeholders who failed to check the requirements as a result of established beliefs and commitments.

The appropriateness of the responsibility of staff is influenced by the established norms which can either lead to compliance or non-compliance. In this case, the initiator of the 'life cycle' of responsibility was perceived as being compliant, so the process was carried out by subsequent staff without questioning, leading to non-compliance. On the other hand, if there was indication that the actions of the initiator of the process was not in line with the established norms, subsequent staff may have challenged their action leading to compliant outcome. Despite staff awareness of the procedures and rules, the established norms influenced staff in non-compliance behaviour. Moreover, because there is reliance on the interpretation of the request, the outcome depends on the skill set, the knowledge and the beliefs. At each stage of the process, there is the tendency for one or more agents to make a non-compliant decision based on how they perceived or interpreted the sign. There is indication that the established norms and beliefs influenced the behaviour of staff and by using the semiotic approach we can make sense of the non-compliant behaviour.

6   Discussion

6.1   Suitability and Benefit of Semiotic Approach

The Semiotic approach allowed for consideration of all the sign structures that exist within the organisation to be analysed and the impact on staff behaviour to be noted. Using the organisational containment analysis, the discrepancies between the formal and informal processes can be ascertained. Essentially, by understanding the conflict between the formal and the informal systems, improved procedures and rules can be formulated to guide activities within the organisation. The analysis allowed for sequential process to be followed to make sense of the reasons behind non-compliance. This also allowed for analysis of the actions performed by the various agents within the responsibility 'life cycle' which can be useful in dealing with non-compliance behaviours.

6.2 Limitations of Semiotic Approach

Although the analysis allowed for the investigation and understanding of non-compliance behaviour, the subjective nature of the analysis makes it difficult to generalise. Also the number of case studies used in this review limits the generalisation of this paper. The interpretation of signs within the organisation may differ depending on the experience, education, knowledge, beliefs, etc. of the staff who are involved in the process. In the case analysed, although it was evident that staff failed to follow the procedure, it is difficult to generalise that all the staff in the department will not be compliant due to the subjective nature of application of norms. Moreover, the perception of one staff member may be different from others and as such the outcome of their interaction with the procedures may be different at any given time which makes generalisation of findings difficult and problematic. Furthermore, although the semiotic approach allows for sense to be made of non-compliance behaviour, to allow for validity of the studies other analytical lens may be useful in future work.

7 Conclusion

Compliance has been shown to be an important aspect of the operations in organisations. Based on the concepts in organisational semiotics, in this paper, failures of compliance to rules, regulations and procedures are attributed to failure by agents to appropriately interpret and invoke the norms when required. The use of semiotic analysis has indicated that the established norms and beliefs in the organisation influences the actions taken to complete the task as noted. Moreover, subcultures within the departments have been shown to play a role in compliance behaviour. Furthermore, the organisational containment analysis points to possible discrepancies between the informal and formal systems that exist within the organisation. This influences how agents comply with rules, procedures and regulations and can influence compliance behaviour. Moreover, the actions of the agent that initiates the process have been shown to influence application of task by subsequent staff and this can impact on compliance behaviour. By establishing a culture that supports staff for compliance, there is indication that the appropriate actions may be compliantly performed routinely. Semiotic approach can aid in making sense of non-compliance behaviour in organisations.

In future work, a further analysis of compliance culture and non-compliance behaviour will be applied to develop a framework for enhancing compliance and monitoring non-compliance in organisations.

Acknowledgments. The authors would like to thank the Quality Assurance Department at NHSBT for their cooperation in this research.

References

1. Solomon, J.N., Gavin, M.C., Gore, M.L.: Detecting and understanding non-compliance with conservation rules. Biol. Conserv. **6**, 2013–2016 (2015)
2. Silveira, P., Rodriguez, C., Birukou, A., Casati, F., Daniel, F., D'Andrea, V., Worledge, C., Zouhair, T.: Aiding Compliance Governance in Service-Based Business Processes, pp. 524–548. IGI Global, Hershey (2012)
3. O'Neill, A.: An action framework for compliance and governance. Clin. Gov. Int. J. **19**(4), 342–359 (2014)
4. Governatori, G.: ICT support for regulatory compliance of business processes. In: Proceedings of 29th World Continuous Auditing and Reporting Symposium (29WCARS), 21–22 November 2013, Brisbane, Australia (2014)
5. Jenkinson, D.: Compliance culture. J. Financ. Regul. Compliance **4**(1), 41–46 (1996)
6. Park, J., Jung, W.: The operators' non-compliance behaviour to conduct emergency operating procedures - comparing with the work experience and the complexity of procedural steps. Reliab. Eng. Syst. Saf. **82**(2), 115–131 (2003)
7. Richard, L.H.-Y., Mande, V.: Factors influencing non-compliance with ASU 2010-06 in the banking industry. Manag. Audit. J. **29**(6), 548–574 (2014)
8. Birse, M.: Blood Consultative Committee New Letter. MHRA, London (2015)
9. Read, A.D., West, R.J., Kelaher, B.P.: Using compliance data to improve marine protected area management. Mar. Policy **60**, 119–127 (2015)
10. Hirschauer, N., Bavorova, M., Martino, G.: An analytical framework for a behavioural analysis of non-compliance in food supply chains. Brit. Food J. **114**(9), 1212–1227 (2012)
11. Hillson, D., Murray-Webster, R.: Understanding and Managing Risk Attitude, pp. 1–6. Gower Publishing, Surry (2004)
12. Daud, S., Mustafa, Z., Mohd Suradi, N.R., Ariffin, A.K., Abu Bakar, N.R., Ramli, R.: Compliance to thesis examination procedure in the ISO quality management system for teaching and learning. Procedia – Soc. Behav. Sci. **18**, 18–23 (2011)
13. Cramer, J.A., Roy, A., Burrell, A., Fairchild, C.J., Fuldeore, M.J., Ollendorf, D.A., Wong, P. K.: Medication compliance and persistence: terminology and definitions. Value in Health: J. Int. Soc. Pharmacoecon. Outcomes Res. **11**(1), 44–47 (2008)
14. Shah, N., Castro-Sánchez, E., Charani, E., Drumright, L.N., Holmes, A.H.: Towards changing healthcare workers' behaviour: a qualitative study exploring non-compliance through appraisals of infection prevention and control practices. J. Hosp. Infect. **90**, 126–134 (2015)
15. Shapiro, B.: Structures that teach: using a semiotic framework to study the environmental messages of learning settings. Eco-Thinking **3**(1), 3–15 (2012)
16. Liu, K.: Semiotics in Information Systems Engineering. Cambridge University Press, Cambridge (2000)
17. Salter, A., Liu, K.: Using semantic analysis and norm analysis to model organisations (1985)
18. Stamper, R., Liu, K., Hafkamp, M., Ades, Y.: Understanding the roles of signs and norms in organisations. Behav. Inf. Technol. **19**(1), 15–27 (2000)
19. Stamper, R.K.: Language and computer in organised behaviour. In: Riet, R., Meersman, R. (eds.) Linguistic Instruments in Knowledge Engineering, pp. 143–163. Elsevier Science, New York (1992)

Semiotic Analysis of E-Document as a Composite Digital Sign: The Case of E-Boarding Pass

John Effah[(⊠)]

University of Ghana Business School, Accra, Ghana
jeffah@ug.edu.gh

Abstract. This study draws on organizational semiotics models to analyze e-document as a composite digital sign. E-documents are increasingly becoming important in contemporary digital world. Yet research specifically focusing on analyzing it as an important information systems component remains limited. Moreover, in organizational semiotics research, semantic relationships between signs, objects and intepretants have traditionally been viewed from a single triangle perspective. This study therefore seeks to analyze e-document as a composite digital sign from multiple triangle perspective, using e-boarding pass as an illustrative case.

Keywords: Organizational semiotics · E-document · Composite sign · Digital sign · E-boarding pass

1 Introduction

The term document generally refers to an identified collection of recorded information [11]. Document is physical when it is on paper or electronic when it is in digital format. An e-document is considered as a composite object because it can contain multiple elements in varied forms, including text, image and diagram. Moreover, each of the individual elements can be considered as an object in its own right.

Following the emergence of the printing press and subsequent diffusion of computers and printers, documents have increasingly become significant parts of organizations and society. Moreover, administrative and governance systems in modern organizations have resulted in increased volume of documents in daily routines [10]. As Latham [2] points out, documents are found in almost every area of human lives.

Documents have traditionally been paper-based. However, the advent of information and communication technologies has created the opportunity for e-documents [4] as digital objects. Compared to paper documents, e-documents are not only cheaper but also more flexible, remotely accessible and easily transferrable. As a result, organizations and society in general are increasingly migrating from paper to e-documents. Yet information systems research specifically focusing on e-document as object of

Published by Springer International Publishing Switzerland 2016. All Rights Reserved
M.C.C. Baranauskas et al. (Eds.): ICISO 2016, IFIP AICT 477. pp. 107–116, 2016.
DOI: 10.1007/978-3-319-42102-5_12

analysis in its own right remains scanty. This study therefore draws on organizational semiotics to highlight e-document as an important information system component for analysis.

The rest of this paper is structured as follows. Section 2 reviews related works on e-documents. Section 3 discusses the semiotic triangle and the semiotic framework as theoretical models for the study. Section 4 uses the two models for the e-document analyses. Section 5 uses e-boarding pass to illustrate e-document as a composite digital sign. Section 6 concludes the paper and offers direction for future research.

2 Related Works

2.1 E-Documents

While physical documents are paper-based, the advent of computers and related networks such as the Internet has afforded the creation and use of e-documents [5, 9] as a collection of binary digits [1]. Paper documents are static and have limited media content. However, e-documents are dynamic and multi-media. Their varied contents and formats can include text, audio, video and animation [5, 11]. With these attributes, e-document can be considered as a composite digital object [11].

2.2 E-Documents Analysis

Information system studies [e.g. 4, 6, 9] on e-documents have largely focused on standards for interoperability. E-document standards were traditionally proprietary and thus restricted interoperability. However, recent development of platform and application-independent standards promotes open exchange and interoperability [6]. The extensible mark-up language (XML) is an example of such open standards [9]. Unlike proprietary standards, XML promotes open document exchange and interoperability [4]. Thus various attempts on e-document analysis have focused more on standardization [6], which in semiotic terms relates to syntax. Less research therefore exists on other human and technical dimensions of semiotics. This study draws on organizational semiotics for e-document analysis beyond syntax.

3 Organizational Semiotics

Semiotics concerns the study of signs. Sign itself refers to anything that stands to someone for something else in a given context [12, 13]. Organizational semiotics is a branch of semiotics that studies development and use of information systems in organizations [3]. This study draws on its semiotic triangle and framework [13] for the analysis of e-document as a composite digital sign.

3.1 E-Documents Analysis

From a triadic perspective, Peirce's version of semiotic triangle presents semantic relationship between a sign, its referenced object and interpretant [8]. The semiotic triangle helps to explain how signs are interpreted by humans in a given context. Figure 1 shows a generic view of the semiotic triangle and its triadic relationship.

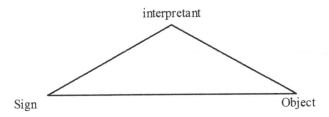

Fig. 1. Semiotic triangle [13]

As Fig. 1 shows, a sign stands not for itself but for something else; the referenced object. Interpretant is the sense made of the sign in relation to the object; the interpreter is the person who makes sense of the sign [3, 8]. The position of this paper is that a single triangular relationship may be sufficient for simple signs with just one referenced object and interpretant. However, composite signs with multiple referenced objects and interpretants/interpreters such as e-documents require multiple triangular relationships.

3.2 The Semiotic Framework

The semiotic framework [3, 13] presents six levels of a sign: physical, empirical, syntactic, semantic, pragmatic and social effects, as shown in Fig. 2. The six levels are further divided into two categories: the technical platform and human information contexts. The technical platform comprises the first three levels, namely the physical, empirical and syntactic; the human information context comprises the remaining three: semantic, pragmatic and social effects.

The *physical* level comprises the material properties and structure of a sign including its storage, communication and access media. For documents, the physical level refers to paper and its properties in the case of physical documents or binary digits and related properties in the case of e-documents. The *empirical* level concerns the technical attributes and quality measures of transmission and communication of signs. For physical documents, the empirical level deals with quality measures of postal and personal delivery systems; for an e-document, the empirical concerns quality attributes and measures of electronic communication media including e-mail and document exchange protocols. The *syntax* layer deals with the technical structure of a sign in terms of rules and standards for its composition.

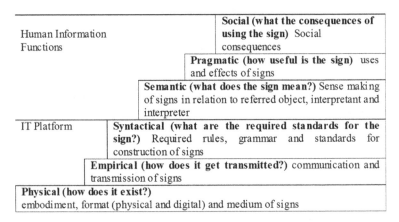

		Social (what the consequences of using the sign) Social consequences
Human Information Functions		Pragmatic (how useful is the sign) uses and effects of signs
	Semantic (what does the sign mean?) Sense making of signs in relation to referred object, interpretant and interpreter	
IT Platform	Syntactical (what are the required standards for the sign?) Required rules, grammar and standards for construction of signs	
	Empirical (how does it get transmitted?) communication and transmission of signs	
Physical (how does it exist?) embodiment, format (physical and digital) and medium of signs		

Fig. 2. Generic semiotic framework, adapted from [7]

For the human information functions, the *semantic* layer concerns the meaning of a sign. For a document, the semantic layer deals with its interpretation. The *pragmatic* layer refers to interpersonal communication and use of a sign in relation to intentions and behavior of senders and receivers as responsible agents. The pragmatic level can be used to analyze the intentions a sender attaches to a document and its content as well as the subsequent reaction of the receiver. Finally, the *social* level concerns the effects of norms that result from the use of signs, such as agreements, commitments and obligations. At this level, a document can serve as evidence of a contract or commitment to an action. This study employs the semiotic framework to analyze e-document as a composite digital sign.

4   Semiotic Analysis of E-Document

This study employs the semiotic triangle and the framework to analyze e-document as a composite digital sign. In this study, digital sign refers to any sign that is electronic and therefore based on binary digit format; composite sign is any sign that contains other signs.

4.1   Semiotic Triangle View of E-Document

The semiotic triangle is used to model e-document as a composite digital sign - a sign of signs. Figure 3 illustrates the triangular relationships between an e-document as a sign and its multiple referenced objects and interpretants.

The figure shows that as a composite sign, an e-document can stand for multiple objects in relation to multiple interpretants. Moreover, while the e-document itself can be a sign, each of its components can also be a sign on its own. Traditionally, semantic analysis in organizational semiotics research has focused on signs with single objects

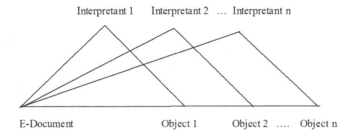

Interpretant 1   Interpretant 2   ... Interpretant n

E-Document   Object 1   Object 2 .... Object n

Fig. 3. Semiotic triangle composite signs

and interpretants. However, the composite nature of e-document calls for a more complex triangular relationships.

4.2   Semiotic Framework View of E-Document

The semiotic framework provides a useful model for representing e-document as digital sign. Figure 4 shows the semiotic framework view of e-document in terms of its technical platform and human/social context. The *physical layer* concerns binary digits as the base constituents of an e-document. It also includes the multi-media forms of e-documents including, text, image, audio, video and more. Other components of the physical layer include computer and network devices that provide the medium for the existence of e-document as a sign. Examples of such devices include desktop, mobile devices (mobile phones, PDAs, tablets and laptops), servers and telecommunication devices (modems, hubs and bridges) that support the display and communication of digital signs.

The *empirical layer* concerns quality attributes of e-document communication via computer displays and telecommunication devices. Examples of such empirical attributes include readability, clarity, brightness, size and software/hardware protocols that affect such qualities during display and communication of e-documents. The *syntactic layer* deals with rules, standards and conventions that govern the structural composition of e-document as a digital sign. For e-documents, such syntactical issues concern the natural language of composing the document, related application/platform standards as well as international, national and industry standards. An example of such standards is XML. Specific industries such as air transportation and international trade also have specified standards for specific documents just as some countries have also defined technical standards for specific documents.

The *semantic layer* deals with the meaning of an e-document in relation to a particular interpreter. Since a digital document can be multi-media, there could be multiple semantics of it at the same time given different interpretants/interpreters. The *pragmatic layer* deals with intention behind the communication of an e-document by a sender and intended effects on a receiver. It concerns the assessment of the effectiveness or otherwise of the intended purpose on the receiver of the e-document. As in the case of the semantic layer, an e-document communication from a sender to receivers can generate multiple pragmatic effects.

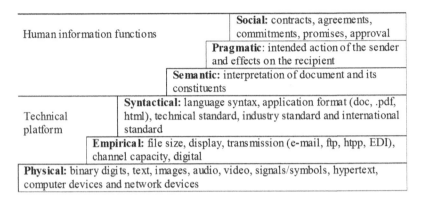

Human information functions				**Social:** contracts, agreements, commitments, promises, approval
			Pragmatic: intended action of the sender and effects on the recipient	
		Semantic: interpretation of document and its constituents		
Technical platform		**Syntactical:** language syntax, application format (doc, .pdf, html), technical standard, industry standard and international standard		
	Empirical: file size, display, transmission (e-mail, ftp, htpp, EDI), channel capacity, digital			
Physical: binary digits, text, images, audio, video, signals/symbols, hypertext, computer devices and network devices				

Fig. 4. Semiotic framework view of e-document as a digital sign

Finally, *social effects* refer to norms that result from using an e-document in a given context. Again, like the semantic and pragmatic layers, the social effects layer can also be multiple for a given e-document. As Fig. 5 shows, an e-document with a single technical platform can have multiple social contexts involving multiple human actors with varied forms of semantics, pragmatics and social effects.

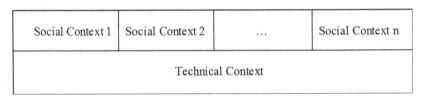

Social Context 1	Social Context 2	...	Social Context n
Technical Context			

Fig. 5. Socio-technical semiotic framework for e-document as a composite digital sign

5   Semiotic Analysis of E-Boarding Pass

Following the semiotic analysis at the generic level, this section provides an illustration of e-boarding pass as an exemplary composite digital sign. The issuing of e-boarding pass is increasingly becoming the norm in air transportation. Figure 6 shows an excerpt of a sample e-boarding pass used for the illustration.

5.1   Semiotic Triangle View of E-Boarding Pass

From semiotic perspective, e-boarding pass can stand for different objects to different people. Figure 7 shows e-boarding pass as a composite sign with multiple interpreters and referenced objects. Examples of relevant interpreters are passengers, ground airline

Fig. 6. An excerpt of e-boarding pass

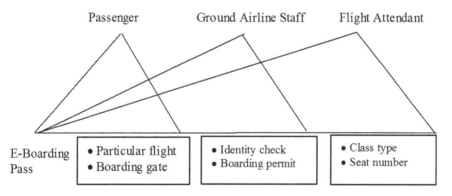

Fig. 7. Semiotic triangle view of e-boarding pass as a composite digital sign

staff and flight attendants. As shown in Fig. 7, each interpreter can interpret the e-boarding pass or any of its constituents differently. For the passenger, the boarding pass can point to the particular flight and boarding gate. For the ground airline staff, it can point to passenger identity check and boarding permit. For the flight attendant, the boarding pass can stand for the class type and seat number.

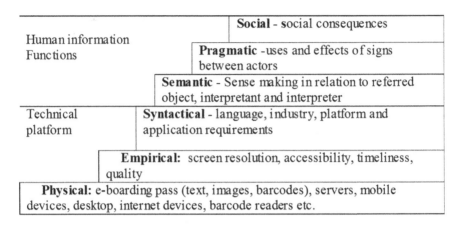

Fig. 8. Semiotic framework view of e-boarding pass

5.2 Semiotic Framework View of E-Boarding Pass

From the technical platform of the semiotic framework, e-boarding pass exhibits various attributes at the physical, empirical and syntactic levels as shown in Fig. 8. The *physical* attributes of e-boarding pass refers to its composition as well as storage, access and communication media. The composition include text, images and barcodes. Storage and access media include disks, servers, mobile devices, desktop, internet networks, and barcode readers; the communication media include electronic display and transmission media. The *empirical* attributes concern display and communication quality measures such as screen resolution, network accessibility, speed and sharpness of applications and devices used for the display and communication. The *syntax* attributes concern the rules, standards and protocols that govern the design of e-boarding pass. Such standards include grammar and conventions of the relevant natural language as well as technical and industry standards including IATA (International air transport Association) regulations.

While the technical level illustrate the physical composition of the e-boarding pass as a single unit, the human information context shows multiple forms of semantic, pragmatic and social effects attributes, given the involvement of multiple interpreters and referenced objects. The *semantic layer* deals with how each of the different interpreters makes sense of the e-boarding pass. For example the passenger, the ground airline staff and the flight attendants may each interpret the boarding pass differently.

The *pragmatic layer* concerns communication of the e-boarding pass from one actor to another. Within the boarding process, there can be multiple communication of the e-boarding pass, such as from the airline's server to the customer's mobile phone, the customer showing the e-boarding pass to ground staff and the customer showing it to a flight attendant. In each of these interactions, there could be counter communication from the receiver to the sender, thus reversing the communication direction.

Hence, there could be several scenarios of pragmatic enactments. Similarly, there could be multiple scenarios of *social effects* depending on the variety user groups involved, including permission to travel, right to travel, right to sit on a particular seat etc.

6 Conclusion

This paper focused on organizational semiotic analysis of e-document as a composite digital sign. It used an extended version of the semiotic triangle and alternative conceptualization of the semiotic framework to analyse e-document as a composite digital sign and illustrated the analysis with an e-boarding pass case. The study contributes to organizational semiotic research in two ways. First, it extends the single triangle view of sign-object-interpretant relationship to a multiple triangle view for composite signs. The extended model can be used for analysis and modelling of information system components that share characteristics of component signs.

Second, the study offers alternative conceptualization of the semiotic framework to account for semiotic analysis of composite digital signs with single technical platform but multiple human contexts. Again, this reconceptualization can be used for organizational semiotics research on individual information technology components with varied human information contexts, given multiple stakeholders' interpretations, intentions and social effects. For practical contribution, the conceptualization of composite digital signs can be used by information systems analysts and designers to account for attributes of entities with different interpretations by varied user groups. Future research can focus on pragmatic analysis of e-document communication in networked organizational environments.

References

1. Buckland, M.K.: What Is a "Document"? J. Am. Soc. Inf. Sci. **48**(9), 804–809 (1986)
2. Latham, K.F.: Experiencing documents. J. Doc. **70**(4), 544–561 (2014)
3. Liu, K., Li, W.: Organisational Semiotics for Business Informatics. Taylor and Francis, London (2014)
4. Liu, O., et al.: E-document management based on web services and XML. Assoc. Inf. Syst. **14**(33), 691–703 (2004)
5. Lund, N.W.: Document, text and medium: concepts, theories and disciplines. J. Doc. **66**(5), 734–749 (2010)
6. Magee, L., Thom, J.A.: What's in a WordTM? When one electronic document format standard is not enough. Inf. Technol. People **27**(4), 482–511 (2014)
7. Mingers, J.: Guidelines for conducting semiotic research in information systems (2014)
8. Mingers, J., Willcocks, L.: An integrative semiotic framework for information systems: the social, personal and material worlds. Inf. Manag. **24**(1), 48–70 (2014)
9. Renear, A., Dubin, D.: Towards identity conditions for digital documents. In: International Conference on Core Metadata Application, Dublin, pp. 181–189 (2003)
10. Sarantinos, V.: Document workflow: modelling and issues for the non-savvy. Int. J. Inf. Technol. **2**(3), 202–209 (2010)

11. Sprague, R.: Electronic document management: challenges and opportunities for information systems managers. MIS Q. **19**(1), 19–24 (1995)
12. Stamper, R.: Organisational semiotics: informatics without the computer? In: Liu, K., et al. (eds.) Information, Organisation and Technology: Studies in Organisational Semiotics. Kluwer, The Netherlands (2001)
13. Stamper, R., et al.: Understanding the roles of signs and norms in organisations - a semiotic approach to information systems design. Behav. Inf. Technol. **19**(1), 15–27 (2000)

Organisational Responsiveness Through Signs

Diego Fuentealba[1,2(✉)], Kecheng Liu[1,3], and Weizi Li[1]

[1] Informatics Research Centre, University of Reading, Reading, UK
d.a.fuentealbacid@pgr.reading.ac.uk,
{k.liu,weizi.li}@henley.ac.uk
[2] School of Informatics and Telecommunications,
Universidad Tecnológica de Chile-INACAP, Santiago, Chile
[3] School of Information Management and Engineering,
Shanghai University of Finance and Economics, Shanghai, China

Abstract. Organisational Semiotics is a discipline that studies signs of organisations, and how these signs aid an analysis and design of technical information systems. The responsiveness of organisations has been discussed as a key feature to adapt the organisational behaviour in turbulent environments, but there are not studies about the implication of these capabilities on Information Systems. Organisational Semiotics can be used as a good approach to understand relationships between living things and organisations in order to develop their responses to the organisation. The purpose of this paper is the proposition of a preliminary model of organisations as living systems, using the concept of organisations as information systems. This paper articulates the information interactions between the border of the system, the environment and the activities of the organisation that maintain this border by methods of organisational semiotics. The future study will focus on the implementation of the proposed framework.

Keywords: Organisational semiotics · Autopoiesis · Responsiveness

1 Introduction

Small and Medium Enterprises (SMEs) are facing constant changes in consumer preferences. A number of competitors and a market size are some factors which impact on how SMEs should respond to changes in the competitive environment [1]. The definition of responsiveness has been used in a wide range of fields as quality to react positively and quickly [2], and responsiveness of organisations has been seen as the ability to recognise changes and act on them [3]. However, the current approaches of responsiveness have been focused on reactions to certain changes, such as customer needs [4], suppliers [5, 6] and supply chain [7], without providing a holistic understanding of which degree of the organisation can support these changes and why. Although responsiveness of organisations is not seen as a competitive advantage like agility, which included the speed of change and the flexibility of infrastructure to change [3], responsiveness should be seen as a basic capability of organisations that allows adaptations and modifications without affecting their current strengths. Autopoiesis as an explanation of life in living systems reveal why living things maintain their

M.C.C. Baranauskas et al. (Eds.): ICISO 2016, IFIP AICT 477, pp. 117–126, 2016.
DOI: 10.1007/978-3-319-42102-5_13

inner-organisations in spite of the environment's changes, and provide a basic expla-nation of which kind of responsiveness can be expected from living systems in order to survive. Current studies about autopoiesis in Information Systems (IS) point out some challenges of preservation of an identity after several changes [8] where the organi-sational image can play a significant role in the definition of the main features of the IS [9, 10]. These definitions explained some properties of an autopoietic system that can be applied to technical IS, e.g. avoiding a concrete analysis of the concept of pro-duction of signs and information to maintain an organisational border that response to the environment with components of IS. This paper provides a preliminary model of organisation based on the definition of autopoiesis to understand why organisations can be seen as living systems, and how their responsiveness should be analysed and designed in order to maintain the autopoietic relationships and structure.

This paper starts with the definition of responsiveness for organisations and living systems, using the definition of autopoiesis as the main engine of responsiveness in Sect. 2. Section 3 analyses the semiosis of organisation as an autopoietic process, followed by the proposition of the preliminary model of organisation in Sect. 4, using the cell-structure as a functional basis. Section 5 discusses the application of this theory, and followed by conclusions and future work in Sect. 6.

2 Responsiveness from Living Systems

Responsiveness of living systems can be defined as the ability of a living-thing to undergo a response [11]. This reaction must maintain the network of processes that allows the life or the autopoiesis of the living system [12]. Autopoiesis can explain why living systems define a set of thresholds to maintain this network of processes. For example, in the case of a cell, its autopoiesis needs a membrane to perform this network, which at the same time produces lipids and proteins to maintain the mem-brane [13]. The responsiveness of a cell could be defined as the threshold of an external stimulus until the cell reacts to maintain the autopoiesis. An example of this threshold is the Heat shock response to avoid protein damage, which is a biochemical response of cells to mild heat stress. In this case, the cell response is the production of the protein HSF1 that repair some protein damage, developing thermos-tolerance [14]. This reaction cannot be explained without the principle of autopoiesis to maintain the membrane. Thus, the definition of autopoiesis in the organisation can help the devel-opment of thresholds and capabilities to improve the responsiveness of organisations.

2.1 Kinds of Autopoietic Systems

According to [15], depending on a level of autonomy and dynamic, autopoietic systems can be classified in first, second and third order. First order autopoietic systems are basic forms of life like a prokaryote or eukaryote cell [13]. They possess the main features of autopoietic systems, which is the capability to produce their components (self-production) as a result of a network of processes. Some features of this kind of systems such as the maintenance of border and the relationship of their components can be found in the autopoietic test proposed by [16]. Second-order autopoietic systems are meta-cellular organisms that are multicellular systems with the same lineage and structural couplings among them. This is possible if the regular interactions among autopoietic systems are sources of perturbations and compensations, where the participated systems do not lose their identity, creating a new unity. Examples of this kind of systems are human beings, animals and plants, which possess their own form of autopoiesis. Meta-cellular organism with nervous systems shows new forms of interactions such as abstract interactions and new inner-states as a result of their self-conscious, which at the same time is able to represent the world with abstract representations. Third-order autopoietic systems are societies of second-order autopoietic systems, which coordinate their acts by language. Communication makes the social coupling by means of linguistic perturbations and compensations among individuals, creating inner-regular interactions in the form of cultural acts [15].

2.2   Minimal Autopoietic Structure

The definition of autopoiesis does not say anything about the components, because autopoiesis emphasises the organisation or the network of processes of production of components over the structure [12]. However, it is possible to describe a basic structure of cells based on the concept of minimal cells, which use the self-production property to define the basic components to self-produce a membrane [17, 18]. The semi-synthetic minimal cell is an extension of this concept that defines the DNA, enzymes, ribosome, RNA, membrane and cytoplasm as basic components for self-maintenance, self-reproduction and possibility to evolve [19].

Additionally, according to [12] there are three kinds of relations of productions that constitute some basic structure. They proposed the following relations:

- Production of constitutive relations: there are components that maintain the topology or physical space. The network of processes of production of these elements constitutes the topology of the autopoietic system
- Production of specificity relations: There are components that specify the creation of other components. The network of processes of production of these elements determines the identity of the components of the autopoietic organisations
- Production of relations of Order: There are components that regulate the points of meeting among processes. The network of processes of production of these elements determines the relations of order among the other processes

These relations describe the following components:

- Topological Components: The main function is the topological deployment of other components. Although membrane is a good example of these components, there are active sites in enzymes that fit with this description
- Creational Components: There are components such as DNA, RNA and enzymes with the capability to produce other components
- Control Components: There are components such as metabolites and enzymes with the capability to control the speed of the production of elements

Table 1. Relation between component and their classification

Component	Function	Kind of component	Specification relation
DNA	Replication	Creational	Specification
RNA	Message of protein synthesis	Creational	Specification
Enzymes	Catalysis	Creational and control	Specification and order
Ribosome	Protein synthesis (translation of RNA into protein)	Creational	Specification
Membrane	Maintenance of cellular environment	Topological	Constitutive
Cytoplasm	Provide a solver system and help the movement of food	Topological	Constitutive

Thus, there are components such as enzymes with more than one function. Table 1 classifies the components of the minimal cell with the components described from the autopoietic relations, and the function of these components into the cell.

Therefore, it is possible to define components based on the three relations of production, where creational and control components can be divided into message, control and production components. The creation of components in an autopoietic system conjugates these three relationships, because it is created a specific component in a specific physical space controlled by components produced by the cell.

3   Information Systems as Organisational Semiosis

3.1   Semiotics Implications of Sign, Data, Information and IS

The understanding of information, data and interpreter can be made with the division of Peirce among interpreter, sign and object [20]. Signs from the perspective of semiotics can be anything determined by an external object and the effect of them upon a person (interpreter). This division defines an object with an independence of the observer and his/her knowledge, where the full understanding of an object can be made with a chain of signs [21]. According to [22], there are intrinsic relations among information, events and signs. Events like objects are independent of an observer, and they can be stored and transmitted as signs by the environment and people. Data of an event can be seen as a collection of signs, which can be stored or transmitted as information. Thus, data is a kind of representation of events. On the other hand, information is a human process of sense making related to semantics, pragmatics and social world, which interprets signs or data as events in the daily life [23]. Figure 1 shows this relationship among events, data, sign and information, where the process of semiosis in the organisation is the process of sense making or understanding of external events, which are perceived as a collection of signs. The organisation has a role of interpreter of these signs to see the events as objects, which could be an abstract representation of the event or another sign that trigger the process of semiosis again. The organisation as the interpreter is affected by previous knowledge, which can be norms, culture and other events that restrict the

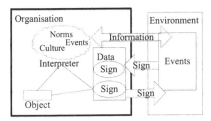

Fig. 1. Organisational semiosis and the responsiveness through signs

behaviour or the possibility for reaction. This background knowledge can be updated as a result of this process and the information about events can open the possibility to react in the form of action or events that at the same time creates new signs. Examples of previous events that can shape the organisational behaviour could be the membership of people in different positions, the acquisition of new technology, changes in the regulation or changes in the competence. For this reason, the responsiveness of external perturbations is limited to the understanding of events or previous semiosis, which restricts or enables this capability for reaction.

According to [20], organisations can be seen as IS, where a set of norms can define the manner of behaving. There are informal, formal and technical norms, where the informal norms are beliefs and goals which are the first definition of the phenomenon named organisation. When a set of clear agreements are made, formal and technical norms formalise the messages of organisations, but in practical terms, they are the understanding and control of this phenomenon. This process of understanding of the organisation as a phenomenon, which starts from the informal layer shapes a set of data from events as formal and technical norms, creating information as a constant process of semiosis.

3.2   First Order Autopoietic System

Responsiveness of organisations depends on capabilities to response through signs, which can be analysed from the biologic perspective of autopoiesis. Organisational onion can simplify the analysis, focusing on the technical and formal layer [23]. The algorithm of six points proposed by [16] can help to analyse systems as an autopoietic system, starting with the analysis of the border and finishing with the analysis of interaction in the network of interactions. Information systems can be seen as autopoietic systems, because the lack of physical boundaries results in a boundary based on the information that is produced by the organisation. Referring to Fig. 1, technical and formal activities are not possible without an understanding (information) of previous events (data). Figure 2 shows the self-definition of identifiable components such as contracts and inventory that can be used in the activities that interact with the environment. These components lead deterministic interactions from previous data or agreements, which can be connected in specific contexts. For instance, the sale activity as a context contains pre-defined signs such as contracts or inventory (norms, tasks or data) that are linked with components of the border, resulting in actions that create signs and information (receipt). Finally, the components that are not self-produced by

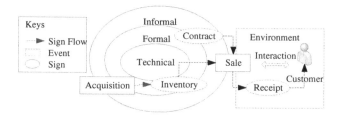

Fig. 2. The role of signs in autopoiesis

the Information System are directly related to the process of generation of information. For instance, the inventory represents the acquisition event and participates in the sales action as a response to customer needs.

Although IS has fitted their features with the autopoietic test, this analysis was made under ideal conditions. For instance, the theoretical division in layers of technical IS can be argued if a technical IS does not have this division. Therefore, the responsiveness of autopoietic systems can be summarised as the capability to maintain its border in spite of environmental perturbations.

4   Preliminary Model of Organisations as Living Systems

Under the assumption that organisation can behave as living systems, Fig. 3 shows an autopoietic model of organisations based on the division of functional components of a minimal cell and the components of an organisation based on organisational semiotics such as the definition substantive, control and communication behaviour.

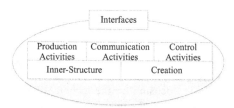

Fig. 3. Autopoietic model of organisation

The main components of the model described as follows.

- Interfaces: These components are inspired in the membrane and represent the interactions that the IS must consider with the external environment such as the interchange of matter and energy. The main sources of interactions are customers, suppliers and other stakeholders such as government (i.e. custom and revenues) and partners. Initially, the border of the organisation is defined by the purpose of the organisation, and the activities that interact with the environment with physical and social consequences. The components of the organisation that participate in the border activity are agents, substantive activity, control and communication.

- Creation Components: These components are inspired on the DNA, and they define the aim of the organisation. Some examples are which product or service is produced, which raw material or organisational product/activity is needed to interact with other stakeholders. It is important to highlight that DNA or creation components control the specification of each component of the organisation and the internal coherence in the form of meta-norms [24]. Meta-norms self-regulate the organisation as a result of the process of adaptation from the environment, because they look the environment in order to prepare or change Meta-norms of organisation for new interactions. For instance, the (re)definition of the strategy is not directly involved in the production, but it would affect the production activities.
- Inner Structure Components: These components are inspired by the Cytoplasm. The inner structure is composed of structural components that define order or hierarchy of the organisation such as hierarchy of communication, the division of departments and the assignation of agents in certain positions. This inner structure is mainly static and defines who the boss of whom is.
- Communication Activities: These activities are inspired by the RNA. These activities are named coordination tasks, because they are not directly involved in the production of product/services, but they are also significant to the organisation. These activities can be basic activities to coordinate processes, but in a complex organisation, there are workflows, which is a composition of communication power and tasks.
- Production Activities: These activities are inspired by the Ribosome. These activities are the substantive tasks that are involved in the creation of product/service of the organisation.
- Control Activities: These activities regulate task and behaviour of the members. There are several classifications of norms, for instance, it is possible to classify according to the control of human behaviour, the effect of execution and the object that is applied [20]. Thus, norms are capable of controlling every aspect of the organisation from their informal conception to their technical application.

These components can create a structure of the organisation, which is based on the minimal components to perform the autopoiesis of a cell. Although, the autopoiesis of organisations have been explained from the perspective of Information Systems and the generation of information, the self-description of these components are the image of the organisation, and their relationships can define a new form of autopoiesis from an abstract perspective. For instance, goals are related to tasks, and the strategy can define new goals. These cycles that generate new organisational signs and new information can be seen as a new perspective of autopoiesis.

5   Discussion

The autopoietic model represents an abstract level of the organisation, but its general features can be applied to any organisations. Companies with several changes during their life can be experimented to study the activity change after different states. An example of this kind of company is Rolls-Royce, which has changed its border activities from a good-dominant (GD) logic to a service-dominant (SD) logic due to the decreasing of the original equipment market. The competitive market with high investment in technology and R&D has pushed to Rolls-Royce into the implementation of the total customer's care system, which means that the business is also focused on the services of aftermarket such as maintenance and repairs of jet-engines [25]. The autopoietic components of Rolls-Royce are:

- Interfaces of Rolls-Royce: Every division of Rolls-Royce provides contracts that include the maintenance, repair and overhaul of their products, making the 50 % of the revenue of the company [26]. The customer's activities are related to the selling of product and services, which are focused on the creation of customer solutions in the form of product and service such as flight hours. The strategy of suppliers of Rolls-Royce is more complex than the procurement of products, but this activity can be seen as a key activity of the border.
- Production Activities: The production of engines is the main activity of civil aerospace division, but also they need goods from the suppliers. For the procurement activity, the supplier selection and segmentation are the activities that can provide new suppliers to maintain this dynamic. The maintenance activity as the border needs the data and strategy from engine health monitoring.
- Control Activities: Part of the control activities are the management of portfolio products, Inventory Management, Inventory Management for Aftermarket service parts and Production Management [26]. All processes of Rolls-Royce are controlled by the flow of cash and financial indicators [27]. Additionally, Rolls-Royce works with several quality standards such as six Sigma, robust design and optimization [28] that measure the production activities.
- Communication Activities: Communication activities can be seen as a part of production and controls activities. For example, production activities are connected with a central ERP system, which spread the current state of inventory [27].
- Inner-Structure: The inner-structure of Rolls-Royce is the division of business units. There is a strong relationship among the production of engines and the maintenance or after service activities.
- Meta-Norms: The meta-norms of the organisation can be seen in the strategy that is focused on the customers, innovation and growth [29]. An example of this application is the innovation, which is reflected in all activities like the collaborative product development.

The autopoietic capabilities of Rolls-Royce are reflected from (1) their management of the suppliers, including the selection and segmentation of new suppliers, in order to maintain this dynamic; and (2) the application of meta-norms, like innovation, to govern their collaboration with the suppliers. Therefore, it is possible to find some behaviour of cells into organisations, and organisations with good practices like Rolls-Royce shows internal activities that maintain the border of the organisation.

6 Conclusion and Future Work

Autopoiesis can explain why living-things have responsiveness, and the definition of autopoiesis from the organisational semiotics can be useful to describe the elements of organisations that are essential in the maintenance of border through the change. The definition of interfaces as the core activities that interchange matter and energy, the set of activities to control, communicate and produce the elements of the border can be seen as an approach to review and understand organisations, their elements and relationships that allow the adaptation. The role of signs is the understanding of organisations as autopoietic systems, which create signs, depending on the current sign structure. Under these conditions, the responsiveness of organisations can be improved with the analysis of the impact of signs and their changes between technical and formal layers, and also among the signs in the interfaces with other kinds of activities in the autopoietic model of organisation. The next stage of this work is the identification of the relationship among these components, and the application of these elements in the analysis of signs of organisations. One of the problems in the design of technical information systems and the analysis of the capability to change is how the connections in the formal layer can be reflected into the technical layer. It is accepted that technical information systems can promote the adaptation, which can be seen in the communication activities, but there are several technical solutions such as three layers architecture or service oriented architecture that promote the flexibility of technical IS, without considering the real capability of the organisation. This work is the first attempt of this understanding.

Acknowledgements. This research is partial supported by CONICYT (BCH72130542/2012).

References

1. Liao, J., Welsch, H., Stoica, M.: Organizational absorptive capacity and responsiveness: an empirical investigation of growth-oriented SMEs. Enrtrepreneurship Theor. Pract. **28**, 63–86 (2003)
2. Stevenson, A.: Responsiveness. In: Oxford Dictionary of English. Oxford University Press, Oxford, p. 2112 (2010)
3. Yaghoubi, N.M., Kord, B., Azadikhah, O.: Assessing organizational agility via fuzzy logic. Int. Bus. Res. **4**, 135–145 (2011)
4. Nidumolu, S.R., Knotts, G.W.: The effects of customizability and reusability on perceived process and competitive performance of software firms. MISQ Q. **22**, 105–137 (1998)
5. Wang, E., Tai, J., Wei, H.L.: A virtual integration theory of improved supply-chain performance. J. Manag. Inf. Syst. **23**, 41–64 (2006)
6. Choi, T.Y., Krause, D.R.: The supply base and its complexity: implications for transaction costs, risks, responsiveness, and innovation. J. Oper. Manag. **24**, 637–652 (2006)
7. Williams, B.D., Roh, J., Tokar, T., Swink, M.: Leveraging supply chain visibility for responsiveness: the moderating role of internal integration. J. Oper. Manag. **31**, 543–554 (2013)
8. Huysman, M., Blonk, H., Van Der Spoor, E.: Autopoiesis and the Evolution of Information Systems. Autopoiesis in Organization Theory and Practice, pp. 1–13 (2009)
9. Bača, M., Schatten, M., Deranja, D.: Autopoietic information systems in modern organizations. Organizacija J. Manag. Inform. Hum. Resour. **40**, 157–165 (2007)
10. Kay, R., Cecez-kecmanovic, D.: Toward an autopoietic perspective on information systems organization. In: Twenty-Third International Conference on Information Systems, pp. 383–390 (2002)

11. Cammack, R., Atwood, T., Campbell, P., Parish, H., Smith, A., Vella, F., Stirling, J.: Responsiveness. In: Oxford Dictionary of Biochemistry and Molecular. Oxford University Press, Oxford (2006)
12. Maturana, H., Varela, F.: Autopoiesis and Cognition The Realization of the Living. Springer Science & Business Media, Berlin (1980)
13. Mingers, J.: Self-producing Systems Implications and Applications of Autopoiesis. Springer Science & Business Media, Berlin (1995)
14. Fulda, S., Gorman, A.M., Hori, O., Samali, A.: Cellular stress responses: cell survival and cell death. Int. J. Cell Biol. **2010**, 1–23 (2010)
15. Maturana, H., Varela, F.J.: The Tree of Knowledge: The Biological Roots of Human Understanding. Shambhala Publications, Boulder (1992)
16. Varela, F.G., Maturana, H., Uribe, R.: Autopoiesis: the organization of living systems, its characterization and a model. Currents Modern Biol. **5**, 187–196 (1974)
17. Fleischaker, G.R.: Autopoiesis: the status of its system logic. Bio System **22**, 37–49 (1988)
18. Luisi, P.L., Varela, F.J.: Self-replicating micelles - a ahemical aersion of a minimal autopoietic system. Orig. Life Evol. Biosph. **19**, 633–643 (1989)
19. Stano, P., Luisi, P.L.: Semi-synthetic minimal cells: origin and recent developments. Current Opin. Biotechnol. **24**, 633–638 (2013)
20. Liu, K., Li, W.: Organisational Semiotics for Business Informatics. Taylor and Francis, Hoboken (2014)
21. Atkin, A.: Peirce's Theory of Signs. In: Stanford Encyclopedia of Philosophy (2013)
22. Mingers, J., Willcocks, L.: An integrative semiotic framework for information systems: the social, personal and material worlds. Inf. Organ. **24**, 48–70 (2014)
23. Stamper, R.: Semiotic Theory of Information and Information Systems. In: Signs of Work: Semiosis and Information Processing in Organisations, pp. 349–398 (1996)
24. Stamper, R., Liu, K., Hafkamp, M., Ades, Y.: Understanding the roles of signs and norms in organisations. Behav. Inf. Technol. **19**, 15–27 (2000)
25. Rolls Royce PLC.: Competing within a Changing World. The Times 100 (2009)
26. Tiwari, M.: An exploration of supply chain management practices in the aerospace industry and in Rolls-Royce. Master dissertation, Massachusetts Institute of Technology (2005)
27. Yusuf, Y., Gunasekaran, A., Abthorpe, M.S.: Enterprise information systems project implementation: a case study of ERP in Rolls-Royce. Int. J. Prod. Econ. **87**, 251–266 (2004)
28. Foden, J., Berends, H.: Technology management at Rolls-Royce. Res-Technol. Manag. **53**, 33–42 (2010)
29. Rolls-Royce Holdings plc: Annual Report 2014. http://ar.rolls-royce.com/2014/assets/pdf/RR_Full_Annual_Report.pdf. Accessed 10 Apr 2016

Research on Association Rules Reasoning and Application of Geosciences Data Based on Ameliorated Trapezoidal Cloud Transformation

Xu Jing[(⊠)]

School of Information Management and Engineering,
Shanghai University of Finance and Economics,
Shanghai 200433, People's Republic of China
13491299@qq.com

Abstract. This paper proposes an association rules reasoning model based on ameliorated trapezoidal cloud transformation. It is aimed primarily at complexity and randomness geosciences data bears. The traditional trapezoidal cloud transformation is improved in order to avoid lack of data mutation information and to finish reasonable and sensitive exchange from qualification to quantification. A set of attributes for simulating faults extraction algorithm is designed, which breaks through limitations of traditional visual interpretation and ensures an effectiveness and completeness of test data. Multi-Level Association Rules (MLAR) model [1] is also adopted to reason and predict unknown faults and fault properties in Chengdu Office zone. The result shows that the MLAR algorithm enhanced an association mining between fault types with their classified attributes.

Keywords: Trapezoidal cloud · MLAR algorithm · Chengdu office

1 Introduction

As a series of systems deep geochemical exploration, space remote sensing and geodetic survey, were established and improved. Vast amounts of data have been gradually accumulated in the area of earth science, and these data need to be made use of by scientists. Association rules is a data mining method. It was first put forward by Agrawal et al. [1] in 1993. Now it has become one of the most widely used algorithms in the field of data mining. Li et al. [2] has proposed a new method for conversion-cloud information instead of "hard" division which divides a cloud environment into several quantitative concepts based on cloud model considering fully fuzziness and randomness of data. Subsequently, the cloud conversion has been used in many fields. Hu et al. [3] proposes a new way of figuring out the weight of land evaluation factors by mapping qualitative linguistic words into a fine-changeable cloud drops and translating the uncertain factor conditions into quantitative values with the uncertain illation based on cloud model. Fang and Yu [4] attempts to evaluate the economics of wind power projects based on the cloud model. Han et al. [5] imports the conceptual

M.C.C. Baranauskas et al. (Eds.): ICISO 2016, IFIP AICT 477, pp. 127–132, 2016.
DOI: 10.1007/978-3-319-42102-5_14

partition algorithm based on cloud model to finish the exchange from qualification to quantification. Expectation of some concept is not just a numeric value but in a sequence, so trapezoidal cloud makes description more accord with contiguous data. Wang [6] uses trapezoidal cloud model to advance the concepts of division, and transforms qualitative data in to quantitative conception which is proved to be effective. Complexity of geosciences data behaves as not only fuzziness and uncertainty but also large amount in quantities and global continuity.

In this paper, a traditional trapezoidal cloud transformation is described in order to avoid a lack of information about data mutation and to carry out a reasonable and sensitive exchange from qualification to quantification.

2   Construction of Association Rules Mining Model Based on Ameliorated Trapezoidal Cloud Transformation

2.1   Concept Partition Algorithm Based on Ameliorated Trapezoidal Cloud Transformation

According to the basic idea of data fitting and a certain rule [5], spatial data of any irregular distribution are mathematically transformed so as to generate a set of atomic concepts and make the distributed spatial data become the superposition of several concept of different size, the basic idea is expressed in Eq. (1).

$$g(x) = \sum_{i=1}^{n} (c_i * f_i(x)) + \varepsilon \ and \ 0 < Max\left(\left|g(x) - \sum_{i=1}^{n} (c_i * f_i(x))\right|\right) < \varepsilon \quad (1)$$

Geosciences data bears global continuity. As the concept is described, its expectation is not just a numeric value but in a sequence, so trapezoidal cloud makes description more accord with the features of geoscience data. In this paper, trapezoidal cloud is adopted to assist concept division, i.e., dividing a concept into atomic concepts in a number field. Figure 1 shows the structure of trapezoidal cloud.

The function Find_En is used to search for entropy and hyper entropy of cloud droplets. The idea of backward cloud generator [2] is applied during the search.

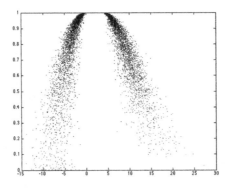

Fig. 1. Diagram of structure of trapezoidal cloud

2.2   Association Rules Mining Algorithm Based on Multi-Level Association Rules Algorithm (MLAR)

Association rules is an important branch in the research area of data mining. It is aimed at mining correlations hidden behind massive data. As a large amount of data is collected and stored, it is increasingly demanded by scientists to discover knowledge from the data.

3   Prediction Model of Fault Property in Chengdu Office Area

In this paper, we will take Chengdu Office area ($28° \sim 32°$ E, $102° \sim 108°$ N) as research zone to determine and predict nature, position and scale of simulated faults by the model of multilevel association rules algorithm based on improved trapezium-cloud model according the geophysical information 1:1,000,000 geologic map of this area conveys.

3.1   Data Preparation and Attribute Extraction Simulation

In this paper, we take fault in Chengdu Office area ($28° \sim 32°$ E, $102° \sim 108°$ N) as the research subject in processing known fault data. Figure 2 presents the spatial data used by this work.

Fig. 2. Satellite image of known faults in Chengdu office zone

Current findings in the field of earth science are built on the fusion of previous space data. According to prior knowledge of experts, subjective judgments on new knowledge are made by using visual interpretation, field measurements and other methods. Rare automated discoveries on new knowledge of earth science are achieved by the degree of inference through association rules, the methods previous adopted are difficult and inefficient.

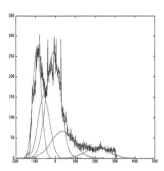

Fig. 3. Line graph of normal distribution fitting data distribution

3.2 Prediction of Faults Property in Chengdu Office Area Based on Ameliorated Trapezoidal Cloud Transformation

According to the data distribution curve of attributes of known and simulated faults (the blue curve in the Fig. 3), the threshold value of error is set at 0.5. It is defined as the input item, when the respective discretization of the number attribute of the 32

Table 1. Association rules

No	Succeeding item	Antecedent item	Support (%)	Confidence (%)	Score
1	ATTR = F	STDMAG_3 = 8 2 3 and AVGMAG0_2 = 5 3*	31.645	95.82	70.15
2	ATTR = F	AVGDEM_3 = 5 2 1 and AVGMAG_2 = 2 9 3 and AVGGRA_3 = 6 3*	27.34	97.89	69.67
3	ATTR = C	AVGGRA_3 = 10 1 3 and STD_GRA0_3 = 21 1 2	26.09	98.54	69.56
4	ATTR = C	AVGMAG0_2 = 5 1* and AVG_GRA45_2 = 12 3*	29.195	94.62	68.45
5	ATTR = D	AVGDEM_3 = 3 1 3 and AVGGRA45_2 = 21 3*	24.01	97.31	67.99
6	ATTR = F	STDDEM_3 = 4 1 3 and AVGGRA45_3 = 15 1 6	28.11	93.81	67.53
7	ATTR = A	AVRGRA_3 = 10 1 3 and AVG_MAG0_2 = 6 1*	35.87	88.12	67.22
8	ATTR = E	AVRGRA_3 = 10 1 3 and AVG_MAG = 6 3* and var_gra451 = 16 2 1	26.35	92.75	66.19
9	ATTR = E	AVGGRA_3 = 3 2 4 and AVGGRA4513_3 = 9 3 2	31.42	89.17	66.07
10	ATTR = F	AVRGRA_3 = 10 1 3 and AVG_MAG0_2 = 7 2* and STDDEM_3 = 5 2 3	35.46	85.66	65.58
11	ATTR = E	STDDEM_3 = 3 1 3	40.17	82.32	65.46
12	ATTR = C	AVGGRA_3 = 6 2 3 and STD_GRA0_3 = 20 2 1	58.705	69.73	65.32

Table 2. Fracture property and direction proportion

Fracture direction	Direction proportion	Fracture property	Property proportion
NE trend (30°–50°)	78 %	General fault	32.46 %
		Klippe	1.36 %
		Thrusting-nappe fault	42.16 %
		Transpressional fault	17 %
		General reverse fault	7.48 %
NS trend (0°)	10 %	General fault	59.32 %
		Transpressional fault	40.68 %
NW trend (270°–360°)	12 %	Thrusting – nappe fault	14.29 %
		General fault	85.71 %

attributes in the table is implemented. After that, the trapezium-cloud concept of every attribute is built.

3.3 Result Validation

In order to judge the quality of association rules, we introduced the scoring mechanism [5]: Score = 40 % * support + 60 % * confidence and the higher score the better quality on simulated faults. Table 1 presents the top 12 association rules used for the experiment on disposal of simulated faults.

Table 2 shows the simulation results. When the length of 40 steps (about 60 km) is chose as a parameter, 42444 simulated faults in each angel were covered. After successive adjustments, it is inferred that 2305 faults are in a north-east direction(35–50°) and most of them are in 40°; 295 faults are in north-south direction; 354 faults are in a north-west direction (270°–360°).

It is important to note that unclassified faults mean that they do not conform to any one of the 12 association rules above. The superposition of the part verified by the simulated faults and the satellite image of this area is shown in Fig. 4.

Fig. 4. Satellite image of simulated faults verified

4 Conclusion

This paper proposed the association rules reasoning model based on ameliorated trapezoidal cloud transformation, which is aimed primarily at complexity and randomness geosciences data bears. The traditional trapezoidal cloud transformation is improved in order to avoid lack of data mutation information and to finish reasonable and sensitive exchange from qualification to quantification. The attributes of simulated faults extraction algorithm was designed to overcome the limitations of traditional visual interpretation to ensure the effectiveness and completeness of the test data. MLAR model was adopted to reason and predict the unknown faults and fault property in Chengdu office zone. The result supports the judgements other academics made for the faults and their attributes in probability perspective, further explains it acts better in association mining between fault types and its attribute data automatically, through which the model's reliability has been testified.

Acknowledgments. Our appreciation goes to Qin Zheng, Wen Wang, Dongmei Han for their valuable comments to improve the quality of the paper.

References

1. Agarwal, R., Imielinski, T., Swami, A.: Mining association rules between sets of items in large databases. In: Proceedings of the ACM SIGMOD Conference on Management of Data, pp. 207–216 (1993)
2. Li, D., Meng, H., Shi, X.: Cloud model and cloud model generator. Comput. Res. Dev. **32**(6), 15–20 (1995)
3. Hu, S., Li, D., Liu, Y., Li, D.: Mining weights of land evaluation factors based on cloud model and correlation analysis. Geo-spat. Inf. Sci. **10**(3), 218–222 (2007)
4. Fang, F., Yu, A.: The Economic evaluation of the wind power projects based on the cloud model. Adv. Intell. Soft Comput. **163**, 443–448 (2013)
5. Han, D., Shi, Y., Wang, W., Dai, D.: Research on multi-level association rules based on geosciences data. J. Softw. **8**(12), 3269–3276 (2013)
6. Wang, Z.: Application of cloud theory in association rules. Int. J. Inf. Technol. Comput. Sci. **3**, 36–42 (2011)

Interactive Data Visualisation: Facilitate the Accountability Disclosure Through the Lens of Organisational Semiotics

Qi Li[1(✉)] and Kecheng Liu[1,2]

[1] Informatics Research Centre, Henley Business School,
University of Reading, Reading, UK
q.li5@pgr.reading.ac.uk, k.liu@henley.ac.uk
[2] School of Information Management and Engineering,
Shanghai University of Finance and Economics, Shanghai, China

Abstract. UK charities suffer from insufficient accountability disclosure regarding different stakeholders, therefore failing to meet their various needs. For the purpose of facilitating an accountability disclosure of the charity reporting practice with interactive data visualisation, this paper, as an extension of the previous research from Liu and Tan [1], is to propose a framework leading the design of interactive data visualisation procedure on the scope of charity reporting practice. It firstly interprets the impact of 'display and interaction' of data visualisation on both semantic and pragmatic levels of data signification, based on the theory of semiosis triangle and semiotic ladder. It then develops a visualisation framework for dividing the information into different degrees of detail and linking each information points to a user's intention. Finally, the developed framework will be applied to a visualisation prototype relating to Age UK.

Keywords: Interactive data visualisation · Organisational semiotics · Pragmatics and visualisation

1 Introduction

Data visualisation, a set of activities to present data or information with the aid of visual representatives, such as a table, map, diagram and chart, allows data to become sense-making in front of various readers [2]. Strecker [3] points out that data visualisation looms as a tool which offers opportunities to transform and display data and information, for the purpose of 'capturing and addressing' complexity of dataset. Segel and Heel [4] point out that an interactivity on data opposed to the traditional static visual display enables readers to filter information according to their reflective interpretation. With the development of cloud computing techniques and data intelligence, interactive data visualisation can be accessed through multi-devices, where the reader can customise content and layout of data dashboard in terms of ad-hoc information requests. To some extent, to compare with traditional 'visual display', the 'interactive' of data visualisation not only enables data to be sense-making, but also fulfils a wide range of information demands from different readers.

© IFIP International Federation for Information Processing 2016
Published by Springer International Publishing Switzerland 2016. All Rights Reserved
M.C.C. Baranauskas et al. (Eds.): ICISO 2016, IFIP AICT 477, pp. 133–142, 2016.
DOI: 10.1007/978-3-319-42102-5_15

Referring to the definition from the Charity Act [5], charity can be defined as the organisation which is established for a charitable purpose and serve the social public with charitable activities. There are 165,231 registered charities in England and Wales, which earn the income of 69.49 billion pound in 2015 [6]. However, Charities have been suffering from low transparency because of insufficient disclosure, since the traditional charity annual report cannot fulfil the information needs from multiple stakeholders was spotted since 1990s [7, 8]. Connolly [9, 10] argues that because of the inadequate efficiency on the charity reporting practice, charities tend to be increasingly 'business-like' – over-emphasise the financial information, such as 'annual income', instead of describing the performance and impact of charitable activities. Influenced by the scandals that happened in the charities section around 2000s, some scholars further discuss that without efficient and understandable reporting practice, it is likely for the social public to gradually lose their 'trust' on charities [11]. Although a series of empirical studies proved that the reporting practice tends to be improved over a period years, since the pressure of regulation and public supervision, lack of awareness, skills and resources still prevent the information delivery of UK charities [8, 12, 13]. Hyndman and McConville [14] and Charity Commission [15] criticise that the transparency of charity operation would be constrained since the reporting practice cannot enable the social public to understand 'where did a charity raise money' and 'how did they use money'.

For the purpose of facilitating the information delivery of charities and enhancing the transparency, the concept of accountability was proposed in the 1970s, which indicates 'be awarded of its conducts and stakeholder's information needs in terms of what has done, is doing and plans to do' [7, 11, 16]. In contrast to the research above, this paper will improve the accountability disclosure in the charity reporting practice with the aid of technical support – interactive data visualisation, for the purpose of enhancing the performance of charity reporting practice in terms of understanding, accessibility and interactivity (Sect. 2). Organisational semiotics, a theory revealing the procedure where information transfers from one party to another on the context of business, will be applied to lead the design of interactive data visualisation (Sect. 3). Instead of purely exhibiting data into 'fancy pictures' [3], this paper will follow the principle of organisational semiotics, regarding data visualisation as a 'procedure' where data should be categorised and displayed in different layers in terms of 'degree of detail' (Sect. 4). Age UK, one of the leading charities, will be selected as a case study to demonstrate how the framework aided their business reporting in Sect. 5. In the final section, a brief summary and a few suggestions will be provided to guide the following studies to progress the research further.

2   Interactive Data Visualisation: Basic Concept and Principle

Information-overload intensifies the complexity of datasets, which causes the static data visualisation to no longer able to fulfil the diversified information demands from different stakeholders [17]. The function of 'interaction', where readers can customise the content and layout of dashboards, and interpret data from their ad-hoc perspective. The development of cloud computing enhances the interaction of data visualisation where readers can drill down the dataset into a detailed extension. In addition, the presentation of data visualisation can be assessed by multi-devices, including PC, tablet and even smart phone [4]. Aligned with business intelligence, interactive data visualisation can address the complexity of dataset and answer the ad-hoc requests from different stakeholders [18], which will be utilised for assisting the accountability disclosure in charity reporting practice.

However, without a proper design and clear definition, data visualisation cannot automatically signify data and reveal the meaning and story behind it. Few [17] indicates that data visualisation is more than just simply displaying the raw data with visual representatives, but a certain procedure which enables data to be sense-making and to fulfil the information needs from various readers. Schoffelen et al. [19] emphases that compared with displaying data in numeric format, the means of data visualisation to enhance the readability of dataset, where visual representatives attract people's attention with different colours and shapes, enabling sense-making in different layers of detail, and facilitating the reflecting interpretation with interactive functionalities. Ware [20] categorises two methods for visualising data, including 'button-up' which perceives the information through observing the patterns shown in the visualisation, and 'top-down' which checks over the data visualisation with pre-defined requests. Two approaches of designing data visualisation procedure is mentioned in Segel and Heer [4], 'author-driven' where the authors predefine the content, format and layout of information presentation and 'reader-driven' where the readers can explore the whole dataset based on the ad-hoc information needs. In 2015, stemmed by the theory of organisational semiotics, Liu and Tan [1] suggest to think of data visualisation as a procedure of 'abduction', where users can search for explanation, generate hypothesis, testify hypothesis, instruct their following behaviour based on the analysis result. This research focuses on display and interact with data which enables users to perform information processing capabilities.

This research puts a focus on the 'author-driven' approach to improve the interoperation between authors and readers towards data visualisation. This approach advances the research outcome from Liu and Tan [1] in terms of building interactive capabilities around data while they are presented.

3 Organisational Semiotics to Data Visualisation

Semiotics is a study of sign which carries information from one party to another. Organisational semiotics shows that information delivery with an organisational and social system should not rely on technology alone and the impacts of procedure and interaction should not be neglected [21]. Liu and Tan [1] suggest under theory of organisational semiotics, data visualisation should be defined as a procedure which signifies data on both semantic and pragmatic levels, covering collecting data, transforming data, mapping visual representatives and displaying (interaction). Instead of discussing displaying visual representatives, this paper will discover how interactive data visualisation signifies data on the semantic level, and enables readers to address their ad-hoc requests and to interpret the author's intentions from different perspectives. Thus, in this section, two theories in organisational semiotics, Semiosis and Semiotic Ladder, will be discussed to inspire the following findings with theoretical supports.

3.1 Semiosis

Theory of semiosis was derived from the work of Peirce in the 1930s, which demonstrates the procedure of information delivery among different parties into a triangle framework [22]. Sign, plays the primary role in this framework which carries information through a physical token, such as written words, graphics and oral language. Object indicates the meaning and information which a sign indicates or links to. In order to link a sign to an object, every individual needs to go through the process of 'interpret', which is more than interpreting the information carried by sign, but also the author's intensions and reflections/impacts on the reader's behaviour. Therefore, both the quality of sign and principles of interpret would influence the information delivery and interpretation.

Data visualisation, as a procedure of information signification and interpretation, can also be demonstrated into the framework of semiosis (Table 1). Visual representatives can be regarded as signs which carries information. On the context of business, the financial or operational performance always counts as object which should be revealed to stakeholders. Different from the previous research which stress design of visual representatives and algorithm, this paper will focus more on the procedure of interactive data visualisation where not only the information would be revealed with the help of a visual representative, but readers will also be empowered to interact with data on the function of interaction.

Table 1. Explanation of semiosis [22]

Roles	Explanation	Data visualisation
Sign	The physical carrier of information, or the raw material where the information comes from	Visual representatives: chart, diagram, table and map
Object	The meaning of sign, which will influence the receiver's understanding and even behaviours	Financial and operational performance: cost-efficiency, customer satisfaction, market growth
Interpretant	A mechanism or a set of activities to process the raw material to the information which fits the demand of information users	Understand the definition of each variable in the visual presentation; Link different variables to the performance measurement; Capture the author's intentions through reflecting ad-hoc requests

In summary, the semiosis triangle demonstrates the procedure of information delivery as an information pathway going through three points, including sign, interpret and object. Moreover it leads this paper to focus on the procedure of interpretant, where the authors and readers can achieve communications in terms of information and intentions. In the following part the process of sense-making 'interpretant' will be discussed further, within the body of the semiotic ladder.

3.2   Perception Towards Information

Following the semiosis triangle from Peirce, Stamper [23] further interprets the procedure of 'interpretant' in semiotic ladder, for the purpose of identifying and removing the barrier of signifying different signs. The procedure of 'interpretant' covers more than just interpretation, but a set of activities, from perceiving the sign from a physical aspect to instructing the following behaviour. Inheriting the research from the traditional semiotics where divisions of syntactic, semantic and pragmatic to indicate grammar, meaning and usage of sign, semiotic ladder extends the basic levels of 'physical world' and 'empiric' to measure the quality and functions of sign, and the premium level of 'social world' to imply the influence of social context [21]. Table 2 provides all six levels and their detailed explanations.

Table 2. Explanations of semiotic ladder [22]

Levels	Explanation
Physical element	The durability and stability of sign
Empirical element	The reliability of channel used to deliver the sign
Syntactic element	Whether the language can be understood by both information senders and receivers
Semantic element	Whether the receiver can figure out the relationship between the sign and object
Pragmatic element	Whether the intention attached to the sign can be perceived
Social element	Whether the interpretation of sign can be linked to some certain social norms

The functions of 'sign' are mainly related to the semantic, pragmatic and social levels. Following the study of Liu and Tan [1] where data visualisation should be regarded as a procedure to reveal the meaning of data and intentions from authors, this research will enhance the information further, to interpret the procedure of data visualisation on semantic and pragmatic levels, and develop a framework to enhance the communication in terms of the meaning of data and even information needs from readers. On the semantic level, compared with the traditional annual report of charities, data visualisation signifies data with visual representatives. On the pragmatic level, the function of 'interactive' allows readers to explore the data based on their information demands.

In charity reporting practice, although previous research points out that the traditional annual report cannot fulfil the information needs, they have never tried to solve the problem with technical solutions. In this research, interactive data visualisation will be utilised as a tool to enhance the performance of charity reporting and to enable the content to be understandable for all stakeholders. Also, it supports the communication between authors and readers on the level of pragmatic. On the one side, all report content will be divided into different levels in terms of the degree of detail and all information can be linked to the whole picture which demonstrates the overall performance of charity operation. On the other side, readers can request a certain theme they are particularly interested in, instead of following the predefined routine. In the following section, a new-developed framework will be introduced for the purpose of leading the design of interactive data visualisation. On the semantic level, it enables data to be sense-making; on the pragmatic level, it allows readers to follow the author's routine and reflect their ad-hoc request at the same time.

4   The Visualisation Framework

Data visualisation is more than displaying raw data with visual representatives, but rather a procedure to enable data to be more sense-making and empower the reader to reflectively interpret data and author's intentions through the function of 'interaction'. Following the principles of organisational semiotics, a design of interactive data visualisation should sufficiently address issues from both semantic and pragmatic levels.

The visualisation framework is depicted in Fig. 1. This framework was inspired by a common challenge when a reporting system offers a presentation of data in a specific structure, in non-profit organisaitons [14]. Such challenge often affects users to easily discover business issues from the data. The framework intends to empower users to have sense making on the data through their pragmatic abilities.

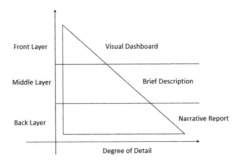

Fig. 1. Framework of visualisation pyramid

On the semantic level, it divides the procedure into three layers in terms of the degree of detail, where authors can present all information from a low to a high degree of detail. Visual dashboard at the front layer is an interactive user interface which presents information to allow users quickly generating facts and views based on meaningful signs through colour, size and shapes of visual representations [20]. On the pragmatic level, interactive visualisation empowers all readers to address their different information requests based on their preference. Other than capturing the pattern of dataset from the dashboard, readers can drill down certain information themes they are particularly interested in and look for further explanations.

5 Age UK: A Case Study and Prototype of Interactive Data Visualisation

This study has chosen Age UK, a leading charity providing services to senior citizens, as a case study. With a reference to Hyndman and McConville [14] and Connolly and Hyndman [12], two themes from Age UK's annual report, such as income and expenditure, are considered to be mostly interested by the readers (Table 3).

Based on such requirements, this study employed the visualisation framework to design an information structure (Fig. 2) which transformed the reporting practices. It feeds the data into the defined business views and governs interactive behaviour for reflective interpretations. For example, a user (i.e. reader) can compare income with expenditure on the top level dashboard, and then look into the cost structure within the theme of expenditure, in order to find out which type of charitable activities Age UK spent money on. Furthermore, the user can choose to view more narrative contents of performance which describe how Age UK invested money to help beneficiaries in terms of their welfare.

Compared with the traditional annual report, the prototype of interactive data visualisation can be utilised as a complimentary tool of charity reporting practice in Age UK. Firstly, instead of showing all contents in one report, this prototype is more flexible for readers to choose the information their interested in and get insight of the overall performance. Secondly, readers are able to drill down the information points they are interested in to a desired level of detail, rather than reading through all contents, which can fulfil their ad-hoc requests in an efficient way.

Table 3. Information categories (charity report)

Theme	Reader's requests	Relevant contents
Income	How did Age UK raise money in 2015?	Five main sources of income Cost of raising money Detail description: narrative description, news, stories, photos
Expenditure	How did Age UK spend money in 2015? How did Age UK serve the social public in 2015?	Five main charitable activities Cost of each main charitable activity and percentage of total cost Performance measurement: case studies and beneficiary stories

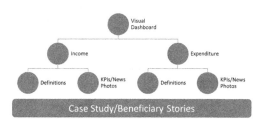

Fig. 2. Information structure for visualisation

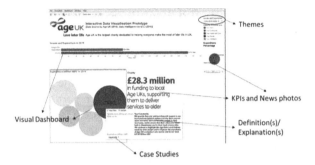

Fig. 3. The dashboard for revealing information (https://public.tableau.com/profile/qi.li#!/vizhome/Book1_8896/AgeUKDashboard)

Figure 3 exhibits all three layers of information points based on the information structure. Themes, setting and visual dashboard, present the front layer of information, which delivers a 'big picture' of financial status. On the middle layer, Definition(s), KPIs and News, provides the complimentary information, which helps readers to understand the concepts and relevant indicators. On the back layer, case studies with extensive information of beneficiary stories, can be accessed through hyperlink, which can trace back to the website and demonstrate the most detailed information in a particular expenditure category that the reader is specifically interested in.

6   Conclusion and Future Work

This paper identifies the research gap where UK charities always suffer from insufficient accountability disclosure since the traditional charity reporting method cannot enable all stakeholders to understand the report content and provide little flexibility for them to address their ad-hoc requests. Instructed by the theory of organisational semiotics, this paper developed the visualisaiton framework which implemented the pragmatic ability in making sense of the data via the interactive data visualization tool. This framework was experimented on the Age UK. This tool enables every single information point to be link in a holistic viewpoint of the business. The functions of the interaction meet the uses' specific information demands and view the content from different perspectives.

In addition, there are a few points where the following studies could be discussed further. Firstly, other than information of income and expenditure, more content can be fulfilled through the framework of visualisation pyramid. Especially, the study from Hyndman and McConville [14], where the information reflecting performance of charitable activities can be addressed by data visualisation, which helps identify the 'high-profile' charity in terms of their performance. Secondly, this paper interprets the procedure of data visualisation on both semantic and pragmatic levels. Referring to the framework of the semiotic ladder, further research is suggested to focus on the level of the 'social world' of interactive data visualisation, where the meanings of data (semantic level) and intentions (pragmatic level) might influence the following behaviour of readers.

References

1. Liu, K., Tan, C.: Semiotics in visualisation. In: Proceedings of the 16th International Conference on Enterprise Information Systems, pp. 5–7. Lisbon, Portugal (2014)
2. Lindquist, E.: Surveying the World of Visualization. Australian National University, Canberra (2011)
3. Strecker, J.: Data Visualization in Review: Summary. IDRC (2012). https://idl-bnc.idrc.ca/dspace/bitstream/10625/49286/1/IDL-49286.pdf. Accessed 2 Feb 2016
4. Segel, E., Heer, J.: Narrative visualization: telling stories with data. Visual. Comput. Graph. **16**(6), 1139–1148 (2010)
5. Ellington, E.H., Guillaume, B., Austin, C.: Using multiple imputation to estimate missing data in meta-regression. Methods Ecol. Evol. **6**(2), 153–163 (2015)
6. Charity Commission: Charity Overview. Charity Commission (2015). http://apps.charitycommission.gov.uk/showcharity/registerofcharities/SectorData/SectorOverview.aspx. Accessed 5 Jan 2016
7. Hyndman, N.: Contributors to charities - a comparison of their information needs and the perceptions of such by the providers of information. Financ. Acc. Manag. **7**, 69–82 (1991)
8. Hyndman, N.: Charity accounting - an empirical study of the information needs of contributors to UK fund raising charities. Financ. Acc. Manag. **6**(4), 295–307 (1990)
9. Connolly, C., Dhanani, A., Hyndman, N.: The accountability mechanisms and needs of external charity stakeholders. In: ACCA (2013)
10. Connolly, C., Dhanani, A.: Accounting narratives: the reporting practices of British charities. J. Public Non Profit Serv. **32**, 73–97 (2006)
11. Dhanani, A.: Accountability of UK charities. Public Money Manag. **29**, 183–190 (2009)
12. Connolly, C., Hyndman, N., McConville, D.: UK charity accounting: an exercise in widening stakeholder engagement. Brit. Acc. Rev. **45**, 58–69 (2013)
13. Dhanani, A., Connolly, C.: Non-governmental organizational accountability: talking the talk and walking the walk? J. Bus. Ethics **129**, 613–637 (2015)
14. Hyndman, N., McConville, D.: Transparency in reporting on charities' efficiency: a framework for analysis. Nonprofit Volunt. Sect. Q. (2015). doi:10.1177/0899764015603205
15. Charity Commission: Transparency and Accountability. UK Government (2004). https://www.gov.uk/government/uploads/system/uploads/attachment_data/file/284721/rs8text.pdf. Accessed 5 Feb 2016
16. Stewart, J.: The role of information in public accountability. Issues Public Sect. Account. **17**, 13–34 (1984)
17. Few, S.: Now You See It: Simple Visualization Techniques for Quantitative Analysis. Analytics Press, Berkeley (2009)
18. Rouhani, S., Asgari, S., Mirhosseini, S.V.: Review study: business intelligence concepts and approaches. Am. J. Sci. Res. **50**, 62–75 (2012)
19. Schoffelen, J., Claes, S., Huybrechts, L.: Visualising things: perspectives on how to make things public through visualisation. CoDesign **0882**, 1–14 (2015)

20. Ware, C.: Information Visualization: Perception for Design. Academic Press, San Diego (2004)
21. Stamper, R.K.: Information, Organisation and Technology: Studies in Organisational Semiotics. Springer, Boston (2001)
22. Liu, K., Li, W.: Organisational Semiotics for Business Informatics. Taylor and Francis, UK (2014)
23. Stamper, R.K.: Semiotic Theory of Information and Information Systems (1996). https://assets.cs.ncl.ac.uk/seminars/101.pdf. Accessed 2 Feb 2016

A Pragmatic Approach to Disambiguation in Text Understanding

Martin Wheatman[✉]

Yagadi Ltd., Withinreap Barn, Moss Side Lane, Thornley,
Preston PR3 2ND, UK
martin@wheatman.net

Abstract. This paper describes a novel disambiguation mechanism for a text understanding system, which utilizes a general correction function, also described. This mechanism is comprised of: contextual ordering; transactional persistent memory; and, interactivity aligning machine action with user intent. The latter clearly demonstrates the use of language at a Pragmatic level – directedness toward user intent is afforded, purely through a speech interface. This work is supported by a Java implementation *enguage* and the *iNeed* app.

Keywords: Machine understanding · Disambiguation · Pragmatism · Semiotics

1 Introduction

Being able to speak naturally to computers would be of great benefit for all, including many hitherto disenfranchised groups, other than, perhaps, the functionally mute or profoundly deaf. Speech-to-text services provided by mobile operating systems can disambiguate with surprising accuracy [1]. However, understanding the resultant text remains problematic, which is exacerbated by the many forms of ambiguity in natural language [2]. Simple command based systems, such as Amazon Fire OS's Alexa [3], can successfully apply an operation to an entity, by support fixed phrases such as "ask...to...". However, such slot-filling does not uncover intended meaning in text.

Structural analysis – syntax and semantics – is not sufficient to provide insight into the intention of the speaker [4]. Two sentences with valid, identical structures may have entirely different meanings: *the Jumbo has landed* is an everyday occurrence; whereas, *the Eagle has landed* is one of the most iconic phrases of the C20th. Linguistic studies, such as modelling concordance with corpora analysis software [5], defer any issues with intended meaning to the researcher. Indeed, text understanding software must be able to differentiate between identical sentences. Further, deducing intentional thrust should also be addressed: while *I have a coffee* is the negation of *I need a coffee*, *I have to go to town* has the same meaning as *I need to go to town*.

Human speech, however, is not unduly plagued by misinterpretation: intentionality can be identified and clarified effectively by interaction aside from the main discourse. It is where written speech is unclear, without recourse to an author that problems occur: the spoken word seems to lose its life on the written page.

M.C.C. Baranauskas et al. (Eds.): ICISO 2016, IFIP AICT 477, pp. 143–148, 2016.
DOI: 10.1007/978-3-319-42102-5_16

2 Enguage

The disambiguation mechanism described has been developed for *enguage*, an experimental text understanding interface for mobile devices [6–9]. It uses the speech-to-text and text-to-speech services of mobile operating systems, allowing utterances to affect a response. To do this it constructs, on-the-fly, a set of potential interpreters for each utterance. Each micro-interpreter, or sign, consist of: a pattern, with which to match an utterance, and a corresponding train of thought, consisting of further utterances. Together, these signs along with persistent contextual data are combined into what is generally referred to as *interpretant* that is constructed during the process of interpretation [10]. Thus, meaning is based upon pattern matching rather than adherence to a syntax, so that *the Eagle has landed* is distinct from *the X has landed*.

A pattern consists of constant boilerplate tokens, represented here in lowercase, and variable hotspots, e.g. *the X has landed*. A hotspot can be flagged as representing a phrase if prefixed with *PHRASE-*, where the terminator is the token following the pattern or the end of utterance, e.g. *may name is PHRASE-NAME*, where NAME would match *Martin* or *Martin Wheatman*. Matched values become part of the overall context, e.g. X = "Jumbo", along with the particular train of thought for this sign.

Signs are organized into *repertoires* each of which supports a computable concept. For example, the *need* concept in the iNeed app [11], in essence, is a list manipulated with the repertoire: *i do not need anything*; *i need X*; *i do not need X*; and, *what do i need*. A sign construction repertoire [12] is built into enguage so that a repertoire itself is also a set of natural language utterances: text understanding is self-constructed, or autopoietic, in the same manner that a C compiler is written in C. Thus, natural language is interpreted in natural language: it is decomposed into more specific terms until an unequivocal conceptualization reached.

3 Disambiguation Mechanisms

Three algorithms are used to disambiguate utterances. Firstly, one gives an objective order to signs, and thus a defined order to meaning. Secondly, two in-built repertoires afford the user the ability to implicitly affect this ordering. The first of these is the ability to re-search the interpretant; second, based on the first, gives the user the ability to choose a meaning by revealing and hiding interpretations, determined by the feedback, or perlocution [4], within the ordered signs.

3.1 Ordering

Signs are ordered in increasing pattern complexity, so the least-complex matching pattern is matched first: *the eagle has landed* is matched before *the X has landed*. Further, *the X has landed* is matched before *the PHRASE-X has landed*. This is to ensure that specialized–singular–variables take precedence.

To achieve this patterns are hashed on their complexity: primarily on the number and complexity of hotspots (i.e. a phrased hotspot is given a higher value) and secondarily on the length of (number of tokens in) its boilerplate. Length of boilerplate is significant where there is a phrased hotspot: the shorter the boilerplate, the higher the complexity values. This is because a phrased hotspot potentially matches an infinite number of tokens, so is given an arbitrarily high value (e.g. MAXINT), then any boilerplate and non-phrased hotspots are subtracted from this, meaning that *i have to PHRASE-X* matches before *i have PHRASE-X*, i.e. (MAXINT − 3) < (MAXINT − 2).

3.2   Correction

While speech-to-text systems are remarkable, they can create unintended translations: speech can be misheard. Because the speech-to-text in iNeed is presented directly to enguage, the ability to correct after the fact is required. Further, and pertinent to this paper, natural language is ambiguous: enguage cannot guarantee the above ordering achieves the intended match.

3.2.1   General Correction

Enguage provides an inbuilt sign for general correction which uses a simple transactional persistent memory system. Changes to persistent memory are written to a provisional overlay. If one utterance is simply followed by another, the current provisional overlay is transferred to the database before it is repopulated. To obtain a correction, the provisional overlay is deleted before a new one is created.

The correctional sign has the pattern *no PHRASE-X*. On matching this pattern, the provisional overlay is removed and the utterance *PHRASE-X* is uttered. This allows the user to retract an utterance. It requires that operations that physically cannot be undone are initiated by several interlocking concepts. Further, there is a commitment to the design of repertoires such that *no PHRASE-X* is not matched to non-correctional (*no son of mine X* springs to mind). Being almost entirely composed of hotspot (one phrased hotspot with very little boilerplate), this will be almost the last pattern to be matched. So, all utterances beginning with *no* must explicitly be matched. However, this will not include the single answer *no* as there is no associated hotspot. Further, many utterances such as *no don't take him to the gallows* will work fine, as this is a natural use of this form.

This ability to affect changes to the operation of the software shows that this system is pragmatic, that the correction mechanism is implicit in the conversation between user and app – based on assessment of perlocution: replies from utterances.

3.2.2   Special Correction

There is also a modification to this correctional mechanism which disambiguates utterances. It is triggered if the new utterance, without the initial *no*, is the same as the last. The first match of an interpretant pattern is then ignored, finding the next one. These signs are then swapped in the interpretant order to maintain this new context on subsequent utterances. If another *no PHRASE-X* is uttered, and the X matches the previous utterance, both the first and second matched patterns are ignored to find the third, and so on. This is dependent on the replies in interpretant – perlocution – to reflect the intentions of the user: it is for the speaker to decide if they have been misunderstood. This is seen as being the natural way that misunderstanding is corrected in human discourse:

user: *The Eagle has landed.*
app: *Ok, we've a bunch of guys here about to turn blue!*
user: *No the Eagle has landed.*
app: *Ok, the eagle has returned to its nest.*

In practice, is has been found that a corrected utterance is automatically chosen by a speaker, rather than repeating the phrase to force disambiguation. For example, in the above interaction, the user reply may very well be *No the Eagle has returned to the nest*. This will not result in any signs being swapped.

3.2.3   Pragmatism

The reflecting of user intent shows that this process is pragmatic, that the actions taken (or proposed as being taken) depend on the interaction of the user and app, not in some hypothetical absolute meaning. It requires that the repertoire unequivocally reflects the app's interpretation: the repertoire should plainly confirm the specific action taken in response to each utterance. So, *my name is X* should have a reply of *ok, your name is X*. There is a minor issue here in the enguage interpreter; there is a obtuse option which returns only up to the comma. So *ok, your name is X* will reply *ok*. This mode can be used if the user is happy with the operation of the app, or if they are sure there is no ambiguity in the repertoire. Otherwise, the default (verbose) mode should be used, which replies the full phrase.

4   The Test

A test repertoire, which doesn't rely on any special cases or context, has been devised to fully demonstrate this disambiguation mechanism. This repertoire includes three signs with identical patterns, each with a separate significant train of thought.

    On "this is a test":
        perform "list add _user needs meaning one";
        then, reply "this reaches meaning one".
    On "this is a test":
        perform "list add _user needs meaning two";
        then, reply "this reaches meaning two".
    On "this is a test":
        perform "list add _user needs meaning three";
        then, reply "this reaches meaning three".

The test pattern, *this is a test*, is ambiguous because it is all boilerplate and used on more than one sign. By reuttering this phrase, the progression through the distinct trains-of-thought is achieved. When the matched patterns are exhausted, enguage will first reply with the default *I do not understand*, before repeating the search. A full demonstration of this can be found at [13], a transcript of which is:

user: *This is a test.*
app: *This reaches meaning one.*
user: *No this is a test.*
app: *This reaches meaning two.*
user: *No this is a test.*
app: *This reaches meaning three.*
user: *No this is a test.*
app: *I don't understand.*
user: *No this is a test.*
app: *This reaches meaning one.*

5   Contribution and Further Work

Enguage is a text understanding interface allowing developers to create context dependent natural language apps. It provides many generic features for the conversation engineer, of which disambiguation is possibly the most important as it provides the key to context dependent processing across all repertoires. To be certain, it is not an AI chatbot designed for the Turing Test [14].

The mechanism overcomes structural issues with syntax and semantics by exploiting, at a pragmatic level, the human ability to detect and direct intent. It builds upon pattern matching so that meaning is determined by the boilerplate and in the interpretation of hotspot values, rather than individual word types and structures comprising a syntax tree. It utilizes a general correction mechanism, aiding its simplicity; it avoids the many individual forms of ambiguity.

This is not a mechanism for avoiding ambiguity; ambiguity will always occur, it simplifies the interaction needed when it is deemed to have occurred. In that it affords the user to direct intent, it is pragmatic. However, it is restricted to a discourse system – where there is interaction between the app and user—it cannot aid applications which are restricted to the structural domain: it will be of no use to the semantic analyses of corpora [5] which does not work within a conversation.

This work also serves to highlight differences between the spoken and written word. Current spoken word speech systems do not, in general, register pauses and intonation which could aid disambiguation. However, working with text, an arbitrary list of strings could also include emojis and other non-vocal ephemera to help identify intent. Written repertoires—including the autopoietic repertoire – use punctuation to express clearly. Further work includes producing a simplified, completely vocal autopoietic repertoire: *X implies Y* works already, but *X is conceptually Y* needs developing. Furthermore, context-free data types, such as *number* and *when*, have been instigated which needs to be enhanced by the concepts of *where* and *class*.

Dedication. This paper is dedicated to my father, James Malcolm Wheatman 11.2.1931 – 7.4.2016.

References

1. Huang, X., Baker, J., Reddy, R.: A historical perspective of speech recognition. Commun. ACM **57**(1), 94–103 (2014)
2. Wikipedia. https://en.wikipedia.org/wiki/Ambiguity. Downloaded 26 Jan 2016
3. Amazon. https://developer.amazon.com/public/solutions/alexa/alexa-skills-kit/getting-started-guide. Downloaded 26 Jan 2016
4. Austin, J.L.: How to Do Things with Words. Oxford University Press, Oxford (1976). Ed. by Urmson, J.O., Sbisa, M.
5. Anthony, L.: AntConc Software (2015). http://www.laurenceanthony.net/software.html. Downloaded 26 Jan 2016
6. Wheatman, M.J.: A semiotic analysis of, "if we are holding hands, whose hand am I holding". J. Inf. Technol. **22**(Special Issue on Logistics), 41–52 (2014)
7. Wheatman, M.J.: https://www.youtube.com/watch?v=HsJyrdtk0GM. Uploaded 8 Jul 2015
8. Wheataman, M.J.: https://www.youtube.com/watch?v=ngdHVV3hwpE. Uploaded 18 Sept 2015
9. Wheatman, M.J.: https://play.google.com/store/apps/details?id=com.yagadi.iNeed. Accessed 22 Feb 2016
10. Peirce, C.S.: Collected Papers, vol. 1–8 (1935–58). Ed. by Hartshorne, C., Weiss, P.
11. Wheatman, M.J.: (2015). https://github.com/martinwheatman/enguage/iNeed/
12. Wheatman, M.J.: An autopoietic repertoire. In: Proceedings of AI-2014 34th SGAI International Conference on Artificial Intelligence, Cambridge, UK (2014)
13. Wheatman, M.J.: https://www.youtube.com/watch?v=Ig2Xd1QDu6E. Accessed 20 Jan 2016
14. Loebner, H.G.: In response. Commun. ACM **37**(6), 79–82 (1994)

A Study of Complication Identification Based on Weighted Association Rule Mining

Zhijun Yan[1]([✉]), Kai Liu[1], Meiming Xing[1], Tianmei Wang[2],
and Baowen Sun[2]

[1] School of Management and Economics, Beijing Institute of Technology,
Beijing, China
{yanzhijun, 2120141521, 2120131555}@bit.edu.cn
[2] School of Information, Central University of Finance and Economics,
Beijing, China
{wangtianmei, sunbaowen}@cufe.edu.cn

Abstract. With the fast development of big data technology, data mining algorithms are widely used to process the medical data and support clinical decision-making. In this paper, a new method is proposed to mine the disease association rule and predict the possible complications. The concept of disease concurrent weight is proposed and Back Propagation (BP) neural network model is applied to calculate the disease concurrent weight. Adopting the weighted association rule mining algorithm, diseases complication association rule are derived, which can help to remind doctors about patients' potential complications. The empirical evaluation using hospital patients' medical information shows that the proposed method is more effective than two baseline methods.

Keywords: Weighted association rule · Complications · Data mining · Neural network

1 Introduction

Many hospitals use the Electronic Health Records system (EHRs) to integrate different kinds of medical data [1, 2]. The data mining technology is widely applied on the EHRs to support clinical decision, including drug supervision [3], complication identification [4], disease prediction [5], patient stratification [6] and other related directions [7]. Among them, medical complication identification gets special attention. Complications refer to diseases caused in the process of another disease. It is difficult to discover the potential relationship between disease and its complication based on a small dataset. The emerging of big data analytic technology makes it feasible to identify the possible complications by mining the massive data in EHRs.

Previous studies on complication identification normally focused on the specific disease and adopted the data mining algorithms to find some potential complications for the specific disease. However, these researches rarely consider the complications of different diseases together and ignore individual disease's features. Aiming to mine the potential complication relationship in the EHRs, this study firstly proposes the concurrent weight of diseases to depict the possibility that one disease will be a

© IFIP International Federation for Information Processing 2016
Published by Springer International Publishing Switzerland 2016. All Rights Reserved
M.C.C. Baranauskas et al. (Eds.): ICISO 2016, IFIP AICT 477, pp. 149–158, 2016.
DOI: 10.1007/978-3-319-42102-5_17

complication of other diseases. Based on the concurrent weight, we adopt the weighted association rule mining algorithm to mine potential complication relationship and predict the possible complications for clinical decision-making.

The rest of the paper is organized as follows. Section 2 introduces the related works on complication identification. Then, the proposed complication mining method is presented in Sect. 3, followed by the experiment results in Sect. 4. Finally, we discuss major research findings and future research of this study in Sect. 5.

2 Related Works

Complications represent the concurrence and association relationships among different diseases. They normally affect the patients seriously and cost much higher medical expenditure. In order to identify the possible complications for the disease, various data mining techniques are applied in complication identification.

Roque et al. [8] uses the text mining technology to analyze the electronic patient records of a Danish Psychiatric Hospital. By extracting phenotype information from electronic patient records, they analyze the disease co-occurrence relationship. Hanauer et al. [9] uses the Molecular Concept Map (MCM) algorithm to mine the electronic medical database and successfully find some interesting new diseases associations. Holmes et al. [10] use Application for Discovering Disease Associations using Multiple Sources (ADAMS) to identify the co-morbidities of the rare diseases Kaposi sarcoma, toxoplasmosis, and Kawasaki disease. By incorporating textual information from PubMed and Wikipedia, they find some rare or previously unreported associations.

As one of the most popular data mining algorithms, Association Rule Mining (ARM) is widely used in complication identification of a certain disease. Tai and Chiu [11] focuses on the complications identification of Attention Deficit/Hyperactivity Disorder (ADHD). By employing the association rule mining algorithm, they find that ADHD case group has apparently higher risk of comorbidity with psychiatric comorbidity than with other physical illnesses. Kim et al. [12] analyze the complications of type 2 diabetes mellitus. Based on the medical data of 411,414 patients from 1996 to 2007, they develop the Dx Analyze tool to clean data and reveal associations of comorbidity. The results show that association rule mining was practical for complication studies. Shin et al. [13] use Apriori algorithm and Clementine program to analyze the data of 5,022 patients with essential hypertension. The strong associations between hypertension, non-insulin-dependent diabetes mellitus and cerebral infarction are mined. Moreover, based on a large amount of data, Wright et al. [14] also use the association rule mining method to find out the association among different diseases and laboratory results. The results show that association rule mining is a useful tool for identifying clinically accurate associations and has a better performance over other knowledge-based methods.

In summary, some prior studies make great efforts to identify complication relationship by adopting association rule mining technique. However, they don't consider the different roles of different diseases on the complication identification, which can improve the mining performance. At the same time, patients' medical history is critical information for disease diagnosis and should be incorporated in mining complication relationship.

3 Methods

In this study, we firstly define the concurrent weight to evaluate the possibility that a disease develops as a complication of other diseases. Then we adopt the Back Propagation (BP) neural network to derive the concurrent weight of diseases and identify the disease complication relationship based on the weighted association rule mining algorithm. Finally, the list of possible complications is recommended to support clinical decision-making.

3.1 The Concurrent Weight of Diseases

Prior medical experience is very helpful to predict the future health status and possible diseases. We assume that some diseases will appear as complication more frequent than others. A concurrent weight is proposed to represent the possibility that a disease becomes the complication of other diseases. The higher the disease's concurrent weight, the more likely it is the complication of certain diseases.

Assume that the disease set is D, and every item in D is one disease. Each disease d_i also has a corresponding set C_i to describe its known complications. So the concurrent weight of the disease d_i can be defined as follows:

$$W(d_i) = \frac{\sum_{j=1}^{n} m_{ij}}{n} \tag{1}$$

where $w(d_i)$ is the concurrent weight of the disease d_i, n is the total number of diseases in the set D, and m_{ij} describes whether the disease d_i appears in the complication set of d_j or not. When the disease d_i appears in the C_j, then m_{ij} is equal to 1, otherwise it is zero.

However, it is impossible to generate a complete complication list for each disease, and we can't directly obtain concurrent weights for all diseases by prior knowledge. Thus we firstly collect the complications of some traditional diseases, then apply some artificial intelligent algorithms to train the collected data and predict the whole set of concurrent weight. For the initial set of traditional diseases and its complications, we used the web crawler to download disease information from domestic professional medical website "Clove Garden" (http://www.dxy.cn/). Then 596 kinds of diseases and their occurrence frequency as complications are collected as the known complication knowledge.

3.2 BP Neural Network Model

The Back Propagation (BP) neural network is one of the most used forward neural networks [15]. We selected the three layer BP neural network to predict the concurrent weight of the diseases. It includes input, output and hidden layer.

Input Layer of the Model. First of all, we describe the disease as a three-dimension vector to characterize the properties of comorbid diseases. The three dimensions include the position of the disease in the International Classification of Disease (ICD) coding schema, the importance of the disease, and the appearing order in diagnosis.

The position of the disease in the International Classification of Disease (ICD) coding schema represents the location of the disease in the ICD list. The importance of the disease represents the impact of the disease on the patient's recovery process. For inpatients, the hospital will normally record all diseases they have and each disease will be assigned an importance value, which describes how it is important for patients' treatment. During the hospital stay, patients may have several diseases. These diseases will be recorded in the appearing order. By converting each disease to a vector, we used the 596 kinds of diseases and their weights as the input of the BP neural network model. At the same time, each dimension of the disease vector is normalized to makes sure that each value is ranged from 0 to 1.

Output Layer of the Model. The output layer represents the learning result of the BP neural network model. In this study, BP model is adopted to predict the disease concurrent weight. Thus the output layer is the disease concurrent weight.

We firstly discretize the concurrent weights of diseases. The discretization process can effectively avoid the hidden defects in the training dataset and make the model more stable. Moreover, the values of the concurrent weights of diseases are commonly very small considering the large number of diseases, thus we amplify the concurrent weights to get significant results. The discretization calculation formula of the concurrent weights is given as follows:

$$
f(w) = \begin{cases} 0.2, & w \leq 0.022 \\ 0.4, & 0.022 < w \leq 0.044 \\ 0.6, & 0.044 < w \leq 0.066 \\ 0.8, & w > 0.066 \end{cases} \tag{2}
$$

where $f(w)$ is the discretization result of the concurrent weight w of a disease.

Then the number of neurons in output layer is set to 2, and the output value of each neuron cell is 0 or 1. Four output values of two neurons: $(0,0)$, $(0,1)$, $(1,0)$ and $(1,1)$ are mapped to four kinds of weights: 0.2, 0.4, 0.6 and 0.8 respectively. Thus we establish the direct connection between input layer and output layer.

Hidden Layer of the Model. The hidden layer of BP model is responsible for the information transformation. It can have one or several layers. As a single hidden layer BP neural network can approximate any nonlinear function with high precision [16], only one hidden layer is set in this study. The number of the neuron in the input and output layer is determined according to the input data and output data. For the hidden nodes number in the hidden layer, although many approaches have been proposed, no one works efficiently for all problems. The most common method is to determine the appropriate number of hidden nodes by experiments performance comparison. Thus we do experiments on a set of values as the number of the neuron in the hidden layer. The value that brings the least training time is the final number of hidden nodes.

3.3   The Weighted Association Rule Mining

Differences among diseases are significant and different disease will have different roles in identifying complications. Thus the weighted association rule mining method [17] is adopted in this study. It attempts to provide a weight to individual items that are not based solely on item support. And thresholds of weighted support and confidence are also defined to measure the significance of the association rules mined.

Similar with the traditional association rule mining algorithm, the support of the item set X is denoted as support(X), if the number of items in X is n, the weighted support of X is:

$$\text{Wsupport}(X) = \text{support}(X) \times \left(\frac{1}{n} \times \sum_{j=1}^{n} w_j \right) \tag{3}$$

The item set X is weighted frequent if the weighted support of X is greater than a predefined minimum weighted support threshold (*wminsup*):

$$\text{Wsupport}(X) \geq wminsup \tag{4}$$

The weighted support of a rule $X \rightarrow Y$ can be defined as:

$$\text{Wsupport}(X \rightarrow Y) = \text{support}(X \rightarrow Y) \times \left(\frac{1}{m} \times \sum_{i_j \in (X \cup Y), j=1}^{m} w_j \right) \tag{5}$$

in which m is the total number of items in the set of $(X \cup Y)$.

The weighted association rule mining algorithm will retrieve all rules $X \rightarrow Y$, where $X \cup Y$ is weighted frequent and whose confidence is greater than or equal to a minimum confidence threshold [18].

In order to improve the algorithm efficiency, we adopt the frequent pattern (FP) tree structure to optimize the weighted association rule mining algorithm [19]. At first, by scanning transaction database and define the minimum weighted support threshold (*wminsup*), the weighted FP-tree is constructed with the weighted potential frequent 1-itemsets. Then the list of potential rules is mined by the weighted association mining approach.

3.4   Complication Prediction

The mined complication association rules among diseases provide valuable information for patient diagnosis. Based on patients' medical history, we can predict patients' possible complication by applying the mined complication rules.

When a patient has a new visit to the hospital and the doctor identifies his/her disease, the patient's main diseases in several latest visits are considered as a disease set, which includes patients' medical history information. The antecedents of mined complication association rules will be browsed to identify whether it contains all diseases in the set. If some rules are matched, the consequents will be displayed as the possible complications. If no rules have antecedents that contain all diseases in the set, the oldest diagnosis will be excluded. Suppose there have n diseases in the original set, the set will be $n-1$ diseases after the exclusion. Then the antecedents of mined complication association rules will be browsed again to find the matched rules. Iterate the above steps until some complication rules are matched or the set is empty. If the set is empty, no prediction will be given. Because only few rules include more than 6 diseases, we consider patients' 6 latest visits for prediction in the first step. For the matched rules, the possible complications are listed in the order of confidence of the complication association rules.

4   Evaluation

We have conducted an empirical evaluation of the proposed approach by using electronic medical records from a hospital in China and using the methods proposed by Wright et al. [14] and Hoque et al. [20] as the benchmarks.

4.1   Data Preprocessing

The medical dataset we used is from a hospital in China. The dataset includes the information of inpatients and outpatients. Each patient gets a descriptive and longitudinal record to describe what happened during each visit. The record covers the information of diagnoses, lab test results, medications and procedures. The total number of records is about one million. Because we focus on the disease comorbidity relationship mining, we exclude the patients' data with only one visit to the hospital.

Before mining complication association rules from the dataset, we firstly clean the data. First, the outpatient information is excluded. In the dataset, some medical information of outpatients is missing or incomplete. Moreover, the treatment outcome of outpatients is not recorded and the correctness of the diagnosis can't be evaluated. Second, some doctors may fail to diagnose patients' diseases and patients don't get better after the inpatient treatment. Thus we remove the inpatients information with unclear or uncured treatment results. Third, for those records that missed some important information, we mark them as invalid and exclude from the experiment.

After the data preprocessing, the final qualified diagnosis data includes 253,271 records, and it is related with 24,754 patients and 6,698 diseases.

4.2   Metric and Benchmarks

We used precision (P) as the metric to assess the effectiveness of the proposed approach. Specifically, precision is the fraction of complication predictions that are correct. Higher value of P indicates better performance.

We use the diagnosis with the complication information as test dataset. The dataset includes 1,410 diagnosis records, which include the main disease and complication information. Based on the mined complication association rules, a list of possible complications for each patient can be generated. If the list includes the actual complications, we count that as a correct predication. Thus, the metric P is defined as:

$$P = \frac{Number\ of\ corrected\ prediction}{Number\ of\ test\ data} \times 100\% \tag{6}$$

To evaluate the effectiveness of the proposed approach, the association rule mining (ARM) algorithm introduced by Wright et al. [14] and a rare association rule (RAR) mining approach proposed by Hoque et al. [20] are chosen as benchmarks. Wright et al. applied the tradition association rule mining algorithms in the medical data and confirmed the validity of the association rule mining algorithms. Hoque et al. focused on the improved low-frequency association rule mining and the effectiveness of the generated rules has been validated over several real life datasets.

4.3   Data Analysis and Results

Derive the Concurrent Weight. In the process of deriving disease concurrent weight, there has one important parameter which influences the effect of the BP network. It is the number of neurons in the hidden layer of BP network. Therefore, we choose the training time of the BP network as the evaluation metric and compare the performances with different values of the number of neurons in the hidden layer. By comparing the training time, the number of neurons in the hidden layer is set to 7.

After determining the parameters of BP network, we predict the concurrent weight of the whole 6,698 diseases. The known weights of 596 diseases are inputted to train the model. The weight of other diseases is predicted through the trained model. Finally, the weight of 3,340 diseases is calculated. For those diseases whose weights failed to be predicted, we set their weight as 0.

Weighted Association Rules Mining. Based on the derived concurrent weight, we develop the weighted association rule mining approach by Java language and mine lots of interesting complication relationship. For the mined complication association rules, the number of items in rules is varying. Figure 1 demonstrates the distribution of the number of items in mined rules. Obviously, most rules include 4 items, which accounts for 21 % of the total association rules. The rules that include 3, 4 or 5 items are more than half of the total rules. Surprisingly, there has a little of rules that only include two items.

We also apply the baseline methods to mine the complication association rules in the experiment dataset. The RAR method is trying the find the rare association rules and the number of generated rules is the biggest, i.e., 96,637. The ARM method derives 42,142 rules. Because some uncommon diseases are weighted, 83,029 rules are mined by the proposed method.

Performance Comparison. We compare three algorithms from two perspectives: processing time and accuracy. For processing time, three algorithms have significant

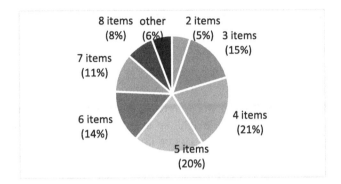

Fig. 1. Number of items in complication rules

differences on the time consumption for complication association mining. All tests were performed on a PC with 3.4 GHz Intel i7-4770 CPU and 12G RAM. The running time of RAR, RAM, and the proposed method are 262, 196, and 27 min, respectively. The predication accuracy of RAR, ARM and the proposed method are 45.3 %, 38.5 % and 80 % respectively. The results show that the proposed method performs better than two baseline methods in processing time and accuracy.

As we mentioned before, the prediction step is to go through all mined compli-cation rules and identify the consequent items of the matched rules as the predicted complications. And the prediction list includes several diseases. However, in the practical scenario, it is important to limit the list length, which can give more insightful suggestions for doctors. Thus we also compare the accuracy of three algorithms with different length of prediction list (Table 1). The results show that the proposed method is better than the baseline methods in three scenarios.

Table 1. The accuracy comparison of three algorithms with different list length

Methods	Accuracy		
	Length = 10	Length = 20	Unlimited length
The proposed method	32.4 %	37.5 %	80 %
RAM	13.1 %	17.5 %	38.5 %
RAR	14.9 %	21.1 %	45.3 %

5   Conclusions

This paper focuses on mining disease complication association rules based on medical information. The concept of concurrent weight of diseases is proposed and defined. And the BP neural network model is introduced to predict the weight for all related diseases. Then, we adopt the weighted association rule mining algorithm and FP-tree structure to retrieve the complication relationship among diseases. Based on the mined rules, the potential list of patients' complication can be generated.

This research provides several research contributions. First, we propose a new index to evaluate the importance of different diseases on complication prediction. The defined index, i.e., concurrent weight, can describe the possibility that a disease become a complication of other diseases. Second, we introduce the BP network to predict the disease weight and design the appropriate input and output data. We define the disease information as a three dimension vector and the output of BP network is described by two neurons. By using the BP model, we can deduce a relatively complete disease knowledgebase. Third, we adopt the weighted association rule approach to mine the diseases association rules. To the best of our knowledge, it is the first time to apply the weighted association rule mining approach in the medical field. And some interesting association rules are retrieved.

There are several limitations of this study, which provide opportunities for future research. First of all, we only focus on the mining of relationship among diseases, which can't describe the complication relationship accurately. Second, due to the scope and complexity of this study, we do not invite medical professionals to evaluate mined complication association rules. Although the derived rules are surely helpful for doctors' decision-making in the real practice, some rules maybe not meaningful or even wrong from the view of clinical research. Third, this research only uses the predication accuracy as the metric.

Acknowledgments. This paper was funded by National Natural Science Foundation of China (Grant No. 71272057, 71572013) and Beijing Natural Science Foundation (Grant No. 9152015).

References

1. Esfandiari, N., Babavalian, M.R., Moghadam, A.M.E., Tabar, V.K.: Knowledge discovery in medicine: current issue and future trend. Expert Syst. Appl. **41**(9), 4434–4463 (2014)
2. Shea, S., Hripcsak, G.: Accelerating the use of electronic health records in physician practices. New Engl. J. Med. **362**(3), 192–195 (2010)
3. Coloma, P.M., de Bie, S.: Data mining methods to detect sentinel associations and their application to drug safety surveillance. Curr. Epidemiol. Rep. **1**(3), 110–119 (2014)
4. Murff, H.J., FitzHenry, F., Matheny, M.E., Gentry, N., Kotter, K.L., Crimin, K., Dittus, R.S., Rosen, A.K., Elkin, P.L., Brown, S.H.: Automated identification of postoperative complications within an electronic medical record using natural language processing. JAMA **306**(8), 848–855 (2011)
5. Eshlaghy, A.T., Poorebrahimi, A., Ebrahimi, M., Razavi, A.R., Ahmad, L.G.: Using three machine learning techniques for predicting breast cancer recurrence. J. Health Med. Inf. **4**(2), 124 (2013)
6. Jensen, P.B., Jensen, L.J., Brunak, S.: Mining electronic health records: towards better research applications and clinical care. Nat. Rev. Genet. **13**(6), 395–405 (2012)
7. Kwon, J.H., Lee, N., Park, J.Y., Yu, Y.S., Kim, J.P., Shin, J.H., Kim, D.S., Joh, J.W., Kim, D.S., Choi, K.Y.: Actionable gene expression-based patient stratification for molecular targeted therapy in hepatocellular carcinoma. PLoS ONE **8**(6), e64260 (2013)
8. Roque, F.S., Jensen, P.B., Schmock, H., Dalgaard, M., Andreatta, M., Hansen, T., Søeby, K., Bredkjær, S., Juul, A., Werge, T.: Using electronic patient records to discover disease correlations and stratify patient cohorts. PLoS Comput. Biol. **7**(8), e1002141 (2011)

9. Hanauer, D.A., Rhodes, D.R., Chinnaiyan, A.M.: Exploring clinical associations using '-omics' based enrichment analyses. PLoS ONE **4**(4), e5203 (2009)
10. Holmes, A.B., Hawson, A., Liu, F., Friedman, C., Khiabanian, H., Rabadan, R.: Discovering disease associations by integrating electronic clinical data and medical literature. PLoS ONE **6**(6), e21132 (2011)
11. Tai, Y.M., Chiu, H.W.: Comorbidity study of ADHD: applying association rule mining (ARM) to National Health Insurance Database of Taiwan. Int. J. Med. Inform. **78**(12), e75–e83 (2009)
12. Kim, H.S., Shin, A.M., Kim, M.K., Kim, Y.N.: Comorbidity study on type 2 diabetes mellitus using data mining. Korean J. Intern. Med. **27**(2), 197–202 (2012)
13. Shin, A.M., Lee, I.H., Lee, G.H., Park, H.J., Park, H.S., Yoon, K.I., Lee, J.J., Kim, Y.N.: Diagnostic analysis of patients with essential hypertension using association rule mining. Healthc. Inform. Res. **16**(2), 7–81 (2010)
14. Wright, A., Chen, E.S., Maloney, F.L.: An automated technique for identifying associations between medications, laboratory results and problems. J. Biomed. Inform. **43**(6), 891–901 (2010)
15. Kuo, C.F.J., Hsu, C.T.M.Z., Liu, X., Wu, H.C.: Automatic inspection system of LED chip using two-stages back-propagation neural network. J. Intell. Manuf. **25**(6), 1235–1243 (2014)
16. Wang, L., Zeng, Y., Chen, T.: Back propagation neural network with adaptive differential evolution algorithm for time series forecasting. Expert Syst. Appl. **42**(2), 855–863 (2015)
17. Cai, C.H., Fu, A.W., Cheng, C., Kwong, W.: Mining association rules with weighted items. In: Proceedings of Database Engineering and Applications Symposium. IEEE (1998)
18. Pears, R., Yun, S.K., Dobbie, G., Yeap, W.: Weighted association rule mining via a graph based connectivity model. Inf. Sci. **218**(1), 61–84 (2013)
19. Li, T., Li, X.: Novel alarm correlation analysis system based on association rules mining in telecommunication networks. Inf. Sci. **180**(16), 2960–2978 (2010)
20. Hoque, N., Nath, B., Bhattacharyya, D.K.: A new approach on rare association rule mining. Int. J. Comput. Appl. **53**(3), 1–6 (2012)

A Study on the Individualized Information Service Mode and Its Application in the Manufacturing and Supply Chain

Ni Yingzi[1(✉)] and Qin Zheng[1,2]

[1] School of Information Management and Engineering,
Shanghai University of Finance and Economics, Shanghai 200433, China
niyingzi@foxmail.com, qin.z@sustc.edu.cn
[2] South University of Science and Technology of China,
Shenzhen 518005, China

Abstract. Customer, information and functions are in the same level in the traditional computer application systems, and all customers are treated by the same interface to implement the standardized service functions. However, in general, 80 % of the profits come from 20 % of the key customers. These key customers should deserve better services. Therefore, the enterprises have to response quickly to their needs of individualized information service. In this paper, a detailed case of individualized information service in the field of iron and steel manufacturing supply chain is introduced, and valuable content is extracted and pushed from mass data to constitute a business environment of information sharing that creates value for the customers. The individualized information push mode for the key customer is studied and a functional frame and an operating system for the information service system based on the workflow are introduced.

Keywords: Individualized information service · Supply chain · Key customer · Enterprise system

1 Introduction

In the era of knowledge-based economy, it is becoming ever-increasingly difficult for organizations to create and maintain their competitive advantage [1]. Certain knowledge owned by an organization forms its competitive advantage, and the lack of certain knowledge weakens this very organization. And usually, the lack of knowledge is caused by demand of knowledge and imbalance between demand and supply [2].

Generally for a manufacturing enterprise, 80 % of the profit is created by the key customers which are 20 % of all customers. These strategic users should be granted outstanding service, but in most enterprise information systems, key customers and common customers are provided with the same information service, and the individualized information service demand from the key customers can hardly be satisfied rapidly. The reason is that customers, information and functions are in the same level in the traditional computer application systems, and all customers are treated by the same interface and standardized service functions [3].

© IFIP International Federation for Information Processing 2016
Published by Springer International Publishing Switzerland 2016. All Rights Reserved
M.C.C. Baranauskas et al. (Eds.): ICISO 2016, IFIP AICT 477, pp. 159–168, 2016.
DOI: 10.1007/978-3-319-42102-5_18

This paper analyzes the features of collaborative operation of key customers, discusses the technical features and technical key points, and provides the functional framework of a collaborative business system for key customers and a collaborating case between an iron and steel enterprise and an automobile enterprise based on the collaborative business platform for key customers.

2   Background of Theories

2.1   About Information Push Service

Along with the advent of intelligent information era and ever-improving web data, "matching plus push" comes to replace "search", and is becoming the core of future information service. Information push technology is basically classified into two categories: automatic pulling technology and event-driven technology. In this regard, WU [4] analyzes the application of information push technology in a library system while Tong-Seng [5] carry out an analysis into push service delivery that is based upon wireless technology.

Based on previous studies, we come to notice two distinctive features: one is that one can draw advantages by combing push and pull technologies in order to achieve synergy of push and pull of information, and the other is that push technology augmented with artificial intelligence, which is signified by: Intelligent search agent technology, Automatic classification information processing technology and Intelligent information filtering technology. And particularly for the latter feature, those academic observations were applied into the study of Push technology.

2.2   About the Individualized Push System

The individualized information push system introduced by Zhang [6] and Qiu et al. [7] consists of an intelligent and complicated decision making and reasoning feedback mechanism which is used to help the user fix the information so that the user can obtain the most updated information without visiting the fixed website repeatedly, and it has solved the defects in the search engine and retrieving tool by which usually excessive but not exact enough information can be found. By making the user the key focus and providing customized information push service to the user, this individualized information push system connects the user with more affinity and bridges the gap between the enterprise and the user, which is key to the improvement of user satisfaction [8].

The individualized information push system described by Wei et al. [9] basically consists of six modules: data integration, data normalization treatment, information analysis, information matching, and user utilization evaluation.

2.3   About the Information Push Application

According to the related references about information push, the practice of information push in most Chinese and foreign enterprises is supported by the push technology and realized by the information push system. Based upon observations on the performance of data service of The Johns Hopkins University of the U.S. by Shen and Varvel [10], Davidson et al. [11] analyzes data management programs that are currently carried out in the U.K., and concludes that the information push takes the dominant place in individualized libraries, but less so in the supply chain of the manufacturing industry.

3 Features of Collaborative Business for Key Customers

A strategic cooperating partnership is created by the enterprise with key customers to reduce the operation cost and improve the management efficiency, and a collaborative business platform is built for key customers with the electronic business technology. By the information exchange between strategic partners, barriers of information communication in the business flow are pushed down, the capability of rapid response is enhanced, the processing cycle of each business link is shortened, the management cost is reduced, the operating efficiency of the mutual supply chain is heightened, and the satisfaction degree of key customers is improved by the individualized and all-around customer service and business collaboration. The collaborative business of key customers is all-around and involved in many fields including research, development, distribution, manufacturing, material circulation, and service, e.g.,

1. Highly effective product research and development: the enterprise studies the technology for using, and participates in the customer's research and development workflow so that the products can be matched with the device, design and production workflow in downstream enterprises to improve the "using quality" of products.
2. Dynamic plan collaboration: the customer's plan is also the enterprise's plan, by sharing the strategic customer's production plan and production achievement and creating a material demand computing model of the supply chain between the enterprise and the customer a reasonable and exact stock quantity for varies products can be obtained, the net demand for each type can be known, and a reliable basis for material purchase can be provided to key customers.
3. Convenient information tracing: the customer can inquire about the production progress, material circulation, quality information and settlement information of the contract related in the office via electronic business. Such transparent operating mode can standardize the internal management of the enterprise.
4. High quality after-sales service: in case of any product quality problem, the customer can trace all information from project establishing, processing, claiming for compensation, correcting and completing.

4 Individualized Information Service Mode

4.1 Main Features of Individualized Information Service

The individualized information service demand from key customers is presented on the individualized interface design, business collaboration and information push service.

1. Individualized operating interface: the computer interface design is individualized according to the business features of the key customer in consideration of the way orders are placed, operating time and interface distribution, etc. For example, Shanghai Baosteel has two key customers: Guangdong Galanz Group (the largest microwave oven manufacturer in China) and FAW (a large automobile manufacturer in China). As steel material ordered by Galanz is usually transported along the water way, Galanz may ask to select water way preferentially other than the railway on the ordering interface; but FAW usually asks to select railway transportation to Changchun Station. Furthermore, the interface distribution and menu settings are optimized, frequently used information can be searched by clicking a key once, the functional menu is arranged in a flow chart, and the correlation among all service functions can be known by the user conveniently. In all, the operating interface is simple and clear with minimal operating time and clicking times.

2. Individualized service information collaboration: a shared data collection interface is created for both cooperating parties, the product research, development and production plan and production achievement from both parties are acquired timely to organize business collaboration. For example, steel is researched and manufactured with the upgrading with car types in FAW. Once the demand for car model is fixed, a steel material certification plan with material type classified will be created in the system, the process design plan will be adjusted rapidly, and production will be spread effective to provide new steel material product for trial using. And meanwhile, shearing, punching and welding of steel in FAW can be traced by the system so that the product quality can be continuously improved before the whole car is certified.

3. Timely information push service: an individualized information space opened for each key customer all related information and functions are centralized as per the business flow, and the customized service is provided via the Internet (Web or special SLD). For example, if the globally most updated information about steel research and development is needed by Shanghai Volkswagen, information about new material and new technology released by major steel corporations and major steel magazines (e.g., Metal Abstract or Metal Engineer, etc.) can be automatically searched before confirmed and pushed to the individualized information platform of Shanghai Volkswagen.

Modern communication technology such as short messaging can be used by the system to inform the related person of processing the information at the first time when a demand (opinion or query) is delivered from the customer via the collaborating business platform automatically so that the time delay in information transmission and communication can be reduced and rapid response can be realized effectively.

4.2   Key Technology in Individualized Information Service

The front operating interface must be a customized system to satisfy the individualized information service demand from the key customers, but how to design the back-end application processing system? It will not be economical and cannot be managed effectively if a background system is independently customized for each key customer. In fact, the customers' demand for information can be satisfied by the current system data resources except there are some tiny differences in interface mode, arrangement, function and content. Therefore, it is necessary to create a uniform background information processing center by which information push service is provided, all customers' demands are further concluded into workflows and forms for format conversion, bill exchange and workflow control to realize the flexible system management.

1. Format conversion: automatic conversion between individualized bills and standard bills for each enterprise can be realized in the bill format conversion center so that each partner in the supply chain can only focus on his own related data content and format during the data interface development.
2. Bill exchange: when the address code to be delivered with the business data is given from the application system, the data can be transmitted to the system at the other end by the exchange center via the function of "address registering and automatic address searching", the difference in data integration is shielded, and the system expandability is improved effectively.
3. Workflow control: format bills are described by business bills and definitions so that they can be transferred among different partners and the business information can be transferred more timely, reliably and intelligently. The relationship of information transfer is maintained by the workflow control center to follow the change of business rules and information demands among enterprises.

5 Functional Frame of the Collaborative Service System for Key Customers

5.1 Core Functions of the Collaborative Service System for Key Customers

The collaborative service system for key customers is highly different from the traditional information system. The internal information is extended to the customer and supplier via an electronic business platform to promote the informationization of the whole supply chain, realize the information integration and share among enterprises, reduce the process management cost between the upstream and downstream units, and create value for all customers. Based on the original internal business system, three core application supporting systems including an electronic business system, a supply chain decision making and supporting system and a client service knowledge base system.

Electronic business system – create a bridge between the enterprise and the customer. An electronic business platform is created for the enterprise by the electronic business technology to realize the connection from the internal system of the enterprise to the customer. Firstly, products can be ordered via the Internet conveniently. Secondly, inquiring via the Internet can be realized, the contract with customer, production progress, material circulation and transportation, quality information and settlement information of the customer's contract can be inquired by the customer in his own office. Such transparent operating mode constitutes the supervision by the clients for internal employees and standardizes the internal management. For example, if the customer finds no production is timely arranged for this contract, he can urge the arrangement via the "Hotline for Customers" so that products can be delivered on time. Thirdly, once any dispute on product quality happens and a dispute on product quality is submitted by the customer, the whole course from dispute establishing, processing, claiming for compensation and correcting can be traced.

Supply chain decision making and supporting system – support rapid responses to the customer. An order from the customer usually involves small batches and many types which must be actualized in a short time but frequently changes. In the past, such demand was usually from the least customers, and it can be treated fully in a manual mode. But now, such demand becomes frequent for the enterprise. To solve the contradiction between "individualized customer's demand" and "scaled enterprise production", it is necessary to develop an enterprise information system for supply chain management. The enterprise will actively participate in the customer's organization's production, estimate the customer's demand exactly, create a B2B information connection, and use the model technology to optimize the own organization for production. Information technology is used to create a system collaboratively operated with the customer's business, the scale advantage of industrialized production can be realized by the enterprise, the customer's contract can be completed and all customers' demands can be satisfied in quality, quantity and time. A model for estimating the customer's demand is developed to analyze the integrated optimization of supply chain between the customer and manufacturer, for example, what material and when it will be used by the customer's production line, and how to ensure the supply for production before optimizing the stock structure timely, i.e.: the own sales plan is fixed according to the customer's production plan, once the customer's plan is modified, the steel sales plan will be adjusted correspondingly. A production model will be developed and optimized, the internal ordered production and optimized organization will be studied, the contradiction between the "individualized customer's demand" and the "scaled enterprise's production" will be solved to realize the large scale customization. The production for the contract will be reasonably arranged according to the customer's demand and the own production conditions by optimized computer tools to realize the dynamic response of the delivery period.

Customer service knowledge base system – integrate the customer service information resources for knowledge sharing. To support the customer's query for ordering, the salesman has to know the product's sales history, price information, production capacity, quality assurance capacity, claim for compensation and customer's credit, etc. The information is controlled by the sales, manufacture, financial and other departments separately, the salesman in the past can only master the sales information and other information has to be replied by other departments in a long time and low efficiency. Information technology is used to integrate and share the information, a knowledge base is created for customer consultancy, any information can be inquired by the front sales and service men timely on line, the customer's demand for ordering can be replied at the first time, and thus rapid response and scientific decision making can be realized effectively.

5.2   Information Correlation Between the Electronic Business Platform and the Internal Management System

The spatial and temporal distance between manufacturer and the customer is shortened by the application of the Internet and electronic business technology. The online marketing service provided by the electronic business platform for the enterprise has created an information bridge between the enterprise and the customer. The electronic business platform is closely integrated with the integrated manufacture subsystem, data warehouse subsystem, rapid response subsystem and other special management subsystems in the enterprise to answer the customer's demand and share manufacture information with the customer. For example of steel products, the main information exchange is involved with:

Sales management: customers can directly query for ordering and order on line, by the connection between the network and integrated manufacture subsystem, data warehouse subsystem and rapid response subsystem, the interaction between business and information can be realized effectively, and the management efficiencies for both parties can be improved.

Material circulation management: GPS/GPRS technology is used to position and trace the truck or ship, share the sales and material circulation information with the customer, and realize the informationized management for the transporters. The transferring speed of packet data, work instructions, coded bill information, transportation bill information and contract settlement speed are accelerated by the electronic transmission of bills based on the code bar technology of steel products.

Service management: the service system of the online marketing subsystem is functioning through the whole business flow before, during and after distribution, involved with production introduction, standard inquiry, contract trace, quality assurance inquiry, quality dispute, user's hotline, satisfaction degree investigation, and provides all-around service to the customer. In the collaborative business for key customers, the satisfaction degree of key customers is improved by the fully individualized and all-around service and business collaboration, a closer strategic partnership is created between the enterprise and the customer, and a powerful support is provided. Case of application.

5.3   Collaborative Business Between Baosteel and FAW-Volkswagen

Baosteel is one of the largest iron and steel group in China, and one of the major products is the cold rolled steel panel for automobiles. FAW-Volkswagen is a key customer of Baosteel, the automobile steel panels of Jetta, Bora and Audi, etc. are mainly from Baosteel, more than 6,000 tons of steel is supplied from Baosteel monthly.

In 2003, a strategic cooperation agreement was signed between Baosteel and FAW to create a collaborative business platform, to reduce the material circulation cost and improve management efficiency. The management of the steel sheet roll warehouse of FAW-Volkswagen is authorized to Baosteel. Therefore, the management of Baosteel is extended from the plant to the customer, the warehouse is created at the door to the customer, as shown in Fig. 1.

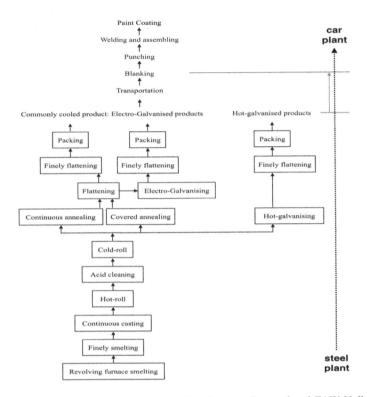

Fig. 1. Schematic drawing of business workflow between Baosteel and FAW-Volkswagen

A steel supply chain computing model is created between Baosteel and FAW-Volkswagen by the computer system, by sharing the car production plan and achievement with FAW-Volkswagen, the steel stock in the whole supply chain from Changchun to Shanghai can be dynamically balanced, the steel production plan can be adjusted timely, the contract actualization, manufacture, and finished product transportation in Baosteel can be reasonably arranged, and the demand for car production from FAW-Volkswagen can be satisfied. A "Just In Time" supply mode is realized to solve the trouble back at FAW-Volkswagen.

By the mutual effort, the steel stock in FAW-Volkswagen becomes more reasonable, the material purchase cycle is highly shortened, and the delivery accuracy is effectively improved. By the high efficiency supply chain management and informationized collaboration platform, the cooperation level between both parties is improved, and a promising benefit is brought to both parties. In this way, a stable and reliable strategic customer is obtained by Baosteel with value is created for the customer.

5.4   Production Plan Collaboration Between Baosteel and FAW-Volkswagen

The core of production plan collaboration is a material demand management system for the supply chain, and the system is used to calculate the net demand (from

FAW-Volkswagen). The core modules are supply chain material circulation information model, production demand calculation model and purchase demand calculation model, etc. All business links including car production plan, net material demand calculation, purchase plan confirmation, steel purchase contract generation, manufacture, contract trace, material circulation, transportation and product delivery are realized on the collaborative business platform for key customers between Baosteel and FAW-Volkswagen, and the effective contract data can be directly accepted by the internal business system of Baosteel.

1. The customer's stock information is integrated with the steel stock information of Baosteel production, delivery, and transportation, and a material circulation information model for the whole supply chain is created between Baosteel and FAW-Volkswagen.
2. A production demand calculation model is created according to the car production plan and fixed consumption of FAW-Volkswagen to obtain the corresponding steel demand via conversion.
3. A net demand for purchase is fixed by the purchase demand calculation model according to the safe stock days, railway transportation cycle and steel stock deducted, and finally a purchase plan is reviewed, approved and fixed.
4. The purchase plan is automatically converted into a steel ordering contract and transmitted into the internal business system of Baosteel via electronic processing.
5. The manufacture information and railway transportation achievement of Baosteel can be timely fed back to the collaborative business platform, and the stock structure of the whole supply chain can be dynamically traced by both parties.

6 Conclusion

The individuality of any customer is not specially treated in the traditional information system, the positions of key customers and ordinary customers are same and same functions are used in the system. Therefore the individualized customer's demand is restricted by the common system functions. Differentiated information service will become more and more popular with the improvement of customer's level. A customized and individualized information service system is created for FAW-Volkswagen by Baosteel based on the supply chain collaboration theory for business collaboration and information share. From the case of production and material circulation collaboration between Baosteel and FAW-Volkswagen, we find: the material demand calculation for the whole supply chain is more accurate than the independent MRP calculation in the enterprise because of the expansion of calculation range and the improvement of information transparency, and the customer's raw material stock becomes more reasonable. And meanwhile by the mutual all-around information collaboration, paperwork is greatly reduced, the production plan flexibility and response level are improved, and the operation is simplified effectively. Therefore, a larger value space is created for both parties by the individualized information service for key customers.

References

1. Zack, M.H.: Developing a knowledge strategy. Calif. Manag. Rev. **41**(3), 124–125 (1999)
2. Fan, Z., Sun, Y.: Enterprise knowledge management strategy based on SWOT analysis. Nankai Bus. Rev. **5**(4), 4–6 (2002)
3. Zhang, X., et al.: The study on information service for strategy customer in B-B e-business model. In: Proceedings of International Conference on Service Systems and Service Management, Beijing, China, pp. 769–772 (2004)
4. Wu, J.: Principle of information push technology and its application in the library. Sci-Tech Inf. Dev. Econ. **14**(3), 19–21 (2004)
5. Tong-Seng, J.: Push selling-multicast messages to wireless devices based on the publish/subscribe model. Electron. Commer. Res. Appl. **1**, 235–246 (2002)
6. Zhang, Y.: Individualized knowledge push system based on search engine. Inf. Technol. **6**, 60–61 (2004)
7. Qiu, Y., Pan, X., Qiu, J., Gu, X.: WEB-based knowledge management and design of its software system structure. Manuf. Autom. **24**(14), 15–18 (2002)
8. Li, Y.: Study on quality assessment system of client-focused digital information push service. Liaoning Normal University (2011)
9. Wei, C., et al.: On measuring cloud-based push services. Int. J. Web Serv. Res. **13**(1), 53–68 (2016)
10. Shen, Y., Varvel Jr., V.E.: Developing data management services at the Johns Hopkins University. J. Acad. Librariansh. **39**, 552–557 (2013)
11. Davidson, Y., Jones, S., Molloy, L., Kejser, U.B.: Emerging good practice in managing research data and research information within U.K. Universities. Procedia Comput. Sci. **33**, 215–222 (2014)

Trends, Challenges and New Issues in Education, Health and eScience Systems

Using Stakeholder and Pragmatic Analyses to Clarify the Scenario of Data Sharing in Scientific Software

Alysson Bolognesi Prado[✉] and Maria Cecilia Calani Baranauskas

Institute of Computing, State University of Campinas, Campinas,
São Paulo, Brazil
{aprado,cecilia}@ic.unicamp.br

Abstract. Scientific communities can be seen as highly focused organizations, composed of people performing strict patterns of behavior. The growing body of scientific data available digitally, as well as new infrastructure of distributed access, has given to funding agencies, politicians and scientists in general the foresight of novel possibilities of discovery and innovation reusing those data. Many stakeholders now expect the data to be released, although relevant sharing rates are not always verified. In this paper, we propose a method to bring forward and represent these interests. Applying this method, we investigated how the availability of software capable of data storage and sharing can act upon their users, and whether it makes them more suitable to share research byproducts. Results show that, although current software empowers the scientists to carry out their own research, it still does not create a path through which users can make their interests spread among other stakeholders.

Keywords: Scientific communities · Actor-Network Theory · Norm analysis · Stakeholder analysis · Data sharing · Collaborative systems

1 Introduction

Over the last two decades, scientists have increasingly relying on computers to store and manage research data. This trend has given rise to a whole field of knowledge called e-science [6]. Several software have been developed in order to support researcher activities, for instance, SEEK [27], openBIS [2] and PEDRo [10].

As a consequence of this higher availability of digitally stored data, some began to advocate the possibilities of other scientists to reuse these data [4]. However, data sharing did not reach the expected rates [1, 3]. Faniel and Zimmerman [9] have raised some questions to be answered in order to achieve data sharing and reuse in a larger scale. For instance, *"What other types of social interaction beyond that with the data producer can facilitate data reuse (e.g., colleagues, third party experts)? How can social exchange and documentation be combined to support data sharing and reuse on a large scale?"* [9, p. 61].

Scientific communities can be seen as highly focused organizations [26] performing tasks strictly conformed to their accepted methods. Therefore, we argue that the tools

© IFIP International Federation for Information Processing 2016
Published by Springer International Publishing Switzerland 2016. All Rights Reserved
M.C.C. Baranauskas et al. (Eds.): ICISO 2016, IFIP AICT 477, pp. 171–180, 2016.
DOI: 10.1007/978-3-319-42102-5_19

provided by Organizational Semiotics [19] are suited to capture the systemic features of scientific work, in particular, the ones related to intentions, interests and behavior, that is, the pragmatic level. Associated to a stakeholder analysis, it could also be used for understanding the cultural reverberations, either beneficial or disadvantageous, of an innovation among the involved parties [25].

In this paper, we outline and apply a method to capture the social and pragmatic aspects of the interaction of scientists with one another as well as with technological artifacts, and the interests involved with data sharing. Given the important social facet involved in use and reuse of scientific data, we draw upon the sociological framework provided by Actor-Network Theory [16, 17] in order to improve the understanding of how non-human entities, such as software and data but not limited to them, participate in the processes performed by scientists.

This paper is organized as follows: Sect. 2 brings a summary of other studies contributing to the theoretical and methodological support of our analysis, while Sect. 3 shows the sources of information that fed it. In Sect. 4 we propose a method to capture how the interested entities articulate in a social scenario involving people and technology in order to achieve mutual benefit, and apply it in Sect. 5 to existing software. In Sect. 6 we discuss the findings and add our final remarks in Sect. 7.

2   Theoretical-Methodological Background

The Actor-Network Theory (ANT) is a theoretical as well as methodological framework that emerged from Social Studies of Science and Technology. It proposes to see social phenomena as chains of associations distributed in time and space, dependent of the continuous agency of their participants on each other [17]. Its origins on empirical studies of scientists performing their daily activities make it very suitable to help understanding social aspects of science making.

An *actor* is defined as any entity, whether human or not, capable of changing a certain state of affairs Human actors encompass people involved and interested in a certain state of affairs, along with their embodied knowledge and know how. ANT claims that purely human relations are short ranged and fast decaying. Non-human actors, although not provided of intentionality, have the potential of mediation and interaction, either by physical or cognitive means. Participants of social activities create associations among themselves, with the intention to get support, propagate forces and interests as well as mobilize other partners to achieve their goals.

An actor is an *intermediary* in a chain of associations when propagate the actions received without change. The behavior of an intermediary is predictable and the outputs are determined by the inputs. On the other hand, an actor is a *mediator* when it modifies, distorts, amplifies or translates incoming stimuli, being creative and showing variability and unpredictability to act on others. During a scenario analysis, intermediaries often fade out whereas mediators stand out as solvers of asymmetries and conflicts between other actors.

From the ANT perspective, normative behavior can be seen as the sum of social forces generated, stored and replied by actors and conducted through the associations between them. One actor acts upon the others affording some behavior, trying to mold it to his own interests and benefit. The more these forces are stable, the more community's behavior seems homogeneous [18]. Knowing the source and path of these influences, as well as the reservoirs of the rules, examples, laws and models [17], is fundamental when someone is interested in understanding or changing them.

Prado and Baranauskas [23, 24] proposed a method for representing the social forces involved in a social phenomenon, introducing the idea of *intended norms*, that is, desired or expected patterns of behavior. These norms can be scored using the following proposed syntax, where each one receives an identification (ID) and the source of the norm, that is, the actor who is acting upon the other, shaping its behavior, is identified: **Norm** `<norm-id>`**: whenever** `<condition>` **if** `<state>` **then** `<target-actor>` **is** `<obliged | permitted | prohibited>` **by** `<source-actor>` **to do** `<action>`. These IDs can be applied in a graphical representation of the actors and their relationships, labeling arrows that show the path of mediators and intermediaries they travel.

3 The Conundrum of Sharing Research Data

Borgman [3] studies in depth the intricate subject of data sharing among scientists, producing a clarifying discussion about the involved interests, benefits and the difficulties to overcome. For her, sharing covers a variety of acts as varied as announcing the existence of data, posting them on a website, or contributing them to a richly curated repository.

There are four main rationales driving the requests for sharing research data: reproducibility of experiments, publicity of the outcomes of public funded research, reuse of data for asking new questions, and innovate the way science is made. The reproducibility is desired, for instance, by the peer reviewers of publications, who can make better judgments of the submitted papers. Other scientists are also interested in reproducibility, since they can validate the references on which they are basing their own research. Publications add value to data and vice-versa [20].

Public funded research is a target of legislators, representing the taxpayers, who wants to make available all research data produced using governmental grants, as a direct return to the society of the invested amounts. Researchers are also willing to have access to third-party data to ask new questions over the existing datasets, particularly when those are expensive or difficult to obtain. The reuse of data raises the question of assessing the veracity and integrity of a given dataset, and the need for documentation [4, 8]. At last, it has been argued about the existence of a scientific "fourth paradigm", a new way of doing science where algorithms for data crunching and mining are applied to massive datasets to produce scientific knowledge, therefore being highly dependent of availability of data.

However, there are also reasons for limiting data sharing. For instance, researches involving human subjects must be concerned with privacy issues and not all data could be disclosed. Scientists may also be unwilling to provide their data to other researchers, particularly when they are not related to the same project or institution. That happens because researchers compete for grants, jobs, publication venues, as well as for students, and access to data is a competitive advantage in this scenario. In private funded research projects, a lower rate data sharing could be observed.

Studying how scientists interact with one another, with technology and with nature during the production of a scientific fact, Latour [16] proposes to understand this process as a progressive effort to strengthen claims by means of mobilizing other entities. These may be other person, but mostly are non-human of semiotic or material nature, which provide support to the arguments, allowing certain statements to be held against inquiries.

One of the main allies a scientist can resort is the previously published scientific literature, because claims are harder to be refuted when adequately associated to citations widely accepted. The same rationale can be applied to inscriptions and other visual records produced by laboratory instruments or derived from their data, which can go along with texts to permit their authors to sustain their point of view about a subject. The validity of these arrangements, however, cannot be measured by its intrinsic characteristics. Once approved by the scrutiny of other scientists, the hypothesis can be gradually strengthened as a scientific fact as it is used by others, who become interested in its correctness.

4   A Method to Trace Interests of Stakeholders

Understanding that the behavior of users towards a piece of software can be affected by the resultant of the forces propagating on the network of associations that surround and reach them, we need to clarify the intricate set of influences each actor exerts and receives in this scenario. To perform this task, we envisioned a method that identifies the involved parties and represents their relationships and interactions, as well as the patterns of behavior they expect or desire from the others.

The Stakeholder Diagram [15] is widely used in problem articulation, serving as a good starting point to clarify the scenario under study. It provides visual representation of the roles of the participants, also showing how closely related they are to the system under study. Pouloudi et al. [22] suggest the conjoint use of stakeholder analysis and ANT as a generic, context free, guidance to identify the involved humans, as well as other relevant non-human actors.

We adopted this method to elicit the participation of actors of both nature, and employed the concepts described in Sect. 2 to capture the interest each actor has in the behavior of the others. In our proposal, human actors will be drawn as round rectangles, while the non-human as the ones with straight corners. They are bound by lines whenever they have some kind of interaction or association. Norm statements, representing a behavior not necessarily observed but sometimes desired or intended, are attached to arrows depicting the path from the source actor to the target, that is, from the one who will benefit from the pattern of action to the actor who should perform it accordingly.

Whenever a non-human actor is software, we must inspect its user interface in order to capture some affordances for the users. As intended norms, these can be traced back to discover, or at least hypothesize, their sources. For example, consider a system that requires the user to select the project a given dataset belongs to, being otherwise denied to upload files. It may indicate a need or intent of the institution, which provides the

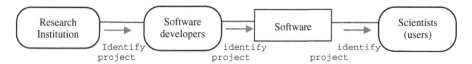

Fig. 1. Software and its developers acting as intermediaries, propagating the interests of the institution and molding the repertoire of actions of the users: they are obligated to identify the project a new dataset belongs. Arrows show the path of the influences and actions needed to promote such affordance

software to its scientists, to keep data files properly categorized. This can be captured as the following norm and diagram elements shown in Fig. 1.

Norm "identify project": **whenever** uploading a file **then** the scientists **are** obliged **by** the institution they work for **to** relate it to a previously registered project

In another example, consider the interests the general public have as taxpayers and as people being studied by scientists. They are stakeholders with distinct expectations about how the researchers should behave, expressing themselves through their representatives by means of legislation. The interest of the taxpayers is exerted by means of the taxes which willingness to be paid by the citizen can influence the legislators. On the other hand, the human subjects can only rely on their contacts to legislator and personal pressure. We must notice that the taxes are acting as a non-human actor – an intermediary forwarding the intended norm. In their turn, the legislators shall act as a mediator, finding a half term solution, for instance, creating legislation regulating the concession of grants. This can be recorded in the following set of norms plus the diagram sketched in Fig. 2.

Norm "funding": **whenever** funding research **if** with public taxes **then** the scientists **are** obliged **by** taxpayers **to** share their research products

Norm "privacy": **whenever** publishing data **if** it involves human subjects **then** the scientists **are** prohibited **by** human subjects **to** disclosure sensitive information

Norm "public/ethic": **whenever** funding researches **if** from public taxes **and** no sensitive data involved **then** the scientists **are** obliged **by** regulation law **to** make available their research products

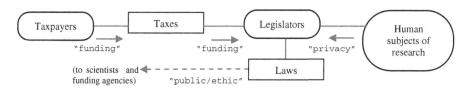

Fig. 2. Legislators acting as mediators of conflicting interests, since "funding" and "privacy" are balanced and issued as another distinct desired pattern of behavior

5   Inspecting a Software for Scientific Data Management

We have studied SEEK (v.0.16.3), a scientific web-based software intended to be used by systemic biology researchers, designed and developed by a team of e-science researchers funded by a consortium of research institutions. It supports the management, sharing and exploration of data and models [25]. The user can store biology-specific information, such as records of specimen, as well as research outcomes of generic type, such as publications and presentations. The user is always obliged to associate these items to one of the projects she is affiliated – as the "identify project" norm defined previously.

SEEK allows users to standardize and organize their digital assets, as well as to define access permissions for each one, ensuring the scientists have the final word about who can access those files. When defining these access rules, developers provide a default value that allows anyone to know the existence of the file, but not its content. All uploaded items have a persistent URL that allows data citation, as well as a reference to its authors, rewarding the contributions of each individual. Put in norm syntax, this means:

Norm   "control": **whenever** data is uploaded **then** scientists **are** allowed **by** developers **to** choose access rules

Norm   "default": **whenever** data is uploaded **if** user does not control permissions **then** other projects' members, anonymous visitors **are** allowed **by** developers **to** view data summary

Norm   "request": **whenever** viewing data summary **then** other scientists **are** allowed **by** developers **to** request full access to file owner

Norm   "cite": **whenever** writing a paper **if** used data files **then** scientists **are** allowed **by** developers **to** add a link referencing data

Norm   "access": **whenever** data is stored on SEEK **if** paper cites data **then** other scientists, peer reviewers **are** allowed **by** scientists **to** view, use or download the file

To describe the broader context in which the software operates, we used the previous studies summarized in Sect. 3, as well as the complete reports of Latour [16] and Borgman [3]. In addition to the actual examples presented in Sect. 4, we scored some other following intended norms, representatives of the main involved interests. The main goal of scientists is to produce scientific content, mainly in the form of publications, which are expected to be accepted and cited. All these interests are placed on the stakeholder diagram, and the result is shown in Fig. 3.

Norm   "funding policies": **whenever** receiving grants **then** scientists, institutions **are** obliged **by** funding agencies **to** produce scientific knowledge, mainly in the form of publications, following public/ethic laws

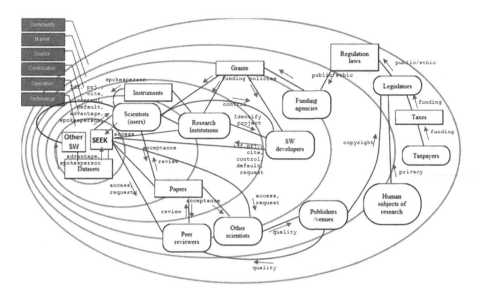

Fig. 3. Expanded stakeholder diagram eliciting the role of actors as the path of interests in certain patterns of behavior

Norm "copyright": **whenever** sharing resource products **then** scientists **are** prohibited **by** publishers **to** disclosure copyrighted material

Norm "quality": **whenever** publishing papers **then** publishers **are** obliged **by** other scientists **to** evaluate quality and veracity of its contents

Norm "review": **whenever** submitting paper for publishing **then** scientists **are** obliged **by** peer reviewers **to** provide related data

Norm "reuse": **whenever** possessing data difficult to be obtained **then** scientists **are** obliged **by** other scientists **to** publish data

Norm "advantage": **whenever** possessing data difficult to be obtained **if** they are kept private **then** scientists **are** allowed **by** those data **to** publish new relevant papers

Norm "spokesperson": **whenever** writing a paper **then** scientists **are** allowed **by** data, instruments, SEEK, other software **to** make claims and statements

Norm "acceptance": **whenever** writing a paper **then** other scientists, peer reviewers **are** obliged **by** scientists **to** accept their claims and statements based on data, instruments, references

6 Analyzing the Outcomes

The ANT rationale of the proposed method demands an inquisitive stance from the analyst of a given scenario, requiring the identification of in-between actors and finding or guessing how they receive and propagate interests. The search for a path for the influences, represented graphically by the arrows on the diagram, leads to a more complete set of involved entities and points out possible gaps. For instance, no path was defined for the norm "reuse", unless exists a missing link between the scientists and any – or several – other actor to promote some sort of influence. Other issues are brought forth by the arrangement provided by the stakeholder diagram; for instance, the funding agencies and the publishers are the main "bridges" to the more external social world, while the inner layers remain self-regulative. As a drawback, to guess the source of an interest can be a tricky task; for instance, "default" is attributed to the developers, only because they are the most probable responsible for that choice. Deontic operators also need to receive more attention, since the restrictions of "obliged" and "prohibited" have a different actuation than the possibilities given by "allowed".

Regarding the particular scenario in which the method was applied, the analysis reveals that software developers may play a major role as mediators. Despite of being often kept aside of the stakeholders list, their engagement to the subject in this case is not neutral. They capture the funding agencies' intentions issued as funding policies, the institutions' management requirements, the scientists' needs of using data, and finally their own interests of making some software capable of promoting data sharing; the resultant of mediation being expressed through the software affordances. Empirical validation of this finding will require further research, in situations with conflict of interests that are neither self-regulated prior to software development, nor solved during the analysis phase – for instance, using participatory design workshops.

Analysis also show that "other software" is an alternate path to provide to scientists certain possibilities of action – despite of these systems to have no social features, but instead good data visualization or manipulation – and therefore "SEEK" does not poses itself as an obligatory passage point [17] of interests. This raises as an interesting research question of how to better design these software, which should be addressed by research proposals such as the Human-Data Interaction informed by Organizational Semiotics [11]. Software has the capability of embed complex rules, also being able to act as mediator. Particularly in a social scenario where it can receive clues about the heterogeneous set of interests of the persons operating him [12]. For instance, "request" captures the interest of other scientists in datasets and mediates users, institutions, developers and other scientists' interests without exposing any file details.

There are other studies of the factors affecting data sharing and reuse among scientific communities, such as surveys based on questionnaires applied to scientists of different fields of knowledge such as health sciences [14], STEM – science, technology, engineering and mathematics [13], or social sciences [5]. They conclude that journal publishers have a statistically significant influence on such behavior, while normative pressure by other scientists and regulative pressure by funding agencies are not perceived. Our proposal complements these measures of perception by showing paths pressures travel, and pointing out possible inconsistencies. For instance, the value given to a published paper is coherent to the strength of the norms it mediates. On the other hand, the low perception of pressure by funding agencies is not compatible to previous studies and discussions [3, 16], requiring a deep checking of the actual actuation of grants onto researchers. As stated by Eze et al. [7], the adoption of technology is not a one-off action that can be precisely captured by quantitative methods such as questionnaires; therefore a qualitative approach as provided by ANT also contribute to a broader analysis and comprehension of the phenomena.

7 Conclusion

The effectiveness of software when different interests – sometimes conflicting – are involved is not only a matter of its technical features but also a social [21] and pragmatic challenge. Scientific software intended for data sharing are not an exception, and despite of their capacity to store huge amounts of data, its publishing and reuse rates could be improved.

By asking who is potentially benefited from a certain behavior imposed or allowed by software, and the path this influence takes, responsible agents can be pointed out. Many of the patterns promoted by the system targets the users, while other external stakeholders seem barely influenced. As software is the direct point of contact of the scientists to data, its potential as mediator to resolve asymmetries and conflicts between converging interests could be better explored. Further research includes adding existing generic scientific social software such as Mendeley or ReserchGate to the diagram, to enrich the analysis with other possible social interactions between scientists mediated by technology.

Acknowledgments. We thank the Brazilian Research Foundation CNPq (Grant # 308618/2014-9). The opinions expressed in this work do not necessarily reflect those of the funding agencies.

References

1. Appelbe, B., Bannon, D.: eResearch – paradigm shift or propaganda? J. Res. Pract. Inf. Technol. **39**(2), 83–90 (2007)
2. Bauch, A., Adamczyk, I., Buczek, P., et al.: openBIS: a flexible framework for managing and analyzing complex data in biology research (2011)
3. Borgman, C.L.: The conundrum of sharing research data. J. Am. Soc. Inf. Sci. Technol. **63**(6), 1059–1078 (2012)
4. Carlson, S., Anderson, B.: What are data? The many kinds of data and their implications for reuse. J. Comput.-Mediated Commun. **12**(2), 635–651 (2007)
5. Curty, R.G.: Beyond "data thrifting": an investigation of factors influencing research data reuse in social sciences. MSc dissertation. Syracuse University (2015)
6. DeRoure, D., Jennings, N., Shadbolt, N.: Research agenda for the semantic grid: a future e-science infrastructure. Report Commissioned for EPSRC/DTI (2001)
7. Eze, S., Duan, Y., Chen, H.: Factors affecting emerging ICT adoption in SMEs: an actor network theory analysis. In: Khachidze, V., Wang, T., Siddiqui, S., Liu, V., Cappuccio, S., Lim, A. (eds.) iCETS 2012. CCIS, vol. 332, pp. 361–377. Springer, Heidelberg (2012)

8. Faniel, I.M., Jacobsen, T.E.: Reusing scientific data: how earthquake engineering researchers assess the reusability of colleagues' data. J. Comput.-Support. Coop. Work **19**(3–4), 355–375 (2010)
9. Faniel, I.M., Zimmerman, A.: Beyond the data deluge: a research agenda for large-scale data sharing and reuse. Int. J. Digit. Curation **6**(1), 58–69 (2011). doi:10.2218/ijdc.v6i1.172
10. Garwood, K., McLaughlin, T., Garwood, C., Joens, S., Morrison, N., Taylor, C.F., Paton, N. W.: PEDRo: a database for storing, searching and disseminating experimental proteomics data. BMC Genomics (2004)
11. Hornung, H., Pereira, R., Baranauskas, M.C., Liu, K.: Challenges for human-data interaction– a semiotic perspective. In: Kurosu, M. (ed.) Human-Computer Interaction. LNCS, vol. 9169, pp. 37–48. Springer, Heidelberg (2015)
12. Jensen, C.J., Dos Reis, J.C., Bonacin, R.: An interaction design method to support the expression of user intentions in collaborative systems. In: Kurosu, M. (ed.) Human-Computer Interaction. LNCS, vol. 9169, pp. 214–226. Springer, Heidelberg (2015)
13. Kim, Y., Stanton, J.M.: Institutional and individual influences on scientists' data sharing behaviors: a multilevel analysis. In: ASIST (2013)
14. Kim, Y., Kim, S.: Institutional, motivational and resource factors influencing health scientists' data-sharing behaviours. J. Sch. Publ. **46**(4), 366–389 (2015)
15. Kolkman, M.: Problem articulation methodology. Ph.D. thesis, University of Twente, Enschede (1993)
16. Latour, B.: Science in Action: How to Follow Scientists and Engineers Through Society. Harvard University Press, Cambridge (1987)
17. Latour, B.: Reassembling the Social: An Introduction to Actor-Network-Theory. Oxford University Press, Oxford (2005)
18. Law, J.: Actor-network theory and material semiotics. In: The New Blackwell Companion to Social Theory. Blackwell Publishing Ltd
19. Liu, K.: Semiotics of Information Systems Engineering. Cambridge University Press, Cambridge (2000)
20. Pepe, A., Matthew, M., Borgman, C., Sompel, H.: From Artifacts to Aggregations: Modeling Scientific Life Cycles on the Semantic Web (2010)
21. Pereira, R., Baranauskas, M.C.C., Silva, S.R.P.: A framework-informed discussion on social software: why some social software fail and others do not? In: 11th International Conference on Enterprise Information Systems, ICEIS (2010)
22. Pouloudi, A., Gandecha, R., Atkinson, C., Papazafeiropoulou, A.: How stakeholder analysis can be mobilized with actor-network theory to identify actors. In: Kaplan, B., Truex III, D. P., Wastell, D., Wood-Harper, A.T., DeGross, J.I. (eds.) Information System Research, vol. 143, pp. 705–711. Springer US, New York (2004)
23. Prado, A., Baranauskas, M.C.C.: Perspectives on using actor-network theory and organizational semiotics to address organizational evolution. In: The 15th International Conference on Enterprise Information Systems, ICEIS (2013)
24. Prado, A.B., Baranauskas, M.C.C.: Capturing semiotic and social factors of organizational evolution. In: Hammoudi, S., Cordeiro, J., Maciaszek, L.A., Filipe, J. (eds.) ICEIS 2013. LNBIP, vol. 190, pp. 264–279. Springer, Heidelberg (2014)
25. Rambo, K., Liu, K.: An organisational semiotics approach to multicultural requirements engineering: stakeholder's analysis of online shopping for Saudi Arabian female consumers. Int. J. Inf. (IJI) **4**(1/2), 473–483 (2011)
26. Wenger, E.: Communities of practice and social learning systems. Organization **7**(2), 225–246 (2000)
27. Wolstencroft, K., Owen, S., du Preez, F., Krebs, O., Mueller, W., Goble, C.A., Snoep, J.L.: The SEEK: a platform for sharing data and models in systems biology. Methods Enzymol. **500**, 629–655 (2011). PUBMED: 21943917

Meaning Construction and Evolution: A Case Study of the Design-in-Use of a System for Inclusive Education Teachers

Heiko Hornung[1]([⊠]), Roberto Pereira[2],
and M. Cecilia C. Baranauskas[1]

[1] Institute of Computing, University of Campinas, Av. Albert Einstein,
1251 Cidade Universitária, Campinas, SP 13083-852, Brazil
{heiko,cecilia}@ic.unicamp.br
[2] Department of Computer Science, Federal University of Paraná, R. Cel.
Francisco H. dos Santos, 100 Centro Politécnico, Curitiba, PR 81531-980, Brazil
rpereira@inf.ufpr.br

Abstract. Evolution in the digital technologies has changed the way people interact with others mediated by those devices. In this paper, we argue that systems design needs to go beyond the meaningful interaction of people with computational systems, and include meaningful interaction among people that is mediated by computational artefacts, by rules and norms that guide people's actions, as well as by culture, values, and intentions. This paper presents a case study of design-in-use of a system for inclusive education teachers. The design process for the system is participatory and based on Organisational Semiotics, i.e., explicitly considers collaborative meaning construction and negotiation. We illustrate and discuss examples of meaning construction and evolution from the perspective of interface and interaction design.

Keywords: Meaning construction · Meaning evolution · Pragmatics · Human-Computer Interaction · Interaction design

1 Introduction

There are different theoretical and methodological frames of reference for understanding, studying and designing for "meaningfulness". The notion of what constitutes "meaningful interaction" in a system, as well as what constitutes the "system" in which this interaction happens, and what or who takes part in this interaction have changed over the years. Consequently, the notion of how a system mediates interaction has also changed, making the subject even more relevant to research about Information Systems (IS) and Human-Computer Interaction (HCI).

Digital technology has permeated all aspects of life [3]. People use devices of a wide variety of forms in a wide variety of contexts or situations. When designing an application or a system, the traditional definitions of "user" and "task" do not hold up anymore. "Users" today have diverse characteristics and diverse motives for using applications, consequently "tasks" can no longer be seen in a singular context. For instance, a simple app for managing a to-do list might be used by a team of professional software developers for project managing or by a single user for creating a shopping list. "Meaningfulness" in this case relates to people's practices, and design needs to focus on facilitating these practices. Systems design then needs to go beyond the meaningful interaction of people with computational systems, and include meaningful interaction with people, i.e., interaction mediated by computational artefacts, by rules and norms that guide people's actions, as well as by people's culture, values, and intentions.

In this paper, we present the case of a system that is being designed-in-use with its users and other stakeholders since 2010. After briefly describing the context in which this system is being created, we present and discuss examples of meaning construction and evolution from the perspective of Pragmatics [6] and Values [11].

2   Todos Nós em Rede (TNR; English: "All of Us Networked")

In the last decade, the Brazilian public policies for inclusion of disabled students in regular schools created the Specialized Educational Services (SES). The SES services regulate and provide support for teachers' activities with students in multifunctional resources rooms, i.e., special rooms in regular schools equipped with specialized resources [10]. In order to qualify professionals in this field, teachers from all over the country started specialization courses through e-learning environments. These courses had a limited period of duration and, after them, teachers are alone in their places for accomplishing their daily activities.

The case study presented in this paper is situated within the context of the research and design project named *"Redes Sociais e Autonomia Profissional"*[1] (English: "Social Networks and Professional Autonomy"). This project investigates how to facilitate continuing learning of teachers in the field of inclusive education in Brazil's public school system and how to support them in their professional activities. Within the project, TNR[2] (*"Todos Nós em Rede"*, English: "All of Us Networked") is a system where inclusive education teachers can socialize, share experiences and discuss matters related to work practices. As of February 2016, the TNR system has more than 800 registered users. More than 1400 contents (articles, documents, questions, pictures) were shared by teachers and received around 4000 comments. TNR is being designed according to the socially-aware process outlined in [1]. Cornerstones of this process are stakeholder participation during all stages of design and semio-participatory practices that are informed by Organisational Semiotics [9] and Participatory Design [12]. During these practices, stakeholders construct and negotiate meanings [1].

The core research and design team comprises professors, researchers and PhD/MSc students from Unicamp's Faculty of Education and Institute of Computing, as well as inclusive education teachers from different parts of the country. For some activities, people with necessary skills are temporarily brought into the project, e.g., the team

---

[1] http://www.nied.unicamp.br/tnr.

[2] http://tnr.nied.unicamp.br.

already collaborated with a journalist, a lawyer, and a Web developer. When the project started in 2010, inclusive education teachers were recruited by sending a questionnaire to a list of registered special education teachers. From the about 300 respondents, 28 have been invited. One selection criterion was the access to and use of technology (computer, smartphone, etc.) and software such as e-mail, social networks, or other online communication systems. All 28 teachers, who are geographically dispersed all over Brazil, accepted the invitation. One reason for the selection criterion was that access and use of computers and online systems was deemed the most viable option for participatory activities. Given the continental dimensions of Brazil, bringing in all members to regular face-to-face meetings is not practical. Another reason for the selection criterion was that digital inclusion was not the focus of the project.

The project started without limiting possible outcomes, i.e., at the beginning, it was not clear that the computational system that is part of TNR would be developed. The main guiding principle was the objective to promote professional autonomy of inclusive education teachers by creating a system for socializing, sharing experiences and discussing matters related to inclusive education work practices. The main input for understanding teachers' work practices was given by a university course offered by the Ministry of Education where a 5-step process was taught, and by the diverse local practices of inclusive education teachers, which varied from ad-hoc processes using no or low-tech tools to custom-structured processes using e.g., electronic spreadsheets or mind maps. All participating teachers had attended the course offered by the Ministry of Education.

Along the first 4 years of the project, we conducted various synchronous and asynchronous online activities as well as two face-to-face one-day workshops. Details of the project and the process have been described in [11]. In the following, we present aspects related to meaning construction and evolution, taking a perspective informed by Pragmatics and Values.

3 Meaning Construction and Evolution in TNR

Inclusive education teachers provide attendance to children with special needs in order to facilitate their participation in regular classes. A core practice of this attendance is the so-called "case discussion" which comprises elements such as understanding the specific requirements of a child for participating in regular class, the elaboration of an attendance plan, as well as the implementation and evaluation of this plan. At the outset of the project, different understandings of the "case discussion" practice existed. Some of the team members from the Faculty of Education had participated in the creation of the university course offered by the Ministry of Education. The course is a representation of the practice as understood by the course creators. The course attendants in turn constructed their understandings of the practice, which probably differed somewhat from the understanding of the creators, given that the course was delivered via an online learning platform with tools that differed from the tools the participants usually had access to. Furthermore, the course was supported by monitors and tutors as well as by course schedules that e.g., determined when to proceed from one phase of the attendance process to the next. Transitions between phases were linear. In actual practice, teachers adopt different methods that vary from unstructured ad-hoc methods with limited tool use to more structured approaches with computational support tools.

In order to understand how inclusive teachers would use a collaborative online system for case discussions, we created prototypical practices where teachers explored and evaluated existing systems regarding the way they could support their professional activities. Four practices were created, and each practice discussed a case based on real cases submitted previously by the participants. The 28 participating teachers conducted the case discussions sequentially during a four to six-week period in existing online systems that afforded different styles of textual communication (a question-answer system, a forum-like system, a system with tool support for explicit meaning construction, and a blog-like system with social networking elements). The case discussions were a rich source of information where teachers gave their feedback by: (i) interacting through the systems in order to solve fictitious cases; (ii) answering evaluation questionnaires for each system, pointing out features they liked, disliked, missed, etc.; and (iii) participating in semi-structured online interviews.

Analyses of aspects related to pragmatic meanings of the four prototypical case discussions revealed how the four different systems influenced the case discussion in different ways [6]. A pragmatic function analysis showed that the participants employed a limited set of illocution types in the question-answer system (mainly affirmations), which hints at a conversation style that might be less beneficial to critically analysing a case and to learning from a case discussion than a conversation in which also valuations or inducements occur.

The analyses also revealed individual differences in practice conduction, e.g., a preference towards a linear sequence of discussion phases versus a parallel elaboration of phases [6], and cultural values related to the teachers' practices [11]. Concepts like collaboration, reputation and privacy were clarified and understood as values with meanings substantially different from the researchers' initial views. These values influenced the way teachers reacted to different features of the systems and to others' behaviour promoted or inhibited by each system. E.g., in a system that permitted synchronous and collaborative editing, teachers revealed a strong valuation for authorship, disapproving editing of "their" content by others and requiring the individual contribution to be preserved.

The users did not conclude the case discussion (phase four in the process) in three of the four systems. We attributed this to a certain artificiality of the discussions: although cases were based on actual cases and experience of the participants, there was no real "case owner" who had an interest of pushing the discussion forward.

The four prototypical practices also revealed an evolution of practice ([2, 7] for more detailed analyses). During the last prototypical practice, which was conducted in the least formal blog-like system, the count of "non-substantial" messages with a socializing intent was highest. It is unknown whether this was due to participants getting to know each other better, or due to the lower level of formality of the system.

All the material produced during the previous activities was synthesized and discussed by the researchers and the teachers in a face-to-face workshop. Once a common understanding about the system and its requirements was achieved, participatory practices were conducted to generate different proposals for implementing the solution. These proposals inspired the design of the TNR system, including the development of

"*Nossos Casos*" (Portuguese for "Our Cases"), an area within TNR to facilitate case discussions. Goals of designing "*Nossos Casos*" included allowing flexible practice and evolution of practice, as well as simplifying the process compared to the discussion taught in the university course. Formulating these goals was a result of the analyses described in the previous paragraph and the follow-up interviews. Although one goal was to enable flexibility, another goal was to provide some structure, since we perceived that the discussions through the previously described systems that provided no or little structure had a tendency to peter out.

Structure is provided by separate tabs for separate moments of the case discussion, clearly demarcated areas for content about the case and comments/discussions of this content, and by some form fields in the content area (Fig. 1). Flexibility is provided by the freedom to fill in and discuss content in the tabs in any order or to even not use some of the tabs. Most of the form fields are optional, and none has restrictions regarding input formats. Furthermore, there are very few explicit, technical norms or rules for conducting the discussion, e.g., the content area can only be edited by the case creator and all registered users can participate in the discussion through non-anonymous comments.

Figure 2 summarizes the meaning evolution of "case discussion", i.e., the different answers to the question of how to discuss a case. The gray areas symbolize that there

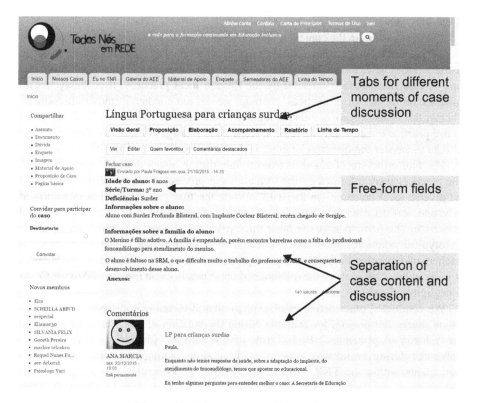

Fig. 1. Flexible structure in *Nossos Casos*

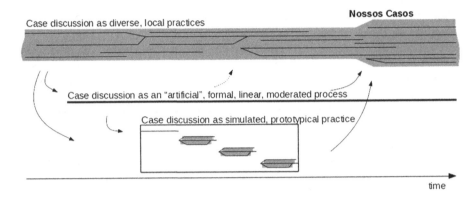

Fig. 2. Timeline of different ways to discuss cases

are many alternative ways to conduct a case discussion. A horizontal line represents a way to discuss a case. Regarding the diverse, local practices at the top and the prototypical practices at the bottom of the figure, different ways might exist in parallel, independent of each other, or be created as a branch or variant of an existing way. It is also conceivable that two ways of discussing a case converge. The introduction of *Nossos Casos* possibly makes new ways to discuss cases possible, hence the expansion of the gray area.

Case discussions in the context of the university course are conducted in exactly one way, as prescribed in the course curriculum ("exactly one way" is a simplification, since instructors and other factors have an influence on the conduction). The definition of this type of case discussion is inspired by the diverse local practices. It probably has an influence on further local practices, although we did not conduct a study to investigate whether this influence exists and how it alters actual practice conduction. The university course practice directly and explicitly influenced the design of *Nossos Casos*. We have no data to answer the question whether it also influenced the use of *Nossos Casos*.

The four prototypical practices existed only during a well-defined interval in time. The practices were informed by the formal, linear process of the university course and the diverse local practices "in the wild". While the first prototypical practice allowed only one way to discuss a case (an exchange of questions by the case owner and answers by the participants), the other three practices allowed for some variance. The prototypical practices influenced the design of *Nossos Casos*. Since the number of teachers participating in the prototypical practices was small compared to the number of users in the TNR system, the influence of these practices on the use of *Nossos Casos* is negligible if existent at all.

We conducted other activities of explicit shared meaning construction and negotiation during the project, for example during the creation of the "Terms of Use" and the "Charter of principles". Both Terms of Use and the Charter of Principles were elaborated during an iterative process of discussions among researchers and project participants within the TNR system. The Charter of Principles was a result of the discussion of the Terms of Use. A value-driven analysis of this discussion revealed values such as autonomy or collaboration that the participants felt should be made explicit in order to influence the constitution of the culture of interaction within the system. The Charter of Principles was also made available as the system home page for non-logged-in users.

4   Discussion

As illustrated by the "*Nossos Casos*" tool presented in this paper, meaning construction and negotiation starts at choosing the theoretical and methodological frame of reference, which in our case is based on and inspired by Organisational Semiotics [9, 13], Participatory Design [12], Activity Theory [8], the Building Blocks of Culture [1, 5, 6, 11]. These frames of reference are compatible with the view that meaning construction is a participatory and bottom-up process. Had we employed other frameworks that for example subscribe to an objectivist world view, the design of *Nossos Casos* would have been different and probably resulted in a tool with less flexibility and more explicit formal and technical norms.

Defining which stakeholders participate in which way and identifying stakeholder representatives has repercussions on meaning construction. Had we recruited teachers from our home state where smartphone diffusion and cell phone signal coverage are considerably higher than in many other parts of the country, the result might have been a mobile platform with dramatically different characteristics regarding meaning construction. Defining the stakeholders also has an influence on which values will be prioritized. For instance, although accessibility affects teachers directly, it was not a concern they manifested, but identified by Education and Computer Science researchers. Similarly, autonomy is another value directly related to teachers, but it was a concern manifested by researchers in the Education field. Teachers are used to adopt a narrow range of activities and approaches to the different cases face; researchers hope that by exchanging ideas and experiences, teachers may become more proactive and creative in their day-to-day work, developing and adopting new practices and activities. Furthermore, it is also desired that teachers become more autonomous using computer technology as they gain experience with the designed system. Had we ignored the existence of other key stakeholders, the results might have been an oversimplified system offering what the teachers already new or learnt during the practices.

Starting with prototyping practices in existing systems instead of prototyping user interfaces contributed significantly to keeping the design space wide open and facilitated the investigation of meaning construction of and about the "case discussion". This kind of prototyping evidenced explicit and implicit meaning making, explicit during follow-up interviews and implicit during the case discussions. Of course, this kind of prototyping has its limitations, e.g., the cases proposed for the practice within TNR had no case owner in the sense of a person who experienced the situation at the time of the practice and who would have a personal interest in concluding the case. However, the benefit of seeing prototypical practice right at the beginning of the process instead of having to wait to create a working prototype of a system safe enough to discuss the highly sensitive cases of children with special needs greatly outweighed the limitations.

Collaborative meaning construction and evolution does not necessarily result in meanings uniformly shared by all stakeholders. As described in the previous subsection, *Nossos Casos* permits different ways of conducting a case discussion, and users in fact use the tool in different ways. Interestingly, at the time of writing this paper, many users use *Nossos Casos* in ways that are different from what the team of researchers, designers and end-user representatives understood would be good practice. For example, with very few exceptions, case owners do not post an attendance plan (tab "*Elaboração*" in Fig. 1) or provide feedback about attendance (tab "*Acompanhamento*" in Fig. 1). This does not mean that the teachers do not use attendance plans or do not document the attendance of a child; they just do not (yet) use *Nossos Casos* for these activities. Using a system in a way different than that intended by the designers or developers is called appropriation in HCI vocabulary [4] and often considered a positive phenomenon. In TNR, appropriation is desired to some extent, although the participating researchers desire that eventually as many teachers as possible converge to an understanding of inclusive education and of how to discuss cases similar to theirs.

Inclusive education is a polemical subject and it would most probably not be feasible, much less desired, to design a system that imposes or even enforces the researchers' views. In terms of affordances and norms, the question arises how to design a system that allows for different understandings of affordances and different, maybe even conflicting norms, but that enables meaning evolution and convergence towards shared norms.

The strategy employed during the design of *Nossos Casos* in order to allow different understandings of affordances and different norms in parallel can be summarized as follows (Fig. 3): involve different stakeholders, conduct participatory design and prototypical practices in order to get a grasp of the diversity of understandings of a case, a case discussion and related concepts; restrict the use of explicit formal norms in order to promote diverse practices; and restrict constraints of the technical system in order to enable diverse practices.

Our strategy for promoting convergence towards shared understandings is anchored at the informal level. It involves dialogue with users within the technical TNR system, e.g., involving discussions in the comment sections of content, as well as outside, e.g., involving personal visits at teachers' schools and homes. This strategy is in line with the view that meaning construction in TNR is a participatory and bottom-up process.

The success of strategies for allowing different understandings can be evaluated within a relatively small time frame conducting pragmatics-driven content analyses (e.g., [7]) or qualitative analyses of group discussions or interviews (e.g., a comment during a group session: *"These are different realities. And sometimes a small nudge*

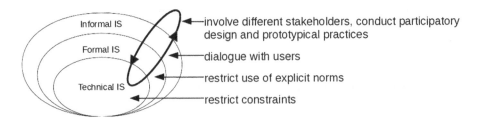

Fig. 3. Strategies for allowing different understandings and promoting convergence [2]

from a colleague who made the comment above yours [in the *Nossos Casos* tool] *already makes you think in other things. It's a support. Various ideas.*"). We believe that in general, these analyses can be conducted by evaluators with little domain knowledge and good knowledge in content analysis methods, e.g., in the TNR case, these evaluations were conducted by HCI-specialists experienced in different qualitative research methods. On the other hand, the success of strategies for promoting convergence of different meanings, at least in the TNR case, requires a much more cost-intensive, longitudinal approach and the involvement of domain experts. In the case of TNR this means to evaluate the success of continuing learning processes, which is a topic with many open research challenges.

Another important open question is how methods for problem understanding can support design for pluralistic meaning constructing and possible convergence more explicitly. In our case, the adoption of Organizational Semiotics and its epistemological position facilitated the consideration of these topics. HCI's "design for appropriation" might also provide some pointers. However, we believe that the design of TNR and *Nossos Casos* might have been more a result of the research team than that of the used methods. Many methods for problem clarification end with a single problem statement. A suggestion might be to investigate whether and how problem clarification might generate diverse or multi-faceted problem statements.

5 Conclusion

We presented a case of a system designed for and with inclusive education teachers, to illustrate how meaning construction and negotiation occurred during design and use, and how user practices and design were interrelated. We illustrated and discussed how pragmatic aspects affected the design of a tool to support teachers' practices.

We illustrated the importance of understanding the stakeholders' cultural context in its broadest sense. When dealing with concepts such as reputation or authorship, the cultural context explains why these concepts are desirable and necessary to different stakeholders. The conducted practices revealed situations where the lack of understanding about why such concepts are important to teachers could have led to the design of features that would not make sense to them, or that would trigger a negative impact on their interaction. They also revealed important and necessary design decisions that would not be made if other stakeholders had not been put into consideration.

We showed how meaning construction and evolution is a bottom-up process, and that at any point different interpretations of an issue might exist. These different interpretations might but do not necessarily have to converge. Designing systems that permit diverging meanings and promoting convergence of meanings poses methodological challenges that start with the problem clarification and definition. Diverging and converging meanings in TNR appeared in different uses of the *Nossos Casos* tool. In general, this problem is relevant to lifelong learning systems and other domains of creative problem solving. We described possible strategies anchored at the different levels of an information system. Further work is required to evaluate and refine these strategies and to identify additional ones.

Acknowledgments. We thank our colleagues from InterHAD and LEPED, and the teachers participating in this project. This work is supported by CNPq (grant 308618/2014-9) and FAPESP (2014/01382-7; 2013/02821-1), and is part of a project approved by Unicamp Institutional Board on Ethics (CAAE 0647.0.146.000-11).

References

1. Baranauskas, M.C.C.: Social awareness in HCI. Interactions **21**(4), 66–69 (2014). http://doi.acm.org/10.1145/2621933
2. Bonacin, R., Hornung, H., dos Reis, J.C., Pereira, R., Baranauskas, M.C.C.: Pragmatic aspects of collaborative problem solving: towards a framework for conceptualizing dynamic knowledge. In: Cordeiro, J., Maciaszek, L.A., Filipe, J. (eds.) ICEIS 2012. LNBIP, vol. 141, pp. 410–426. Springer, Heidelberg (2013)
3. Bødker, S.: When second wave HCI meets third wave challenges. In: NordiCHI 2006: Proceedings of the 4th Nordic Conference on Human-Computer Interaction, pp. 1–8. ACM, New York (2015)
4. Dix, A.: Designing for appropriation. In: Proceedings of the 21st British HCI Group Annual Conference on People and Computers: HCI…but not as we know it (BCS-HCI 2007), vol. 2, pp. 27–30. British Computer Society, Swinton (2007)
5. Hall, E.T.: The Silent Language. Anchoor Books, New York (1959)
6. Hornung, H.: Interaction design in the pragmatic web – reducing semiotic barriers to web-mediated collaboration. Ph.D. thesis, University of Campinas, Brazil (2013)
7. Hornung, H., Bonacin, R., dos Reis, J.C., Pereira, R., Baranauskas, M.C.C.: Identifying pragmatic patterns of collaborative problem solving. In: Proceedings of the IADIS International Conference on WWW/Internet, Madrid, Spain, pp. 379–397 (2012)
8. Kaptelinin, V., Nardi, B.A.: Acting with Technology: Activity Theory and Interaction Design. The MIT Press, Cambridge (2006)
9. Liu, K.: Semiotics in Information Systems Engineering. Cambridge University Press, New York (2000)
10. MEC: Brazilian National Policy on Special Education in the Perspective of Inclusive Education (2009). (Portuguese), http://portal.mec.gov.br/arquivos/pdf/politicaeducespecial.pdf. Accessed 12 Feb 2016
11. Pereira, R., Baranauskas, M.C.C.: A value-oriented and culturally informed approach to the design of interactive systems. Int. J. Hum.-Comput. Stud. **80**, 66–82 (2015)
12. Schuler, D., Namioka, A. (eds.): Participatory Design: Principles and Practices. Lawrence Erlbaum Associates, Mahwah (1993)
13. Stamper, R.K., Althaus, K., Backhouse, J.: MEASUR: method for eliciting, analysing and specifying user requirements. In: Computerized Assistance During the Information Systems Life Cycle, pp. 67–115 (1988)

SIERA: Improving Data Visualization for Learning Assessment in Educational Organisations

Manuel J. Ibarra[✉], Cristhian Serrano, and Juan C. Muñoz

School of Informatics and Systems Engineering,
Micaela Bastidas National University of Apurimac,
121 Arenas Av., Apurimac, Peru
manuelibarra@gmail.com, cristhiansj@gmail.com,
juancarlosmunozmiranda@gmail.com

Abstract. Encouraging a culture of evaluating students' knowledge, makes it possible to promptly discover weaknesses in the teaching and learning process. Once weaknesses have been identified then teachers can apply methodological strategies to reverse this situation and improve the student learning process. This paper describes a proposed strategy that supports the evaluation process. We propose to use an Excel file in which the evaluator fills in the answers provided by the student, then the system processes the data to rate the assessment for each student and generates statistical reports. The data is exported to a CSV file and then uploaded into a database server using the HTTP protocol. To validate this proposal we used focus group and daily meetings with teachers and students in evaluation process in Apurimac-Peru. The results highlight that using the tool makes it possible to have information everywhere and every time.

Keywords: Learning assessment · Educational organisations · Data visualization · Excel VBA

1 Introduction

To meet the *first commitment*, one of the *Eight Commitments School Management* given by the government [1], the school (IE: Institución Educativa in Spanish) organize and propose periodically assessments for students; it means, they implement an evaluation culture for students and propose corrective measures for poor academic performance in the evaluated areas. According to Gonzales et al. [2], an evaluation culture could be defined as the set of values, agreements, traditions, beliefs and thoughts that an educational community attaches to the action of evaluation. Bolseguí and Fuguet [3], point out that the evaluation culture is an evolving concept that refers to the need to evaluate on an ongoing basis; for them, the assessment is a complex and multidimensional process that includes different components: vision, values, behaviours, routines, organizational and social context, past and present experiences, epistemological, theoretical and methodological.

Organisational complexity is very high because the evaluation processes and functions require multi-systems collaborations, and has a high reliance on effective

M.C.C. Baranauskas et al. (Eds.): ICISO 2016, IFIP AICT 477, pp. 191–196, 2016.
DOI: 10.1007/978-3-319-42102-5_21

information communication among DRE (from spanish Dirección Regional de Educación), UGEL (from spanish Unidad de Gestión Educativa), IE, Director, Teachers and therefore faces many challenges regarding pragmatic interoperability such as information collision, policy obstacles, and procedure mismanagement.

Once evaluated, it is necessary to analyze and interpret the results, for which it is important that the data is properly displayed; this topic has been widely discussed by the authors in the area of data visualization [4, 5]. Most frequently, a key feature of such an approach is showing relationships between different data groups of a provided statistical selection: in order to compare relative proportions between various indicators [6, 7].

This article presents a strategy to qualify student test primary and secondary level in *Math* and *Communication* areas in Educational Institutions of Apurimac-Peru, showing the obtained results by statistical charts sharing achievement levels for each student, this information is useful to teachers who can use improvement strategies for underperforming students. In addition, the tool also allows you to display statistical graphs of the results by district, by level, by grade, by area; so that the Directors of DRE, UGEL and IE can make decisions to improve student learning.

Section 2 of this article presents and discusses the work related to the subject of semiotics of educational organizations and data visualization; Sect. 3 explains the design and implementation of the proposed strategy; Sect. 4 explains the evaluation methodology used to validate the proposed strategy; finally, Sect. 5 describes the conclusions and future work of this research.

2 Related Works

Semiotics is the study of meaning of sign processes and meaningful communication. This includes the study of signs and sign processes (semiosis), analogy, metaphor, symbolism, signification, and communication. Within the organisational semiotics literature, three forms of activities are discussed, namely *substantive, communication* and *control* [8]. While much attention has been paid to substantive norms in business process modelling [9], relatively less research has focused on control norms, especially in virtual environments. Process controls are embedded constraints that serve as conditions for performing related activities [10].

Effah and Liu [9] publishes an article titled "Virtual Process Control Modelling in Organisational Semiotics: A Case of Higher Education Admission", this study explores Web-based virtual process control modelling based on organisational semiotics, Web modelling language (WebML), and higher education admission process. The study contributes to organisational semiotics research, which has so far focused more on substantive norm and less on control norm modelling.

On the other hand, *Data Visualization* is a general term that describes any effort to help people understand the significance of data by placing it in a visual context. Patterns, trends and correlations that might go undetected in text-based data can be exposed and recognized easier with data visualization software. There are techniques for facilitating data selection in the data transformation process [11, 12], techniques for selecting chart type and visual components (e.g., line style, point face, axis range) automatically in the visual mapping process [13, 14]; and techniques for changing visual effects to clarify the user's viewpoint and assertion easily [15] in the view transformation process.

Matsushita and Kato [16] make a research titled "Interactive Visualization Method for Exploratory Data Analysis". They propose an interactive visualization method suitable for exploratory data analysis. The method extracts parameters for drawing from a series of user requirements written in a natural language and redraws the drawn chart interactively according to the change in the user's viewpoint. In this type of data analysis, statistical charts are employed to help the user understand the target data, and displayed chart is redrawn interactively according to the user's input inspired by looking at the chart.

3   Design and Implementation

For this work we used the sign-based Semiotic Communication and the System Oriented Approach of Semiotic Organisation which includes Sign System Oriented Approach. Sign System Oriented Approach studies media (spoken language, texts, instruments, computer interfaces) as sign systems, and see the use of these media by people as based on systems of narration and interpretation. User interaction with media (texts, computer interfaces, instruments) is observed, as well as communication between people at work.

We also used a Visual Communication approach to represent the obtained results, which has various types of codes that help determine the message. The argument can be made that visual communication operates similar to a language sign system.

3.1   Educational Business Process Management for Assessment

The process starts when DRE proposes a schedule for evaluations, then Specialists develop indicators and questions for the test. Then each UGEL's Director, print the tests and distributes to each IE. Then The Director of each IE, assign evaluators (students) for each grade and section. The evaluation day, students take the exam, then teachers fill answers in Excel sheet to qualify each test using Excel Macro (just clicking a button). Then, Director and teachers of IE can see the graphical results generated by the system. Then, Excel file is very heavy in size (about 10 Mb), so we convert the data to a lightweight format file "CSV" (about 5 k), so that file is easier to transfer by Internet. Finally, the System processes updated data and generate new reports for users. The process is shown in Fig. 1.

3.2   Input and Output of Data Visualization

Designing Excel File. An Excel File was designed to fill the answers marked by students, as shown in Fig. 2. Every question can be market with "A", "B", "C", "X" (when students mark two or more answers) or " " (blank, when a student did not mark any answer). Mathematics and Communication have 23 questions, every section has from one to forty five students approximately, and in the *primary* level there are six grades named "First", "Second", "Third", "Forth", "Fifth" and "Sixth"; and in the *secondary* level there are five grades named "First", "Second", "Third", "Forth", "Fifth".

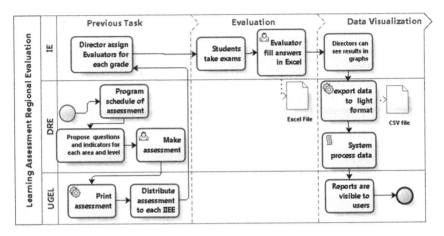

Fig. 1. Business process management for assessment application

Fig. 3. Report using semaphore indicators (Color figure online)

Fig. 2. Sheet to fill answers

Designing Reports. After the teacher fill out the answers, the system use functions in Excel Macro to rate the assessment using values assigned in Table 1. An example of the Report is shown in Fig. 3.

Assigning Reached Level. Each test has 23 questions for each area. To determine the level a student has reached, specialists produce distribution of scores, as shown in Table 1. For example, if a student gets a score of 5, then, the level acquired is "Initiation"; if a student gets a score of 12, then, the level acquired is "In Process"; and if a student gets a score of 20, then, the level acquired is "Achieved".

Table 1. Distribution of reached level according to punctuation and colour assigned

Item	Reached level	Punctuation	Description
0	Initiation	0-8	Red
1	In Process	9-15	Orange
2	Achieved	16-23	Green

4   Evaluation of the Proposed Strategy

The validation of the tool was conducted with Education Specialist (workers) of the DRE-Apurímac through a focus group. The two events took place on: May 15 and September 14, 2015; in a meeting room of the Pedagogical Management Area of DRE. The participants were five specialists in evaluation. All participants had significant years of experience in monitoring and supervising educational schools.

Before starting the activity, the developed system was briefly shown to each specialist in evaluation. A simulation of the software functionality was then done. An operator, using the SIERA system, entered the "modular code" of the IE, then, the System generates the list of students of each grade and sections. The specialist fill out the answers for each student and then the system show the results graphically, then, he exports the result to CSV file and finally sends the result to the datacentre.

After this simulated process, the Education Specialists provided feedback, suggestions and opinions, and agreed that the system can definitely help improve decision making and perception (awareness) of the assessment results. When asked: *"will the use of the designed software help you to make it easier the data visualization of evaluation assessment results?"*, they all answered that in their opinion that assumption was valid. Then they were asked: *"would the decision-making speed and quality of decisions have been better if the Director would have had a support tool that is visual and provides the appropriate suggestions?"*, they all replied that a positive answer would be valid.

There were two evaluations until August 31 2015 using SIERA system; 614 schools and 38338 students were evaluated in the first assessment; 961 schools and 68075 students in the second assessment.

5   Conclusion and Future Work

Education Specialists agreed that having this type of information in the SIERA system would help to know the levels reached (Beginning, In Process, and Achieved) by students in every area, level, grade and district; also, Director could have accurate information when making decisions based on the learning achievement indicators. The time required to have results of the assessment is reduced significantly and the information is available at every time and everywhere whenever Internet connection is available. Likewise the participant Specialists agreed that, a priori, they can expect a significant improvement in the process of student learning and the quality of decisions, because Directors would have accurate information when making decisions.

For the future work, we need to define some key performance indicator to measure the improvement speed and then compare current way of working with the improved way of working. We hope to continue the experimentation process of using the other Departments to improve the application.

Acknowledgments. Thanks to the Education Specialists of Pedagogical Management Area of the Regional Education Apurimac in Peru, especially Edith Montalvo, Alexander Serrano, Dámaso A. Sanchez and José O. Arohuillca.

References

1. http://www.minedu.gob.pe/campanias/pdf/manual-de-gestion-escolar-2015_10marzo_alta. pdf. Accessed 5 Feb 2016
2. González, J.R., Soledad, M., Montoya, R., Rivera, J.A.: Cultura de evaluación en instituciones educativas. Perfiles Educativos 33(131), 42–63 (2011)
3. Bolseguí, M., Fuguet, A.: Cultura de evaluación: una aproximación conceptual. Investigación y Postgrado 21(1), 77–98 (2006)
4. Guchev, V., Massimo, M., Giuseppe S.: Design guidelines for correlated quantitative data visualizations. In: Proceedings of the International Working Conference on Advanced Visual Interfaces. ACM (2012)
5. Keim, D., Kohlhammer, J., Ellis, G., Mansmann, F.: Mastering the Information Age: Solving Problems with Visual Analytics. Eurographics Association, Aire-la-Ville (2010)
6. Spence, R.: Information Visualization: Design for Interaction. Pearson Educational Limited, New York (2007)
7. Wilkinson, L.: The Grammar of Graphics, 2nd edn. Springer, New York (2005)
8. Liu, K.: Semiotics in Information Systems Engineering. Cambridge University Press, Cambridge (2000)
9. Effah, J., Liu, K.: Virtual process modelling informed by organisational semiotics: a case of higher education admission. In: Liu, K., Gulliver, S.R., Li, W., Yu, C. (eds.) ICISO 2014. IFIP AICT, vol. 426, pp. 42–51. Springer, Heidelberg (2014)
10. Brambilla, M., Ceri, S., Fraternali, P., Manolescu, I.: Process modeling in Web applications. ACM Trans. Softw. Eng. Methodol. 15(4), 360–409 (2006)
11. Ahlberg, C., Shneiderman, B.: Visual information seeking: tight coupling of dynamic query filters with starfield displays. In: Proceedings of the SIGCHI Conference on Human Factors in Computing Systems. ACM (1994)
12. Derthick, M., Harrison, J., Moore, A., Roth, S.F.: Efficient multi-object dynamic query histograms. In: Proceedings of the IEEE Symposium on Information Visualization, pp. 84–91 (1999)
13. Mackinlay, J.D.: Automating the design of graphical presentations of relational information. In: Readings in Intelligent User Interfaces (1998)
14. Fasciano, M., Lapalme G.: Postgraphe: a system for the generation of statistical graphics and text. In: Proceedings of the Eighth International Workshop on Natural Language Generation (1996)
15. Mittal, V.O.: Visual prompts and graphical design: a framework for exploring the design space of 2-D charts and graphs. In: AAAI/IAAI (1997)
16. Matsushita, M., Kato, T.: Interactive visualization method for exploratory data analysis. In: Proceedings of The 5th International Conference on Information Visualisation. IEEE (2001)

An Organisational Semiotics Perspective to Co-Design of Technology Enhanced Learning

Aimee Jacobs[1([⊠])], Yu-Chun Pan[2], and Sanaa Askool[3]

[1] Scott College of Business, Indiana State University, Terre Haute, IN, USA
Aimee.Jacobs@indstate.edu
[2] School of Computing and Engineering, University of West London,
London, UK
Yu-Chun.Pan@uwl.ac.uk
[3] Hekma School of Business, Dar Al-Hekma University, Jeddah, Saudi Arabia
saskool@dah.edu.sa

Abstract. While Co-Design approaches have been used in designing technology enhanced learning (TEL) by different scholars, research is needed to understand the relationships between technologies, design and practice. This paper presents organisational semiotics (OS) as an approach for Co-Design of Technology Enhanced Learning. This perspective will provide an insight into the Co-Design of technology and learning in higher education.

Keywords: Technology enhanced learning · Co-Design · Organisational semiotics · Learning design · Learning and teaching · Information systems

1 Introduction

There has been a growing interest and demand in utilising technologies in an educational context to enhance learning and teaching practices [1]. Such practices are often called Technology Enhanced Learning (TEL). Some studies have shown that the use of TEL technologies has a positive impact on learning engagement and outcomes [2, 3]. However, previous research suggests that there is a disconnection between technologies, research, design and practice [4, 5], and therefore the full potential of IT/IS is not fully utilised [6]. Some researchers also argue that the use of technologies does not guarantee the enhancement of learning outcomes [7].

The misalignment of IS and business requirements has resulted in a Co-Design approach. In educational context, this misalignment represents the gap between learning and teaching practices and supporting technological systems. Therefore, designing a TEL application needs to address different challenges ranging from learning theory to software engineering, which can be a key challenge for developers.

The main contribution of this paper is the organisational semiotics (OS) analysis for TEL Co-Design focusing on both technical and social aspects. The article meets this aim by discussing the current research environment for TEL and Co-Design along with the challenges, and proposes OS as a well-suited solution for Co-Design of TEL.

© IFIP International Federation for Information Processing 2016
Published by Springer International Publishing Switzerland 2016. All Rights Reserved
M.C.C. Baranauskas et al. (Eds.): ICISO 2016, IFIP AICT 477, pp. 197–202, 2016.
DOI: 10.1007/978-3-319-42102-5_22

2 Context and Motivation

2.1 Technology Enhanced Learning

Despite the popularity, there is no universally agreed definition of what TEL means. TEL emphasises on the learning experience of learners and the teaching experience of staff [8]. Although different parties have different definitions of TEL [9, 10], the various definitions all address the use and effect of technology in an educational environment. Therefore, this paper adapts other researchers' views and defines TEL as *"the use and effect of any kind of IT applications in learning and teaching environment"*.

TEL has been increasingly adopted in educational organisations ranging from primary schools to higher education. Many researchers [9, 11–13] identify the drivers and benefits of TEL, including inclusion and diversity, stakeholder engagement, personal development, performance improvement, and innovation. It is important to consider the drivers and benefits which play a crucial role in the development and deployment of TEL applications.

2.2 Co-Design and Technology Enhanced learning

The development of TEL applications has continuously attracted plenty of initiatives. The motivations behind this development include improvement of learning and teaching quality, fulfilment of learner expectations, and improvement of administrative processes [10]. Co-Design is one of the most popular participatory development methods that actively involves users for IS development [14, 15].

Co-Design has been used for the collaborative nature of designing activities that tackles the development of IS which includes the change of business requirements. Yet, existing requirements for IS development cannot be considered for Co-Design [16], as they do not consider the changing nature of requirements. Moreover, Co-Design research has been criticised by different scholars [17]. First, it is considered as "expensive" in the design process as it needs numerous meetings and discussions. Second, it is complex to deploy due to its lack of formalisation. Moreover, it focuses on the early design stage and puts few efforts on the later stages.

Current Learning theories support the importance of the social aspects in an organisational domain, however, Siemens [18] suggests that these theories lack the ability to capture the cognitive operations that are now performed by technology such as information storage and retrieval that were previously performed by learners. This indicates the disconnection between learning and teaching practice and supporting technological systems. Educational organisations should emphasise the quality of the technology use and the way it supports achieving learning objectives, rather than only use of technology [19].

Based on these challenges, OS methods could improve the understanding of the requirements for TEL design. Additionally, OS provides a framework to bridge the gap left by current learning theories and the social aspects of technology. The following section introduces OS and the OS methodologies used as a framework.

3 Theoretical Background: Organisational Semiotics

OS is the study of organisations using concepts of semiotics [20]. OS is positioned to meet the needs of both the technical and social aspects in an organisational domain [21]. These aspects make it well suited to meet the needs lacking in current design and theories for TEL. OS is first introduced by Stamper [22] based on Peirce [23] 's work on semiotics. Signs are formulated through a sign mediation process known as semiosis [24]. OS has been applied in various domains, e.g. IS design [25], knowledge management [26], and social media readiness assessment [27].

The OS perspective, which concentrates on the relations between the IT system, and organisation, offers a range of methods to analyse and design organisations [20]. The OS framework, also known as the semiotic ladder, supports the view of inseparability of technical and social aspects of an organisation (or an information system) through the use of the six branches of semiotics diagnosis [20]. This framework aids in classifying signs within the multi-layers of an organisation from the two views of human information functions and IT platform. The OS framework allows an investigation into the human as well as the technological aspects of TEL, as many researchers [18, 28] suggest it is necessary to capture the learning process as well as the social and contextual factors and the value of what is being learned through technology. The following section provides the OS analysis for TEL Co-Design.

4 Organisational Semiotic Perspective to TEL Co-Design

The current TEL design approach focuses on how to create technologies to support learning and teaching environment. As previously discussed, there are two major issues in this approach. Firstly, technologies and human behaviours have the capabilities to influence and shape each other. Secondly, Co-Design method has been applied to TEL application development, however, the current level and scope of user involvement might not necessarily be sufficient, as there are more participants than teachers and learners. This research addresses these two issues by applying OS to further analyse the activities in educational environment where technologies are used.

4.1 Learning System and Technical System in TEL Environment

In order to fully understand the relationship between human agents and technologies in TEL environment, this paper establishes the definitions of informal and formal learning system and technical system. Informal and formal learning systems refer to the culture, structure, process, people and information in learning and teaching environment. It includes all the human activities, controlled by either formal or informal norms, performed by participants in order to achieve the learning objectives. On the other hand, technical system refers to the IS that supports and enhances the operations of learning systems. As shown in Fig. 1, technical system is part of informal and formal learning system. Human participants utilise the data and information stored and processed in the technical system in order to perform in learning system. Through the lens of OS, the environment can be considered as a meta-system including all the six layers of the semiotic ladder.

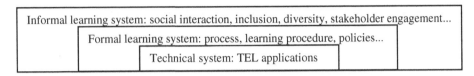

Informal learning system: social interaction, inclusion, diversity, stakeholder engagement...

Formal learning system: process, learning procedure, policies...

Technical system: TEL applications

Fig. 1. Informal and formal learning system and technical system

4.2   Organisational Semiotics Analysis for TEL Co-Design

Co-Design emphasises community and research as part of the participatory process. It focuses on participant involvement, perceptions and the feedback loop. Developers have created the co-design processes based on their need to obtain users' new ideas and feedback, however, the user feedback will be designed from users' perspective. The attractiveness of OS viewpoint for CO-Design is that it can offer analysis of the community interlinks to technology. OS offers a systematic way to analyse the design requirements including what is being designed, purpose of the design, resources needed, and mechanisms required to foster communication among the community. It also helps identify the activities around the students and instructors, which helps identify participant roles within the design process.

	Social World: Wider access to education, inclusion and diversity, stakeholder expectation, learner employability, government requirements...
Human Information Functions (Informal and Formal Learning System)	**Pragmatics**: Motivated autonomous learning, engaging learners, improving learning outcomes, enabling learners to learn, facilitating virtual group discussion...
	Semantics: Requirements for progression, course description, learning objectives, ability to communicate with others...
The IT Platform (Technical System)	**Syntactics**: Learning progression procedure, assignment submission guidance, semester schedule, teaching materials...
	Empirics: Website, learning platform, portal, internet connectivity, connection speed and liability, archives, network of devices, structured data...
Physical World: PC, laptop, mobile phone, tablet, server, cables, database...	

Fig. 2. Organisational semiotic framework for technology enhanced learning

The OS analysis of the TEL environment can be categorised into six distinctive layers (Fig. 2). The analysis of the learning system and technical system identified the requirements for TEL in the human information functions and the IT platform respectively. This analysis of TEL may provide the foundation for TEL Co-Design.

5   Discussion and Conclusion

TEL changes how learning and teaching processes can be managed and delivered. However, the use of IT/IS to enhance learning can lead to some challenges in the communication and interaction process between students and instructors. Moreover, using technology to enhance learning creates a lack of ownership of design, because participants with diverse responsibilities and tasks influence the common paradigm in the classroom. This could be due to a lack of requirements engineering methods that could reflect negatively on the system's analysis and design.

The use of technology and its effects in the educational context has prompted significant interest in the development of TEL applications. However, there is a gap between learning system (learning and teaching practice) and technical system (TEL applications), as many TEL developments fail to recognise learning system and technical system as one integral unit. Co-Design approach has also been deployed in the development of TEL applications. However, Co-Design itself presents challenges, as it is expensive and lacks formality for users to follow. Considering these challenges, OS can be considered a suitable perspective to investigate the TEL environment and its application development because it concerns both social and technical aspects of IT/IS.

By applying OS perspective, the OS framework analysis for TEL provides a comprehensive insight into the key requirements for TEL Co-Design. The analysis identifies the interlinked requirements at the six OS layers. The requirements at higher layers need to be supported by the requirements at lower layers for the IT platform to support the human activities. The understanding of how requirements at different OS layers support each other could allow TEL requirements to be analysed in this manner. Furthermore, Co-Design requires the collective effort of participants at various levels in order to maximise the effectiveness of the design product.

A limitation, however, is that the research framework is based on literature review without empirical studies. However, the proposed demonstrates the relationships between technologies, design and practice which will allow greater integration of technical system into the process of learning system and it is expected to offer guidelines for analysing TEL solutions. Further research can be applied to a case study of an organisation in higher education.

In summary, this paper focused on the improvement of TEL grounded in OS as it applies to both higher education as an organisation and TEL. The analysis highlights TEL requirements through the six layers in OS framework focusing on semantic, pragmatic and social aspects of teaching and learning without ignoring the technical aspects. OS could foster researchers and practitioners understanding of the systems requirements by driving the analysis and Co-design of TEL tools.

References

1. Selwyn, N.: The use of computer technology in university teaching and learning: a critical perspective. J. Comput. Assist. Learn. **23**(2), 83–94 (2007)
2. Shieh, R.S.: The impact of technology-enabled active learning (TEAL) implementation on student learning and teachers' teaching in a high school context. Comput. Educ. **59**(2), 206–214 (2012)
3. Shieh, R., Chang, W., Liu, Z.: Technology enabled active learning (TEAL) in introductory physics: impact on genders and achievement levels. Aust. J. Educ. Technol. **27**(7), 1082–1099 (2011)
4. Hannafin, W.: Design-based research and technology-enhanced learning environments. Educ. Technol. Res. Dev. **53**(4) (2005)

5. Keppell, M.: Assuring best practice in technology-enhanced learning environments. Res. Learn. Technol. **23** (2015)
6. Manca, S., Ranieri, M.: Is it a tool suitable for learning? A critical review of the literature on Facebook as a technology-enhanced learning environment. J. Comput. Assist. Learn. **29**(6), 487–504 (2013)
7. Fewkesa, A.M., McCabea, M.: Facebook: learning tool or distraction? J. Digit. Learn. Teach. Educ. **28**(3), 92–98 (2012)
8. University of the West of England: Technology Enhanced Learning Strategy and Implementation Plan 2012–2017. University of the West of England, Bristol (2012)
9. HEFCE: Enhancing learning and teaching through the use of technology: a revised approach to HEFCE's strategy for e-learning. HEFCE, Bristol (2009)
10. Walker, R., Voce, J., Nicholls, J., Swift, E., Ahmed, J., Horrigan, S., Vincent, P.: 2014 Survey of Technology Enhanced Learning for Higher Education in the UK. Universities and Colleges Information Systems Association, Oxford (2014)
11. Quentin-Baxter, M., Kelly, J., Probert, S., MacMahon, C., Ferrell, G.: A model for evidencing the benefits of technology enhanced learning in higher education in the UK. In: Proceedings of ASCILITE (2008)
12. Keller, J., Suzuki, K.: Learner motivation and e-learning design: a multinationally validated process. J. Educ. Media **29**(3), 229–239 (2004)
13. Law, K.M., Lee, V.C., Yu, T.: Learning motivation in e-learning facilitated computer programming courses. Comput. Educ. **55**(1), 218–228 (2010)
14. Steen, M.: Human-centered design as a fragile encounter. Des. Issues **28**(1), 72–80 (2012)
15. Sanders, E., Stappers, P.: Co-creation and the new landscapes of design. Co-Design **4**(1), 5–18 (2008)
16. Liu, K., Sun, L., Bennett, K.: Co-Design of business and IT systems - Introduction by Guest Editors. Inf. Syst. Front. **4**(3), 251–257 (2002)
17. Tollmar, K.: Towards CSCW Design in the Scandinavian Tradition. Tekniska högsk, Stockholm (2001)
18. Siemens, G.: Connectivism: a learning theory for the digital age (2014)
19. Marshall, S.: Change, technology and higher education: are universities capable of organisational change. J. Asynchronous Learn. Netw. **15**, 22–34 (2011)
20. Liu, K.: Semiotics in Information System Engineering. Cambridge University Press, Cambridge (2000)
21. Liu, K.: Virtual, Distributed and Flexible Organisations. Springer, Berlin (2004)
22. Stamper, R.: Information in Business and Administrative Systems. Wiley, New York (1973)
23. Peirce, C.S.: Collected Papers of Charles Sanders Peirce: Pragmaticisms and Pragnoaticism and Scientific Metaphysics. Belknap Press, Cambridge (1935)
24. Nauta, D.: The Meaning of Information. Mouton, Hague (1972)
25. Stamper, R., Liu, K., Hafkamp, M., Ades, Y.: Understanding the roles of signs and norms in organizations-a semiotic approach to information systems design. Behav. Inf. Technol. **19**(1), 15–27 (2000)
26. Pan, Y., Tan, C.: Three dimensional norm-based knowledge management for knowledge intensive business service organizations: an organizational semiotics perspective. Int. J. Knowl. Eng. **2**(1), 50–55 (2016)
27. Jacobs, A.: Assessing organisational readiness for enterprise social media in information intensive organisations. Ph.D. thesis, University of Reading, Reading, UK (2013)
28. Chen, Y., Lin, Y., Yeh, R., Lou, S.: Examining factors affecting college students' intention to use web-based instruction systems: towards an integrated model. Turk. Online J. Educ. Technol. **12**(2), 111–121 (2013)

Design of Therapeutic Information Systems as Indicating Through Signs

Vânia Paula de Almeida Neris[(✉)] and Kamila R.H. Rodrigues

Federal University of São Carlos (UFSCar), São Carlos, SP, Brazil
{vania, kamila_rodrigues}@dc.ufscar.br

Abstract. Therapeutic information systems are tools to support healthcare professionals to treat their patients, aiding on their rehabilitation, helping them to understand their condition and the treatment procedures, or even motivating themselves to persist on ongoing treatments. Although the importance of digital therapeutic systems, the design of this type of system is still a challenge. Inspired by the Organizational Semiotics, Baranauskas and Bonacin proposed a framework to conduct work in interactive systems design. In the proposed approach, these authors argue in favor of designing as a social process which focuses on problem setting as well as on problem solving. This paper brings reflections of an instantiation of this framework in the context of therapeutic systems and presents the results of an application in a real scenario with patients affected in their mental health.

Keywords: Therapeutic information systems · Semiotics · Organizational semiotics · Human-computer interaction

1 Introduction

Digital therapeutic information systems are tools to support healthcare professionals to treat their patients. These applications may help patients in different ways, such as aiding on their rehabilitation, helping them to understand their condition and the treatment procedures, or even motivating themselves to persist on ongoing treatments. Healthcare professionals may use therapeutic applications to help the patients express their feelings, relax, or improve their own abilities and personal relationships [1].

Although the importance of digital therapeutic systems, their design is still a challenge. The proposal of a design solution cannot be done without considering the individuals in treatment, their physiological and physical conditions, their relationships with family and society and the medical and health care protocols. Semantic, pragmatic and social issues should also be considered. The nature of therapeutic systems demands a sociotechnical approach to its design and development.

We share with those that understand design as an activity to solve problems in a scenario that is socially and dynamically constructed [2–4]. Therapeutic systems, in particular, are generally in an evolutionary scenario with patients with specificities, health care professionals with different backgrounds, medium and long term treatments. Moreover, according to Cheung [1], the involvement of different stakeholders – such as family – results in more effective treatments, often with better results.

© IFIP International Federation for Information Processing 2016
Published by Springer International Publishing Switzerland 2016. All Rights Reserved
M.C.C. Baranauskas et al. (Eds.): ICISO 2016, IFIP AICT 477, pp. 203–208, 2016.
DOI: 10.1007/978-3-319-42102-5_23

Inspired by the Organizational Semiotics (OS) and by a sociotechnical view, Baranauskas and Bonacin [4] propose a framework to conduct work in interactive systems design. In the proposed approach by these authors, designing is a social process which focuses on problem setting as well as on problem solving. It involves a dialogue not only with design materials, but primarily among individuals (designers, developers, users and other stakeholders) in which different views of designing and different ways of framing design situations are contrasted. Several artifacts (informal, formal and technical) are used as communication and mediation tools with the participants during this process of designing the interactive system.

This paper brings reflections of an instantiation of this framework in the context of therapeutic systems and presents the results of an application in a real scenario with patients affected in their mental health.

This paper is organized as follows: Sect. 2 comments about the socio-technical view to the interactive systems design. Section 3 describes an academic extension project that has allowed the conduction of studies using Organizational Semiotics and Therapeutic Systems in the mental health context. Section 4 describes a design as indicating through signs to Therapeutic Systems. Section 5 presents conclusions and future works.

2   Theoretical References

Baranauskas and Bonacin [4] take Semiotics beyond the study of how we use signs for communication to include the shared knowledge and mutual commitment derived from communication in designing. These authors understand that design is about being engaged directly in a specific design situation. This "situatedness" locates the design process in a nested structure in which the informal, the formal and the technical layers of information and interaction co-exist [4].

Figure 1 is based on the "Organizational Onion" from OS and illustrates the Baranauskas and Bonacin [4] proposal. According to the authors, a problem setting is part of the design situation understanding and requires articulation in forms that can be appropriated and assessed by people involved in designing. The design process involves exploring the reality that constitutes the design situation. Ontology is an important aspect of what the involved group understands as constituting reality. The ontology charting allows a discussion on meaning and on what the group considers to be important aspects of reality in that particular design situation. System prototyping refer to the group's idea on how to shape their intervention in the situation, based on their ontology and problem articulation.

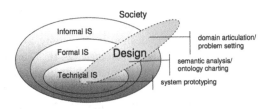

Fig. 1. The structure of design as indicating through signs from different layers [4]

Prototyping overcomes some of the problems of requirement specification oriented methods, which usually assume that system design can be based solely on observation and detached reflection [4]. Moreover, there is very little account of how prototypes are related to the current and future work practices of users. It is equally important that the people involved share a representation model of the work domain to be supported by the prospective system. Meaning-making is constructed as a result of cooperation between designers, developers, interested parts and prospective users of the technology being designed [4].

The design work in these three layers is established in parallel and co-evolves; a problem understanding is revealed as the group works on the semantics and solution ideas. Therefore, design is conceived as a social process of expressing meaning, communicating intentions and constructing knowledge, to be carried iteratively and interactively by designers and a group of stakeholders in a participatory style [4, 5].

3 A Design Challenge in the Context of the Mental Health

The Spiritist Hospital of Marília (in Portuguese *Hospital Espírita de Marília* - HEM) is a philanthropic hospital whose primary objective is to offer tranquility and welfare for its patients for 66 years. A multidisciplinary therapeutic team – with psychiatrists, psychologists, social workers, nurses, and occupational therapists – work together to treat the patients [6, 7].

In 2013, the HEM's board invited us, computing researchers, to develop a computational solution that could assist therapeutic treatments conducted at the hospital. Since then, we have conducted collaboratively studies with the health professionals of the HEM. The teams have been meeting at least three times a year to discuss, evaluate and validate the artifacts generated during the project.

Two therapeutic games were defined collaboratively between stakeholders and are in development for the HEM: one to be used to support the treatment of patients with depression and the other to support the treatment of teenagers chemical dependency.

Considering the framework proposed by Baranauskas and Bonacin [4], we have been studying its adoption and instantiation to the design scenario described here. Next section presents our current view.

4 Design as Indicating Through Signs to Therapeutic Systems

The framework proposed by Baranauskas and Bonacin [4] serves to interactive systems in general and we acknowledge with their ideas. Our proposal here is based on our experience in the specific scenario of therapeutic systems and aims to instantiate their proposal to support further therapeutic systems design processes.

Since we have been working in this scenario, we have identified three main aspects as essential for these systems:

(1) Therapeutic systems are complementary tools to support the therapists' work. They may contribute to the treatment, many times supporting only one aspect of the felling better process. Therefore, they should have a well-established

therapeutic objective to be defined by the health care professionals and clarified between the entire design and development group.

(2) Depending on the condition and procedures, it might be difficult to generalize personal characteristics of each patient. Therefore, therapeutic systems should be highly flexible. This is important both to healthcare professionals and to patients. On the one hand, the professionals might want – or need – to customize the system to the treatment goals. Such changes might include modifying the user interface, adding new interaction mechanisms or new functionalities. On the other hand, patients' interaction needs may vary; thus, a single non-modifiable interaction scheme may not suit everyone [6].

(3) One intrinsic characteristic of computer based systems is that they are good on repeating actions and storing data. This can be useful to therapists to recognize even small changes in the patient's behavior. Therefore, logging meaningful patients' actions and report them to therapists may support analysis and decisions in treatments.

Reflecting on these aspects and considering the opportunity we had to work in a very multidisciplinary team, with health care professionals from different background, we propose the instantiation illustrated on Fig. 2.

The informal layer relies, among others, on the customs, values and intentions of each individual. In the therapeutic system scenario, the particularities of each patient should come from a holist view, i.e., considering information from himself, but also from the family and close people, health care professionals, as well as academic and demographical studies. Therefore, the Participatory Design [5] goes further users and designers and may consider a larger spectrum of stakeholders, including professionals from different knowledge areas.

Aiming to know these stakeholders and use their information to support the domain articulation and problem setting, adopting a holistic view but focusing on the individuals, we have proposed a Personas Enrichment Process [6].

Cooper [8] defines Personas as concrete and realistic representations – based on real or fictitious details – to create faithful representations of users of a system. Personas allow designers to document, organize and represent the diversity of possible users of a system [9]. Designers might include demographic, economic, and behavioral data onto a Persona to map relevant data into a detailed representation of users [10]. They may describe physical and mental characteristics of users, their histories, and daily and professional activities.

In the therapeutic systems design scenario, data may encompass, among others, the patient's clinical profile, therapeutic techniques and procedures for the treatment, and

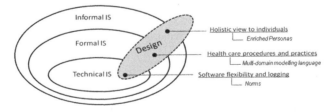

Fig. 2. Design as indicating through signs to therapeutic systems

the expected effects that the application will have on the user. The process uses the Stakeholder Analysis Chart [11, 12] (step 1) and the Evaluation Frame [13] (which one should not confuse with the Valuation Frame) (step 2 with other artifacts), to provide a sociotechnical vision regarding the design problem. Moreover, the process also supports the identification of the therapeutic objectives for the system.

In the HEM context, the stakeholders involved worked collaboratively with representatives of every group of professionals in the hospital to perform steps 1, 2 and 4 of the Personas Enrichment Process. The computer science members of the design team performed the step 3 – the creation of the Personas to represent the focus group for the application. Six different Personas were created. Each persona symbolizes information such as the clinical profiles of the patients, and relations of patients with the stakeholders and technology. Therefore, at this point, the existing Personas are able to aid the design team on making conscious choices regarding the design. The Organizational Semiotics' artifacts explored also provide further information, and allow the team to anticipate problems and work to address them.

In the formal layer, it is important to identify the health procedures and protocols which also underline the therapeutic objectives. Considering the therapeutic scenario, the aim in this layer relies on replace meanings and intentions in the treatment to actions by the actors involved. This leads to interaction scenarios in which the desired action will happen. The scenarios come from a collaborative work with stakeholders having in mind the Personas created. The collaborative work asks for an instrument to formalize the interaction scenarios that could be understood by people from different knowledge domains.

We, therefore, proposed a modeling language (still without a name) with symbols that represent an interaction scenario. It is important that the scenario be not confused with screens or user interfaces. In a further moment in the design, a scenario or sub-scenario may have multiple screens to represent it. For instance, in the proposed language there are stamps indicating flexible aspects, as a number of options that may vary from patient to patient according to the therapist choices. It is also possible to indicate that the patient actions need to be recorded for further analysis by the therapist or explicitly indicates a therapeutic objective, as in this case the memory recovery.

Finally, in technical level system flexibility and data logging aspects need to be addressed. Flexible features can be implemented considering cognitive and physical aspects of the patients that are important to be respected during the interaction.

In the HEM context, we considered patients with vision problems (due to low vision or advanced age) that could have interface elements such as images and texts in an increased size. Moreover, depressed patients tend to have difficulty with choices. Thus, we chose to let the health professionals select the amount of options to choose from, according to the need of each patient. Moreover, the therapist also has the option to print a report with selected information from each patient.

5 Conclusion and Future Works

This paper presented an instantiation of the framework proposed by Baranauskas and Bonacin [4] to the domain of therapeutic information systems. Some particularities of therapeutic systems were considered and reflected in a continuous design process.

Some artifacts, understood as mediator tools, were presented to illustrate the emerged knowledge in this specific domain.

The information systems created are now being used and monitored. We hope they will serve as a complementary tool for healthcare professionals of a HEM. As future work, we plan to apply the framework proposed here in other therapeutic scenarios.

Acknowledgments. The authors would like to thank the healthcare professionals and administrators of HEM on the effective participation and contributions to this research project. We would like to thank the UFSCar's Dean of Extension for their financial support.

References

1. Cheung, M.: Therapeutic Games and Guided Imagery: Tools for Mental Health and School Professionals Working With Children, Adolescents and Their Families. Lyceum Books, Chicago (2006)
2. Fischer, G., Lindstaedt, S., Ostwald, J., Stolze, M., Sumner, T., Zimmermann, B.: From domain modeling to collaborative domain construction. In: ACM Proceedings of DIS, pp. 75–85 (1995)
3. Kyng, M.: Designing for cooperation: cooperating in design. Commun. ACM **34**(12), 65–73 (1991)
4. Baranauskas, M.C.C., Bonacin, R.: Design–indicating through signs. Des. Issues **24**(3), 30–45 (2008)
5. Schuler, D., Namioka, A.: Participatory Design: Perspectives on Systems Design. L. Erlbaum Associates, Hillsdale (1993)
6. Rodrigues, K.R.H., Garcia, F.E., Bocanegra, L.F., Goncalves, V.P., Carvalho, V.G., Neris, V.P.A.: Personas-driven design for mental health therapeutic applications. J. 3D Interact. Syst. **6**, 18–34 (2015)
7. Rodrigues, K.R.H., Bocanegra, L.F., Gonçalves, V.P., Carvalho, V.G., Neris, V.P.A.: Enriquecimento de personas para apoio ao design de aplicações terapêuticas para a saúde mental. In: Proceedings of the 13th Brazilian Symposium on Human Factors in Computing Systems, pp. 51–60. Sociedade Brasileira de Computação, Brazil (2014)
8. Cooper, A.: The Inmates are Running the Asylum: Why High Tech Products Drive Us Crazy and How to Restore the Sanity, 2nd edn. Pearson Higher Education, New York (2004)
9. Aquino Jr., P.T., Filgueiras, L.V.L.: User modeling with personas. In: Proceedings of American Conference on Human-Computer Interaction, pp. 277–282. ACM, New York (2005)
10. Masiero, A.A., Leite, M.G., Filgueiras, L.V.L., Aquino Jr., P.T.: Multidirectional knowledge extraction process for creating behavioral personas. In: Proceedings of The 10th Brazilian Symposium on Human Factors in Computing Systems, pp. 91–99. Brazil Computer Society (2011)
11. Kolkman, M.: Problem articulation methodology. Ph.D. thesis, University of Twente (1993)
12. Melo-Solarte, D.S., Baranauskas, M.C.: Resolução de problemas e colaboração a distância: modelo, artefatos e sistema. Revista Brasileira de Informática na Educação **17**(2), 21–35 (2009)
13. Baranauskas, M.C.C., Schimiguel, J., Simoni, C., Medeiros, C.B.: Guiding the process of requirements elicitation with a semiotic-based approach – a case study. In: Proceedings of the 11th International Conference on Human-Computer Interaction 3, Las Vegas, USA, pp. 100–111. (2005)

Analysis and Representation of Illocutions from Electronic Health Records

Julio Cesar dos Reis[1]([⊠]), Rodrigo Bonacin[2,3],
Edemar Mendes Perciani[2], and Maria Cecília Calani Baranauskas[1]

[1] Institute of Computing, University of Campinas, Campinas, Brazil
{julio.dosreis, cecilia}@ic.unicamp.br
[2] Faculty of Campo Limpo Paulista, Campo Limpo Paulista, Brazil
edemar.mendes.perciani@gmail.com
[3] Center for Information Tecnology Renato Archer, Campinas, Brazil
rodrigo.bonacin@cti.gov.br

Abstract. Electronic Health Records (EHRs) store multiple patients' information, including medical history, diagnoses and treatments. Computer-interpretable representation of meanings and intentions in EHRs content might play a major role for decision making, as well as for medical system integration and information recovery. However, there is a lack of suitable representation models to specify the relations between semantic models and illocutions, which reflect the intentions of medical content producers. In this paper, we propose an analysis to understand how illocutions are expressed in EHRs. We aim to identify domain-specific terms to convey the different dimensions in which illocutions are classified. Furthermore, this research develops a model, based on Web ontology description languages, to encode and instantiate the illocutions in the medical domain. Obtained results point out that some illocution types and associated terms are predominant in the analyzed content. They highlight the potentiality of our model to explore illocutions in several computing tasks.

Keywords: Intentions · Illocutions · Pragmatics · Ontologies · Semantic Web · Pragmatic Web · Knowledge representation · EHRs · Medical data

1 Introduction

Information and communication technologies are essential in complex contexts of medicine and clinical research. These domains are knowledge intensive and require appropriated methods and artifacts for enabling computational representation of knowledge. In this context, Electronic Health Records (EHRs) describe and store patients' information with a great volume of unstructured text. This hinders adequate integration, retrieval of information, as well as access to medical research data.

Aiming to deal with this problem, various studies have devised how to give well-defined meaning to information [1], emphasizing the construction of mechanisms for interpreting digital content through knowledge representation artifacts [2]. However, the communicated intentions affect the understanding of information content.

We understand "intention" as the effects of meanings with a determined purpose in a social context (e.g., a feeling or a judgment), as aligned with the discipline of

M.C.C. Baranauskas et al. (Eds.): ICISO 2016, IFIP AICT 477, pp. 209–218, 2016.
DOI: 10.1007/978-3-319-42102-5_24

Organizational Semiotics (OS) [3]. We argue that dealing with both semantic and intentions (as part of pragmatics[1]) allow to improve medical knowledge management and sharing. Our assumption implies having an underlying model suited to formally represent and link semantic and pragmatic aspects of knowledge.

This model might support both human and machines to interpret and process information. Our research remains under the Semantic Web (SemWeb) vision, which suggests modeling the information in Web ontologies for enabling knowledge interpretation by artificial agents and people [1]. While considering the formal meaning of information may already improve several types of systems, in particular machine-to-machine interoperability, complex settings of medical information systems entail open issues related to human factors. Even simple concept representations may have their interpretation affected by contextual aspects such as intention, users' background and time. Complementarily, the Pragmatic Web (PragWeb) studies meaning negotiation [4], however, there are still open issues on knowledge representation techniques suited to model meanings in a social context with the implied intentions.

Although literature has examined the evolution of meanings and intentions in collaborative problem solving [5], several difficulties still exist to achieve the representation of a complete computer-interpretable model, including alternatives to define the way that intentions are manifested in domain-specific contexts. Moreover, there is a lack of experimentally grounded studies with the focus on investigations of how existing theoretical frameworks can be useful to deal with this issue.

This article proposes an original empirical analysis of dimensions and intention classes in real EHRs data. This investigation relies on Semiotic-based theories and frameworks that structure and classify intentions according to different dimensions of illocutions [3]. The work also contributes with the definition and refinement of an ontology model, specified with SemWeb technologies. The goal of this model is to represent the illocutions materialized in the domain.

This research collected and selected a set of EHRs, which were manually examined to classify the illocution dimensions in their content. On this basis, we performed quantitative and qualitative analyses, which were used as input to the design of a representation model. Our findings reveal the way that illocutions are expressed in the domain-specific text-based content of the medical field. This allows the extraction of commonly used domain terms to represent the illocution dimensions. The proposed model enables to formally explore intentions, in a structured way, in analytics tasks, as well as by information recovery systems. Our investigation demonstrates the potentiality of considering domain-specific terminologies for identifying and classifying illocutions, which represent relevant language expressions of the domain.

The remainder of the paper is organized as follows: Sect. 2 reviews methods for representing meanings and intentions, and describes the adopted theories, frameworks and technical languages; Sect. 3 describes the methods and materials of the study; Sect. 4 presents and discusses the obtained results; Sect. 5 draws conclusion remarks and points out future work.

---

[1] In the context of this work, pragmatics is understood as described in the pragmatic layer of the semiotic framework [3].

2 Background

The Web has progressively evolved towards the SemWeb standing for an extension of the current Web that enables richer information share [1]. The SemWeb aims at making data more accessible and detectable by people and machines. SemWeb has predominantly focused on: (1) turning data machine-interpretable and making the semantic of information explicit at different degrees of expressivity, via formal representations; (2) providing metadata; and (3) integrating well-structured data.

Within the SemWeb proposition, ontology consists of a concrete syntactic structure that models the semantics of a domain [6]. In this paper, we adopt the term "Web Ontology" to refer to ontologies within the SemWeb field. This concept differs from the ontology concept used in OS field. Web Ontologies have specifically been designed to provide rich machine-decidable semantic representations and refers to a formal specification of some domain interpretable by machines. It specifies a conceptualization in terms of classes of domain objects, properties and relationships between classes [7]. This enables knowledge interpretation by artificial agents supporting the correct understanding of shared data. At the core of the SemWeb technology, computational languages, based on logic for knowledge representation and inference, have been designed specifically to define Web ontologies. In particular, according to the SemWeb architecture [1], there exists the *Web Ontology Language* (OWL), which relates to other Web languages, such as *Resource Description Framework* (RDF).

While semantics concerns the study of the meaning, independent of use and context, pragmatics regards the study of the meaning use in context and its purpose. In this perspective, PragWeb has originally been proposed as an extension or a complement of the SemWeb. PragWeb addresses shortcomings and challenges that purely SemWeb approaches fail to tackle with the aim of serving user's needs by making content more accessible. PragWeb emphasizes the relevance of context and purpose of information. Thus, it deals with research issues such as context and meaning negotiation between agents (human or artificial) [4] and issues related to intentions, interests and participation.

Few studies have attempted to represent and recognize intentions and other pragmatic aspects in computer systems. Our investigation indicates studies in natural language processing and computational linguistics that address pragmatic aspects. In the context of discourse analysis, Poesio and Traum [8] have studied a discourse model and different kinds of structure that play a role in conversation. They proposed a theory about the discourse situation, shared by the participants in a conversation, centered on information about the occurrence of speech acts [9]. Dam-Jensen and Zethsen [10] have conducted a linguistic corpus analysis considering pragmatic aspects via patterns. They investigated the relations between lexical meaning and the context where these meanings are inserted.

In addition to modeling pragmatics at the level of natural language, existing researches also emphasize the intentions modeling in other frames. The initial propositions examined logic-based models of intention formation applied to the multi-agent task [11]. They focused on the evolving intentions of agents and the conditions under which an agent can adopt and keep an intention. In contrast, Hawizy et al. [12] argue that the design of a model to produce clear representations of human intentions requires the incorporation of communication studies, such as Semiotics, which encompasses verbal and non-verbal communication.

Some studies have focused on specific domains, e.g., health. Shahar et al. [13] have studied the representation of clinical guidelines, where intentions referred to action patterns or patient states that a system must maintain, achieve or avoid. Other investigations aim at analyzing the users' behaviors in collaborative environments using SemWeb technologies. Kanso et al. [14] present an approach to model intentions by analyzing the authors' acts, focusing on detecting intentions in scientific documents, while Angeletou et al. [15] have proposed a method to represent and compute behavior by inferring roles in online communities. Nevertheless, these behavior roles are not explicitly linked to intentions.

Our previous work proposed a semiotic approach to design ontologies [16]. The investigation adopted OS' concepts and methods to enrich the representation aspects of traditional Web ontologies. In particular, we used the notion of *Agents*, *Affordances* and *Ontological Dependences* from the Semantic Analysis Method (SAM) described as OWL classes. That proposal did not enable representation of intentions, which was initially proposed as a general ontology model to represent pragmatic aspects in a computational way [17]. It encoded the main concepts of the Pragmatics Communication Framework [3] using the OWL language, which included classes, and object and data properties to describe the model.

Although the achieved results already allow correlating the representation of communication acts with ontologies, which demonstrates the initial feasibility of the preliminary model, they have brought up theoretical and practical limitations, which are addressed in the current article. Our research aims to further explore the process of describing the terms by which illocutions are expressed in the domain content. In addition, we contribute with empirical analyses and an extension of the model, encompassing additional classes, terms and instances.

In our study, we adopt an OS view of intentions, which is based on Peircean Semiotics, aiming to represent and study intentions present in EHRs using an *interpretant* dependent communication model. In order to classify and structure types of intentions, this investigation relies on Liu's conceptual framework of Pragmatics Communication [3], which proposes classifying illocutions using three dimensions. Liu's proposal considers communication acts as the minimal unit of human communication. A complete communication act is defined as a structure consisting of three components: performer, addressee, and message. A message contains two parts:

1. The *content* part of a communication act manifests the meaning of the message. The meaning is determined by social construct or human behavior performed by the performer and by the addressee.
2. The *function* part of a communication act specifies the illocution, which corresponds to the intention of the performer.

One dimension distinguishes between descriptive and prescriptive "invention". If an illocution has an inventive or instructive effect, it is prescriptive, otherwise descriptive. Another dimension consists of affective and denotative "mode". If an illocution is related to the performer's personal modal state mood, we call it affective, otherwise denotative. The last one is the "time" dimension, namely past/present and future. The classification of the "time" dimension is based on when the social effects of the message are produced, i.e., in the future or the present/past. The three dimensions result in eight different classes of illocutions including: *Proposal, Inducement, Forecast, Wish, Palinode, Contrition, Assertion* and *Valuation.*

3   Study Design

In this study, we conducted a five-step procedure to attain our objectives as follows:

1. Collect a set of real patients EHRs from hospitals. To make this research viable, we selected from the initial set of EHRs a subset according to a specific disease diagnosis. We only considered this subset of EHRs in our analysis.
2. Perform manual analysis of the EHRs according to the dimensions of illocutions, as proposed by our theoretical frame of reference. This step was performed by the researchers involved in this work with support of physicians. We assign the illocution dimensions to the sentences (messages) of the EHRs content. For this purpose, we consider *Zero* as past/present (time), description (invention) and denotative (mode); we denote *One* as future (time), prescription (invention) and affective (mode) (cf. Table 1).
3. Execute a quantitative and qualitative analyses over the illocutions. In general, we analyzed the occurrences of the dimensions (cf. Table 1) and the frequency of illocution classes detected (cf. Table 2). Furthermore, we examined the representative terms and keyphrases for each illocution class based on the EHR content (cf. Table 3). This allows us to state the domain terms that frequently represent the illocution dimensions.
4. Define an ontology model (cf. Sect. 4.2) based on previous analysis. This model represents illocutions related to domain terminologies. To this end, we rely on the reuse of previous models proposing further extensions and refinements.
5. Instantiate the model with the EHRs contents.

This research considers a set of EHRs available in a public hospital from "Águas de Lindóia" in São Paulo State, Brazil. The total amount of EHRs accounts ∼ 10.200 and all patients' data are anonymous. Our manual analysis effectively used 26 cases regarding the diagnosis of "Dengue fever" disease. We considered free-text notations in pre-consultation and patient's history case, where physicians report on symptoms according to patients' statements, exams results, and suggest treatments.

4   Results and Discussion

In this section, we first present the results concerning the conducted analysis of illocutions in EHRs (Sect. 4.1). Afterwards, we describe a Web Ontology model for representing the expression of illocutions from EHRs content (Sect. 4.2). The results are then discussed in Sect. 4.3.

4.1 Analysis of Illocutions in EHRs

Table 1 presents the occurrence of the values *Zero* and *One* of each dimension according to defined methods (cf. Sect. 4.1). The analysis of 26 EHRs resulted in the identification of 201 illocutions. The results point out that around 90 % of the illocutions are in present/past tense, are descriptive and are denotative. The affective mode is present in less than 80 % of the messages.

Table 1. Distribution of occurrences regarding dimensions of time, invention and mode.

	#Time	#Invention	#Mode
Zero	182 (90.55 %)	182 (90.5 %)	186 (92.54 %)
One	19 (9.45 %)	19 (9.45 %)	15 (7.46 %)

Table 2 presents the frequency of illocution classes in the EHRs' texts. The majority of the illocutions are assertions within 84.58 % of the messages. Proposals (7.96 %), valuation (5.97 %) and inducements (1.49 %) classes are also present in the analyzed messages. Nevertheless, forecast, wish, palinode and contrition did not occur in the analyzed EHRs.

Table 2. Frequency of illocution classes

Illocution classes	Frequency (percentage)
Assertion	170 (84.58 %)
Proposal	16 (7.96 %)
Valuation	12 (5.97 %)
Inducement	3 (1.49 %)

Table 3 presents terms and keyphases used in the messages that indicate their illocution classes. The terms "Refers", "Exhibits" and "Reports" are present in the total of 66 assertions. From a qualitative view, typically, these terms were used to confirm patients' symptoms, characteristics or disease, which are important for medical diagnosis.

Table 3. Analysis of representative terms and keyphases by the illocution classes (A same illocution can be related to more than one term/keyphase.)

Terms	#Assertion	#Proposal	#Valuation	# Inducement
"Refers"	48	-	3	-
"Denies"	82	-	2	
"Exhibits"	12	-	-	-
"Reports"	6	-	-	-
"Requests"	-	12	-	-
"Advises"	-	3	-	3
"There is 'x' hours/days"	24	-	2	-
"Lacks"	3	-	-	-
"Complain"	-	-	2	-
"Improves"	-	-	2	-
Others	7	1	2	-

The terms "Denies" and "Lacks" are present in the total of 85 assertions. Physicians frequently used these terms to report the absence of symptoms or diseases related to the diagnosis. Time related keyphases/expressions (e.g., "There is 'x' hours/days") are present in 24 assertions. The time expressions are frequently used to refer to the presence or absence of a symptom or disease in the days or hours prior to the consultation. Other terms are present in 7 assertions (one occurrence each).

As presented in Table 3, the terms "Requests" and "Advices" are present in 15 proposals. Typically, physicians use these terms to give instructions for the patients. The term "Refers", "Complaints" and "Improves" are present in 7 valuations that consist in subjective judgments about the patients' symptoms, characteristics and conditions (e.g., to say that they are feeling better or to complain about a symptom). The term "Denies" is also present in 2 valuations, which refers to subjective judgments about patients' conditions. The term "Advises" was used in 3 inducements made by physicians to warn patients.

4.2   Web Ontology for Representing Domain-Related Illocution Terminologies

Our Web Ontology representation is based on previous studies and the *Communication Act Ontology* (*CactO*) [17]. The first version of *CactO* was constructed in OWL using the *Protégé tool*[2] with the objective of representing aspects related to intentions in messages of collaborative problem-solving systems. This Web ontology was evaluated in information retrieval scenarios from discussion forums. Despite the promising results substantiated by overall good objective measures of evaluation, the first version of *CactO* is limited when we consider the complexity of medical texts. Thus, based on our reported analyses, we propose a new version of *CactO*, which we named *MedCactO*.

This version of the *CactO* aims at representing intentions in text from EHRs. In *MedCactO*, the *function* part of a communication act is more detailed, including the specification of dimension values and terms used to express these dimensions. The *MedCactO* also links behaviour patterns to standard medical terminologies and existing *Knowledge Organization Systems* (KOS).

Figure 1 presents an overview of *MedCactO*, including the classes inherited from *CactO*. The *Agent* class comprises who (*HumanAgent)* performs (or is the addressee) a communication act. *Physicians* and *Patients* might be subclasses of *HumanAgent*. The *Behaviour_Pattern* class represents patterns that delineate the actions performed by an agent (including meaning interpretation). The *communicationAct* is performed when an agent write a text. One *communicationAct* has a message, which has the function and content parts (cf. Sect. 2).

In *MedCactO*, a *Behaviour_Pattern* is linked to concepts modeled in existing medical KOSs (terminologies, taxonomies, ontologies, *etc.*) (top of Fig. 1). The *MedCactO* also includes the *FunctionAct* class. This class is associated with an illocution type, which has the *Dimensions* of time, invention and mode. Each *Dimension* is

---

[2] protege.stanford.edu.

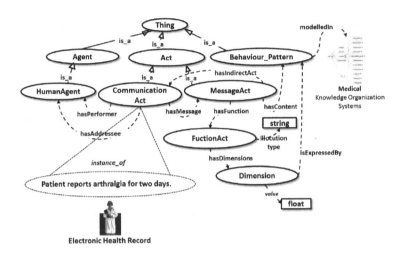

Fig. 1. Overview of the *MedCactO*

described with a value (between 0 and 1) and it is expressed by a *Behaviour_Pattern*, which is linked to terms specified by the existing medical KOSs.

Figure 2 presents an example of communication act modelled according to *Med-CactO*. We extracted the following text fragment from the analyzed EHRs to illustrate the Web ontology instantiation: *"Patient reports arthralgia for two days"*. As shown in Fig. 2, the communication act (*c_act4*) was performed by an agent (*uid_2*) and this act has a message (*m_act4*). Such message has the content part linked to a behaviour pattern (*b_pattern5053*), which is related, for instance, to an UMLS[3] *Concept Unique Identifier* (*C0003862*). The message also contains a function (*illoc_4*), which has an illocution type (*assertion*) and three dimensions (mode and invention dimensions were omitted in the figure for reliability purposes). The "time" dimension (*me_illoc_4*) has the value 0 (i.e., present/past) and is expressed by a behaviour pattern (*b_pattern51*),

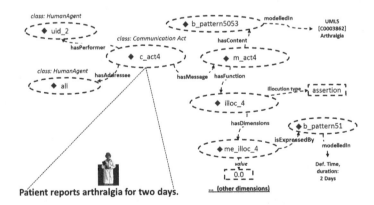

Fig. 2. Example of a communication act modeled using *MedCactO*

---

which is modeled externally in UMLS (for instance) by the concept *C0449238*. The value associated to this concept is *two days*.

4.3 Discussion

The analysis of the EHRs revealed interesting aspects of free-text annotations regarding illocutions in medical records. In general, the analyzed texts are concise and impersonal. This can be observed by the higher incidence of assertions, and the mode 0 (denotative) in more than 90 % of the messages. The majority of the analyzed texts also remains descriptive and in the present/past tense. These characteristics differ from our previous studies [5] in "special education domain", in which there are a wider range of incidence of other illocutions types, including the affective mode.

The analysis also revealed the importance of the terms or expressions that indicate the dimensions of an illocution. For instance, a *coughing* for one day is a different indicator that a coughing for one month. The modeling and computational interpretation of these aspects may result in improvements of medical information tools, including information retrieval tasks and applications for analytical purposes.

Inspired by these results, we proposed the *MedCactO*, which aims at representing the illocutionary acts and linking them to standard terminology and models of the medical field. This Web ontology was constructed using the OWL language, which enables the use of reasoning tools and other Semantic Web technologies that can be used to develop several integration and information retrieval tools.

Neverhteless, this study is limited in terms of size and scope. It was restricted to 26 EHRs of a specific disease (dengue fever). EHRs of other areas of the medical field must be investigated to verify the incidence of illocutions types. RDF/OWL models, as the adopted in this article, are also limited for representing *Agents*, *Affordances* and *Ontological Dependences*. Other methods from OS, such as, the Semantic and Norm Analysis may produce additional and relevant results. Despite these limitations, this study represents a promising and novel initiative for understanding and managing intentions in text-based content of medical records. In a long-term perspective, this might be useful and effective in the definition of further computational tools for supporting clinical research and better medical treatment plans.

5 Conclusion

Medical information, as text described in EHRs, requires adequate computational representation of meanings and intentions. This might be crucial to several organizational and computer supported tasks, including decision making and medical research. However, literature lacks formal methods and models to relate meanings and intentions systematically. Meaning representation and interpretation cannot be considered without context and intention, which can be classified according to several dimensions. In this article, we made explicit how domain terms are used in illocutions related to intention classes. We conducted an analysis to investigate how illocutions are expressed in EHRs using domain terms. This was the basis to expand and refine a model, which formally describes illocution types using standard Web ontology languages. Our findings indicated relevant domain-specific expressions that refer to illocution dimensions and their adequate computer-interpretable representation. Future work involves experimentally investigating the use of the proposed model in larger scale and in specific computing applications such as information retrieval.

Acknowledgments. We thank the São Paulo Research Foundation (FAPESP) (Grant #2014/14890-0), and the CNPq (Grant # 308618/2014-9). The opinions expressed in this work do not necessarily reflect those of the funding agencies.

References

1. Berners-Lee, T., Hendler, T.J., Lassila, O.: The Semantic Web. Sci. Am. **284**(5), 34–43 (2001)
2. Hendler, J., Berners-Lee, T.: From the Semantic Web to social machines: a research challenge for AI on the World Wide Web. Artif. Intell. **174**(2), 156–161 (2010)
3. Liu, K., Li, W.: Organisational Semiotics for Business Informatics. Routledge, Abingdon (2014)
4. Singh, M.P.: The Pragmatic Web. IEEE Internet Comput. **6**(3), 4–5 (2002)
5. Bonacin, R., Hornung, H., Dos Reis, J.C., Pereira, R., Baranauskas, M.C.C.: Pragmatic aspects of collaborative problem solving: towards a framework for conceptualizing dynamic knowledge. In: Cordeiro, J., Maciaszek, L.A., Filipe, J. (eds.) ICEIS 2012. LNBIP, vol. 141, pp. 410–426. Springer, Heidelberg (2013)
6. Uschold, M.: Where are the semantics in the semantic web? AI Mag. **24**(3), 25–36 (2003)
7. Gruber, T.R.: A translation approach to portable ontology specifications. Knowl. Acquisition **5**, 199–220 (1993)
8. Poesio, M., Traum, D.R.: Conversational actions and discourse situations. Comput. Intell. **13**, 309–347 (1997)
9. Searle, J.R.: A classification of illocutionary acts. Lang. Soc. **5**(1), 1–23 (1976)
10. Dam-Jensen, H., Zethsen, K.K.: Pragmatic patterns and the lexical system - a reassessment of evaluation in language. J. Pragmat. **39**(9), 1608–1623 (2007)
11. Grant, J., Kraus, S., Perlis, D.: A logic-based model of intention formation and action for multi-agent subcontracting. Artif. Intell. **163**(2), 163–201 (2005)
12. Hawizy, L., Phillips, I.W., Connolly, J.H.: Intention modeling: a semiotic view. In: Proceedings of International Conference Applied Computing, pp. 478–482 (2006)
13. Shahar, Y., Miksch, S., Johnson, P.: An intention-based language for representing clinical guidelines. In: Proceedings of AMIA Annual Fall Symposium, pp. 592–596 (1995)
14. Kanso, H., Soulé-Dupuy, C., Tazi, S.: Representing author's intentions of scientific documents. In: Proceedings of ICEIS, pp. 489–492 (2007)
15. Angeletou, S., Rowe, M., Alani, H.: Modelling and analysis of user behaviour in online communities. In: Aroyo, L., Welty, C., Alani, H., Taylor, J., Bernstein, A., Kagal, L., Noy, N., Blomqvist, E. (eds.) ISWC 2011, Part I. LNCS, vol. 7031, pp. 35–50. Springer, Heidelberg (2011)
16. Dos Reis, J.C., Bonacin, R., Baranauskas, M.C.C.: A semiotic-based approach to the design of web ontologies. In: Proceedings of ICISO, Reading, UK, pp. 60–67 (2010)
17. Bonacin, R., Dos Reis, J.C., Hornung, H., Baranauskas, M.C.C.: An ontological model for supporting intention-based information sharing on collaborative problem solving. Collaborative Enterp. **3**(2–3), 130–150 (2013)

Characterisation of an Electronic Booking System in the National Health Service: A Semiotic Perspective

Sanjayan Solangasenathirajan[(⊠)] and Keiichi Nakata

Henley Business School, Informatics Research Centre,
University of Reading, Reading, UK
s.solangasenathirajan@pgr.reading.ac.uk,
k.nakata@henley.ac.uk

Abstract. The NHS in England comprises multiple organisations, systems and actors working in co-ordination to deliver healthcare to the population. Transfers of care from primary care organisations is facilitated by an electronic booking system that is provided nationally, and utilised regionally and locally. The success of such system is dependent on the co-operation of actors and organisations in the health economy in affecting its impact and usefulness. Such a system can be seen as an 'artefact' where multiple worlds collide. The theory of boundary objects is approached from a critical realist paradigm to conceptualise the role of the focal system. Organisational semiotics is used to provide an analytical method to interpret the behaviours and perceptions surrounding the artefact. Understanding of these factors provides recognition of the tensions in adoption of the system. Implementation and expert use of systems considering these invisible factors can benefit from greater intellectual buy in and value co-creation.

Keywords: Critical realism · Organisational semiotics · Boundary objects · Computer supported co-operative work · Electronic referrals · National Health Service

1 Introduction

Interoperability of healthcare systems at the macro, meso and micro levels is high on the research agenda and in practice within the National Health Service (NHS) of England. Much of the effort and activity has been focused on the technical integration of systems through core services, linking of datasets, definitions and technical interfaces [1]. Even though, the NHS struggles to achieve effective integration and interoperation locally, within or across organisations in the local health community, or nationally across regions and geographies. Lack of social collaboration in the technical design, development and implementation of systems could be seen as a barrier to healthcare systems interoperation.

An understanding of the interfaces, and the behaviours and perceptions of the stakeholders who take an interactive role within and around these collaborative systems is required, to understand the socio-technical aspects of co-ordinated system utilisation

© IFIP International Federation for Information Processing 2016
Published by Springer International Publishing Switzerland 2016. All Rights Reserved
M.C.C. Baranauskas et al. (Eds.): ICISO 2016, IFIP AICT 477, pp. 219–228, 2016.
DOI: 10.1007/978-3-319-42102-5_25

and the variance of interpretations and barriers to perceived benefits, which result in negative effects. This paper seeks to characterise the role of such a system in its society and the assumed responsibilities of those actors within it. Through the analysis of the human information context it is postulated that a greater understanding of the intrinsic nature is developed to establish the requirements from co-coordinative domains.

2 NHS Electronic Booking System

A number of core national information systems are currently in use by the NHS in England, of which one facilitates the electronic transmission of referral and appointments booking information across NHS organisations nationally. Its fundamental use is to refer a patient from a primary care organisation to a secondary care organisation, and to support the transfer of clinical information, service selection and appointments booking. This information system is based on core clinical Directory of Services, from which referrers and patients can choose and book an appointment date and time of their preference, in a clinical service of their choice. The system is populated by clinical service definitions from providers of NHS services and integrates with the patient administration systems, so that appointment slots can be polled and made available to the referrals and appointments system. Additionally, referrers can initiate the creation of a referral and attach content from within their GP clinical system. Access is based on user roles and governed by Role Based Access Controls on smartcards used to access the system. Users of the system have referring, service provider, commissioning and further supporting roles with the appropriate functionality. The information within this system can be utilised to understand 'future outpatient' activity and the demands and trends of populations on secondary care clinical services.

This information system can be classified as one which acts as a focal point for the interoperation of a number of clinical information systems and co-operative work [2] of a variety of stakeholders in the formal and informal system [3]. The electronic referral and appointments booking system can be treated as an 'artefact' that sits between and forms many 'boundaries' with organisations and their actors. The actors in these organisations take on a number of roles in which they play a part in the function of the system. These use cases can be technical, non-technical, facilitating or beneficiary.

2.1 Design Intentions

The electronic referrals and appointments booking system is utilised in the NHS as part of a core provision of national information services. The core principle was to enable direct access and booking from primary care to secondary care. More specifically: to support patient choice of clinical service and appointment date/time; to support clinical Service Providers to triage and accept referrals that are clinically appropriate only once the patient has been provided an appointment; to facilitate advice and guidance in supporting a referral decision thereby reducing first outpatient appointments through activity diversion and reducing waiting times. Up to date and accurate definition and publication, provides a shop window for Service Providers, for referrers navigating and identifying their services.

2.2   System Characterisation

Figure 1 illustrates the system as a mediating artefact in a network of stakeholders and organisations (indicated the first level), and systems/functions within that organisation.

The system is at the core of interfacing organisations working to co-ordinate activity to facilitate the process of patients 'choosing' and 'booking' an appointment within a Provider service of their choice. Clinical Commissioning Groups play a beneficiary role in the use of management information, delivery of policy and governance over national performance and quality targets. General Practice and the Service Providers play technical and non-technical roles, with the end users acting with the system and management stakeholders playing non-technical roles in the informal system. The Commissioning Support Unit plays a facilitating role in operational support to General Practice, strategic enablement to the Clinical Commissioning Groups and an interfacing role to support and bring awareness of the electronic booking system. With view of the system as an artefact, differences in local and regional norms cause variation in these multiple domains. This leads to a great degree of permutation in use, from design intention.

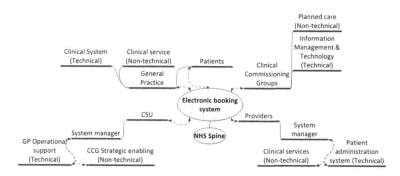

Fig. 1. Stakeholders of the NHS electronic booking system

3   Boundary Objects

The national electronic referrals and appointments booking system can be treated as an artefact, classified as a boundary object [4] in-use, which is comprised of systems acting as repositories and ideal-type concepts provided by definitions. These definitions could be formalised or interpreted to convey different meaning based on the context in which it is being used. A boundary object may be performed differently across multiple sites, times, practices and participants, with varying effects [5]. Boundary objects perform a brokering role [6] involving translation, coordination and alignment between the interfaces and perspectives of specific Communities of Practice [7]. Boundary objects facilitate cooperation between intersecting communities by maintaining a common identity while satisfying the informational needs of each [4, 8] and provide a locus for communication, conflict, and coordination [9] and for actors with diverse goals to work together [10].

The interaction between a user and a system is a conversation in a vocabulary and language determined by the input the system is able to accept and process. Many systems (e.g., help systems, documentation systems) are oriented toward the system rather than toward the user: information is structured around a description of the system, not necessarily around an analysis of the problems users address when using the system [11]. As the electronic booking system is dependent on the co-ordination and collaboration of multiple stakeholders, variation in utilisation and system failure can be caused by neglect by one of the communities it is intended to bridge [12]. Boundary objects require a joint field and incorporation into local practice to become boundary objects-in-use [13] and have material aspects that afford or constrain boundary-spanning practices [14]. They enable knowledge transfer and the translation of meaning and interests, but their boundary-spanning effectiveness or role may vary across settings or time [4, 15, 16].

Studies have shown that artefacts can fail as boundary objects when they do not fully or rightfully capture multiple meanings and perspectives [17]. This interpretive flexibility leads to a misalignment between the IT structure and work process needs and arrangements, and the dynamic between ill-structured and more tailored uses of the objects [18].

Even though the current system has been in operation for approximately 10 years, the utilisation nationally varies to a great extent. Issues from system conception still manifest themselves as ongoing issues to date [19], thus engagement from end users and managers in some places has remained poor and perceptions formed and embedded through bad experience, relationships or interactions [20]. Boundary objects provide a bridging function but additionally need supporting awareness practices [21]. The system is characterised as a boundary object so as to facilitate the conceptualisation of the multiple connected domains, and analysis of their contributory elements.

In this paper we study boundary objects through a semiotic lens. This is appropriate as, for example, the integrative semiotic framework [22] provides a method of analysis of the environmental and social context so that a greater understanding of user requirements can be developed in contribution to gaining intellectual buy in [23]. Moreover, the semantic and pragmatic levels of the semiotic ladder [24] provide aspects of assessment into the characteristics of the boundary object. The pragmatics provide an insight into the communicated intentions of the boundary object and how this influences actors. The semantics looks to uncover individual and the wider collective meaning derived from various signifying factors, in the way so to uncover further issues in the informal system, and contributory factors in domain norms resulting in impedance of innovation and system failures. Subsequently to reveal the gaps between system design, governance mechanisms and situated use.

4   A Semiotic Analysis of NHS Electronic Booking System as Boundary Object

The study was approached by conducting semi-structured interviews to capture the semantic and pragmatic views of the system from its users and stakeholders and to provide a basis for cross examination of these findings with the design intention of the system. This semiotic analysis is to determine the success of the system in fulfilling its design intentions and in highlighting and understanding the causes for failure, where it is not used as intended. Ethnography is used to support or negate this analysis in observing stakeholders in use or co-ordination around the focal system, to provide a basis for highlighting and commenting on the successes and failures from the semiotic perspective.

4.1 Signification

Each has a part to play in the design intention of the system, in that which is signified and that which is interpreted by the various stakeholders. The system as a boundary object artefact signifies its design intentions. The expected use of the system is interpreted and observed by the various actors in accordance with their existing tasks, practice and position, as illustrated in Fig. 2.

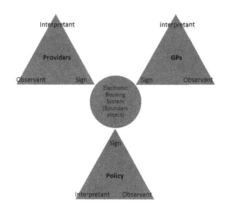

Fig. 2. Signification of system as boundary object

Superficially, the system is observed as merely providing a means to transfer referral information from one organisation to another. However, it serves different meanings and intensions for different stakeholders, e.g., facilitating the strategic objectives of patient choice, waiting time targets, and activity diversion. This is primarily influenced by local governance within the informal system.

4.2 Semiotic Analysis

The semantic and pragmatic perspectives of each system role, as adopted by stakeholders in the information system has been summarized in Table 1.

The system process models the series of tasks that occur for end user interacting with the system from its design intentions. This is described from the GP perspective as illustrated in Fig. 3. In practice, these tasks can be carried out by different users, such as a Medical Secretary at differing time points.

Table 1. Analysis of human information functions

	Semantic	Pragmatic
GP	A comprehensive listing of locally and nationally available services, appointment dates/times. With ability to seek advice from secondary care colleagues	Facilitates the clinically appropriate identification of services for patient referral and appointment booking. Facilitates advice and guidance from secondary care
Medical secretary	Comprehensive listing of locally and nationally available services, appointment dates/times	Facilitates the clinically appropriate identification of services for patient referral, automated digital referral attachments and appointment booking
Practice manager	An electronic referral and appointments system	Monitor and manage referral activity
Consultant	An electronic referral triaging and advice and guidance provision system	Electronically review incoming referrals and advice requests
Outpatients manager	An electronic appointments booking system	Directly book appointments and manage slot availability
Service manager	Digitally define services within specialty	Shop window of services

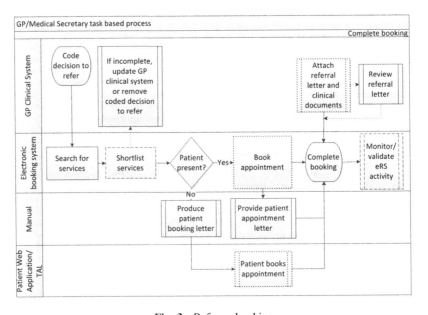

Fig. 3. Referrer booking

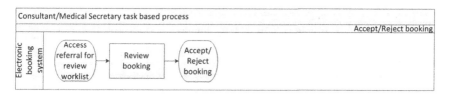

Fig. 4. Service Provider triaging

The 'book appointment' process releases any attached clinical information to the Service Provider, the referral attachments also need to have been attached into the electronic booking system. Due to the variety of clinical systems used in General Practice there are multiple methods by which the letter and clinical documents can be attached. Process variations and the timeliness of working through the process in Fig. 3 directly impact the efficacy of the process in Fig. 4.

In order for the 'review booking' process to take place the 'patient books appointment' and 'attach referral letter and clinical documents' sub processes in Fig. 3 need to have taken place in the time prior to the triaging of the booking. Timeliness of sub processes is key to the success of the system, without which the system fails. Where in Fig. 3 the processes in dashed lines are not carried out completely or routinely, adverse effects such as the GP clinical system recording that a booking has been created when in fact no booking has been created occur. Also, where bookings are rejected these are not picked up and therefore the patient has not progressed in receiving any care.

4.3   Contextualisation of Semantic and Pragmatic Issues

4.3.1   Referrers

GPs view the system as one which can support or impede the day to day clinical duty. Referring a patient is in some cases perceived as a task carried out by administrative staff. This transfer of information is in some cases supported by additional technologies, such as Dictaphones. Referral attachment content is produced by a variety of methods given the variety of up to 5 different GP clinical systems in use by practices, and within a GP clinical system, the particular way in which the patient details and referral prose is added. This leads to inconsistencies in the structure, quality of content impacting on the way that it is accessed and usefully perceived on the Service Provider side.

Where the shortlisting of services takes place there is inconsistency in the number of choices that are provided, and in some cases in merit of the choice discussion having already taken place externally to the system, only one choice would be shortlisted. The directory only publishes planned care services, so accommodates for a proportion of total GP referrals.

If the referral is not made prior to the patient leaving the practice following consultation, then the patient booking letter has to be posted to the patient so that their appointment can be booked. The cost incurred in generating and posting, negates any perceived benefit of the system. In some instances the appointment is booked without consultation with the patient and subsequently removing any requirement to generate the booking letter. This approach heavily relies on the Service Provider contacting the patient with appointment details, and negates intended system use around choice and ability for patients to manage their booking.

4.3.2   Service Providers

In Service Provider organisations the triaging consultant can directly access their referral through the system web interface and accept or reject that particular booking, as illustrated in Fig. 4. They are also enabled to access their 'advice and guidance' requests. Some instances describe where consultants never access the system and have the referrals passed to them in paper format, where they have been retrieved by administration staff. Service Providers do not always (have the capacity) to poll available clinic slots, so this can lead to subsequent manual processes where the patient has to be contacted and appointed manually.

In Service Provider organisations, there is also similar variation in each stage of the activity. Whereby some processes are carried out by clinical or administrative staff, in either centralised or distributed functions throughout the organisation.

Worklists determine the management and administration tasks that occur in the use of the system or in the management of events that have arisen from unintended circumstances. For example, if a referral is rejected as clinically inappropriate by the Service Provider, this then populates on a worklist in the GP practice. This should result in the patient being contacted by the GP practice about this cancellation. The adverse impacts of not monitoring this worklist are unforeseen by practices, and only experienced by the Service Provider and Patient, when a rejected appointment is attended.

In bridging all of this activity the system exhibits behaviour of a boundary object in use, whereby it facilitates an interfacing role. Each of the use cases contributes to a variety of interpretation and use of the artefact. Because of the local variances the sign conveys a different interpretation to observation, as intended. The overall use of the system changes over time and in instances can be influenced by external factors in the informal system. The stakeholder map in Fig. 1 highlights the external composition to a boundary object, in addition to that characterised within.

5   Discussion

The processes and protocols that take place locally are bound to the semantic, pragmatic and social norms of the stakeholders in that particular local instance. This is influenced and constrained by historical and current factors attributed to the signification of the focal system. The malleability of the system from its design intentions, as a boundary object has lent to a multitude of process variations, omissions and workarounds attributed to the ways in which it is interpreted and observed. This flexibility has increased its adoption in tune with local needs, but resulted in deviation from design intention. This also questions whether the design intention was correct, but also for its continuous evolution. Importantly, where beneficiaries as key influencers have least intellectual buy in, resulting interpretations of the system in that instance are subject to greater variation. In these cases, greater facilitation, interfacing and support is required to enable system design intention.

Activity at the boundary is instrumental in shaping the semantics of the system, in setting expectations and resolving misunderstandings. The practical aspects of the system are addressed by collaborating with the group in representation of the system to minimize the emergence of group related issues. The wider social group works in isolation in each organisation, and within an organisation within departments. Internally, the system exhibits its own semiotic characteristics which impact on its wider social use. The greater role of beneficiaries and facilitators is under recognised in the implementation and utilisation of these boundary objects. A subsequent focus is required on the impact of the non-technical stakeholders, and in their use cases that affect the efficacy of the technical system design intentions and innovation governance [25].

6   Conclusion

A system classified as a boundary object signifies that which has varying interpretations and observations, impacted by its semiotic attributes. These affect the way in which the system fulfils its design intentions, and the subsequent effects of system malleability. Activity at the boundary and the stakeholders in the informal system are primary to influencing the instance of the system. The transition to a new open source system provides an opportunity to observe the participation in design. There is a need to bridge natural user protocols, to systems and governance protocols. Where co-design of system intentions takes place there is a reduction in its need for malleability, and co-creation of values based on learned incentives. Further work is required to investigate the factors affecting the efficacy and subsequent utilisation of the system and improving long term acceptance. In uncovering the factors that impact this we can seek to resolve the tensions between the normative values, forms of authority and order imposed by the system.

References

1. Clegg, C., Shepherd, C.: The biggest computer programme in the world…ever!: time for a change in mindset? J. Inf. Technol. **22**(3), 212–221 (2007)
2. Schmidt, K., Bannon, L.: Taking CSCW seriously. Comput. Support. Coop. Work (CSCW) **1**(1–2), 7–40 (1992)
3. Stamper, R.K.: Information in Business and Administrative Systems. Wiley, New York (1973)
4. Star, S.L., Griesemer, J.R.: Institutional ecology, "translations", and boundary objects: amateurs and professionals in Berkeley's Museum of Vertebrate Zoology, 1907–39. Soc. Stud. Sci. **19**, 387–420 (1989)
5. Suchman, L.A.: Human-Machine Reconfigurations: Plans and Situated Actions. Cambridge University Press, Cambridge, New York (2007)
6. Fischer, G., Reeves, B.N.: Creating success models of cooperative problem solving. In: Baecker, R.M., et al. (eds.) Readings in Human-Computer Interaction: Toward the Year 2000, pp. 822–831 (1995)
7. Wenger, E.: Communities of Practice: Learning, Meaning, and Identity. Cambridge University Press, Cambridge, New York (1998)

8. Star, S.L.: This is not a boundary object: reflections on the origin of a concept. Sci. Technol. Hum. Values **35**(5), 601–617 (2010)
9. Yakura, E.K.: Charting time: timelines as temporal boundary objects. Acad. Manag. J. **45**(5), 956–970 (2002)
10. Briers, M., Chua, W.F.: The role of actor-networks and boundary objects in management accounting change: a field study of an implementation of activity-based costing. Acc. Organ. Soc. **26**(3), 237–269 (2001)
11. Arias, E., et al.: Transcending the individual human mind - creating shared understanding through collaborative design. ACM Trans. Comput. Hum. Interact. **7**, 84–113 (2000)
12. Sapsed, J., Salter, A.: Postcards from the edge: local communities, global programs and boundary objects. Organ. Stud. **25**(9), 1515–1534 (2004)
13. Levina, N., Vaast, E.: The emergence of boundary spanning competence in practice: implications for implementation and use of information systems. MIS Quart. **29**(2), 335–363 (2005)
14. Howard-Grenville, J.A., Carlile, P.R.: The incompatibility of knowledge regimes: consequences of the material world for cross-domain work. European J. Inf. Syst. **15**(5), 473–485 (2006)
15. Carlile, P.R.: Transferring, translating, and transforming: an integrative framework for managing knowledge across boundaries. Organ. Sci. **15**(5), 555–568 (2004)
16. Carlile, P.R.: A pragmatic view of knowledge and boundaries: boundary objects in new product development. Organ. Sci. **13**(4), 442–455 (2002)
17. Akkerman, S.F., Bakker, A.: Boundary crossing and boundary objects. Rev. Educ. Res. **81**(2), 132–169 (2011)
18. Star, S.L.: This is not a boundary object: reflections on the origin of a concept. Sci. Technol. Hum. Values **35**(5), 601–617 (2010)
19. Greenhalgh, T., Stones, R., Swinglehurst, D.: Choose and book: a sociological analysis of resistance to an expert system. SSM Soc. Sci. Med. **104**, 210–219 (2014)
20. Peltu, M., Eason, K., Clegg, C.: How a Sociotechnical Approach Can Help NPfIT Deliver Better NHS Patient Care. BCS online, Sociotechnical Group (2008)
21. Schmidt, K.: Cooperative Work and Coordinative Practices Contributions to the Conceptual Foundations of Computer Supported Cooperative Work (CSCW). Springer, London, New York (2011)
22. Mingers, J., Willcocks, L.: An integrative semiotic framework for information systems: the social, personal and material worlds. Inf. Organ. **24**, 48–70 (2014)
23. Edgley, A., et al.: Critical realist review: exploring the real, beyond the empirical. J. Furth. High. Educ. **40**, 316–330 (2014)
24. Stamper, R.K.: Organisational semiotics: informatics without the computer? In: Liu, K., et al. (eds.) Information, Organisation and Technology: Studies in Organisational Semiotics, pp. 115–171. Springer, Boston (2001)
25. Deschamps, J.P., Nelson, B.: Innovation Governance: How Top Management Organizes and Mobilizes for Innovation. Wiley, Hoboken (2014)

Poster Papers

A Preliminary Study on Information Sharing Practice Between Police and Private Security Companies in the United Arab Emirates

Abdulla Alhefeiti and Keiichi Nakata

Informatics Research Centre, University of Reading, Reading, UK
a.alhefeiti@pgr.reading.ac.uk, k.nakata@reading.ac.uk

1 Introduction

The current security system in the private security companies' regulatory department (PSCRD) in the United Arab Emirates (UAE) suffers from inconsistency and inefficiency in communication and information sharing with the private security companies (PSCs). These failings hinder collaborative policing. Therefore, this paper focuses on information sharing practice to support collaboration in policing with the help of PSCs for managing crime prevention and safety. The information sharing within various departments in police is studied in literatures and issues are identified. [1]. On the other hand, the empirical data shows that the mechanism of sharing information does not really work properly and it needs to be improved to fit with the requirements of the effectiveness of information sharing. This is according to S4 "The mechanism of information sharing is required to link all sources in one system while providing a precise context and there is need to have a central call control centre where all security information is coordinated."

2 Activity Theory

Activity theory helps to provide a broad conceptual framework in order to explain the complex development, context, and structure of computer-based activities. It also supports PSCRD and PSCs working on three tenets that ensure its effectiveness [2]. In the theory, there are aspects of modular actions, molar activity, and the components of the two [3]. As a result, it is important to intervene in socially situated practices for offering concrete solutions [3]. According to this theory, observing a realistic situation enables information gathering to identify the conditions of action and implementation [2]. For this reason, it comes out that using a conditioning tool will aid in acquiring this information for use. It provides the theoretical perspective of unification of the computer-human interaction.

© IFIP International Federation for Information Processing 2016
Published by Springer International Publishing Switzerland 2016. All Rights Reserved
M.C.C. Baranauskas et al. (Eds.): ICISO 2016, IFIP AICT 477, pp. 231–233, 2016.
DOI: 10.1007/978-3-319-42102-5

3 Implications on the Design of Information Architecture to Support Information Sharing

The study highlights some obstacles to effective information sharing in the police in the UAE, and the mechanism of information sharing between the PSCRD and PSCs is generally considered ineffective. Therefor, designing Information Architecture (IA) is needed, with further study on the exact processes in sharing information. IA can be described as a collection of design artefacts appropriate for illustrating an object so that it can be produced to suit various requirements and be maintained over time during its useful life [4]. IA can be defined as established regulations that determine the manner, the form and the place where data will be gathered from, kept, processed, and shared and eventually how it will not only be presented but also used. From its definition, information architecture is an imperative for improving and classifying communication, particularly in cases where secrecy is deemed to be very central, such as in the police force control room [5].

The implication of this study is that it is necessary to design IA, which will improve the mechanism of information transference within the police and PSCs, while also supporting the information exchanged between PSCRD, and PSCs.

4 Limitations and Future Work

The attempt has been made to find a suitable method to be proposed and validated by conducting interviews with members of these stakeholders. Basically appropriate technology must be used depending on the need of each issue.

It is important that there are some limitations in this evaluation of the ineffective aspects of the information sharing mechanism within the police and PSCs. One variable is that both sectors have different motivation and purposes as they perform their activities. For example, the police mainly exist to serve the public security whereas PSCs exist for the profit motive in particular. Consequently, the subject of delegating rights to private security concerns that are motivated by profits is an area for future consideration and research. Furthermore, to evaluate how the findings from fieldwork substantiate the requirements of IA. This can help produce a prototype that illustrates how the given information ought to be transformed on a screen as the user proceeds while navigating through the task.

References

1. Kitchen, V., Rygiel, K.: Privatizing security, securitizing policing: the case of the G20 in Toronto. Canada. Int. Polit. Sociol **8**, 201–217 (2014)
2. Engestrom, Y.: Objects, contradictions and collaboration in medical cognition: an activity theoretical perspective. Artif. Intell. Med. **7**, 395–412 (1995)
3. Avis, J.: Engeström's version of activity theory: a conservative praxis? J. Educ. Work. **20**, 161–177 (2007)

4. Buckl, S., Ernst, A.M., Matthes, F., Ramacher, R., Schweda, C.M. Using enterprise architecture management patterns to complement TOGAF. In: Proceedings of The 13th IEEE International Conference on Enterprise Distributed Object Computing (EDOC), pp. 34–41 (2009). doi:10.1109/EDOC.2009.30
5. Jonkers, H., et al.: Concepts for Modeling Enterprise Architectures. Int. J. Coop. Inf. Syst. **1** (3), 257–287 (2004)

The Role of Actors in the Adoption of Emerging ICT in SMEs: An Actor Network Theory Analysis

Sunday C. Eze[1] and Yanqing Duan[2]

[1] Landmark University, Omu-Aran, Kwara State, Nigeria
eze.sunday@lmu.edu.ng
[2] Business School, University of Bedfordhsire, Luton, UK
yanqing.duan@beds.ac.uk

Abstract. This paper aims to understand the role of actors in the adoption of emerging Information and Communications Technologies (ICT) using Actor Network Theory (ANT). The use of ANT helps to identify a diverse range of actors and their role and influence in the dynamic process of emerging ICT's adoption in UK Small and Medium Enterprises (SMEs). This study adopts a qualitative approach to investigate how UK services SMEs are engaged in emerging ICT adoption by focusing on the role of actors in the process. Data were gathered through unstructured and semi-structured interviews with managers, IT experts, government agencies, and customers. Using ANT, the roles of various human and non-human actors at a four-stage dynamic adoption process are examined. The findings reveal the critical and dynamic roles of various actors in the socio-technical network. Although SME managers play the decisional role in emerging ICT adoption, their views and decisions are constantly influenced by various other human and non-human factors. The roles and interactions of all actors are dynamic depending on the adoption stages.

Keywords: SMEs · ICT adoption · Actor Network Theory · Technology adoption

1 Introduction

Although emerging ICT applications offer great opportunities, their successful adoption faces challenges by SME managers and their long-term viability is often uncertain due to the fact that small businesses operate in much more volatile environment with little support on new technology adoption. Very often various stakeholders influence the adoption outcomes. Although ICT adoption has received extensive attention from various researchers, most of research focuses on the factors affecting ICT adoption by treating ICT adoption as a static decision making event and there has been very limited inquiries on how the various actors exert influences that may encourage or inhibit adoption [1]. This research aims to better understand role of diverse actors and their influences in emerging ICT adoption process in UK service SMEs using Actor Network Theory (ANT). This study adopts a qualitative approach aiming to gather rich data. The empirical data collected through interviews are used to first establish a

© IFIP International Federation for Information Processing 2016
Published by Springer International Publishing Switzerland 2016. All Rights Reserved
M.C.C. Baranauskas et al. (Eds.): ICISO 2016, IFIP AICT 477, pp. 234–236, 2016.
DOI: 10.1007/978-3-319-42102-5

dynamic adoption process that has been published in [2]. Based on the process of emerging ICT adoption, this study provides further analysis on the dynamic roles of actors and their key influences at each stage of dynamic adoption process.

This study is theoretically underpinned by ANT because it offers a suitable lends for our investigation and understanding. ANT admits that actors are not restricted to only human beings; rather it is based on how strong the association between human and non-human actors is and tracing such association to a source. Overall, the strength of ANT in understanding ICT adoption lies in its emphasis on studying both the human and non-human entities [3]. The key ANT concepts of inscription, translation, framing and stabilization are adopted for the study.

The research employed a two-round data collection process using unstructured (first round) and semi-structured (second round) interviews. In the first round, the interviewee sample was generated from an online data base and 65 participates were contacted randomly, of which 11 participants were interviewed. In the second round, 15 semi-structured interviews were conducted with a range of key human actors identified from the first round of interviews.

2   Key Findings and Conclusion

Using ANT to examine the process of emerging ICT adoption has helped to unveil the dynamic nature of ICT process and the roles of diverse actors involved in the social-technical network of technology adoption. A number of important findings are emerged from our analysis using ANT as a theoretical lens, including 1. Actors' roles are not static, but dynamic, they plays different roles at the different adoptions stage; 2. Both human and non-human actors influence and are influenced by each other; 3. SMEs managers are the key actor and play a dominant role in influencing and be influenced by non-human actor, i.e. emerging ICT in this context. Overall, emerging ICT adoption has moved from a simple adopters' participation process to involving various actors that constantly interact and influence the process. The findings not only advance our knowledge and understanding on the dynamic nature of emerging ICT adoption and the roles of diverse actors, but also help small business managers to be more strategic and proactive since the adoption of emerging ICT is becoming more challenging. The main limitation of this study is the small sample size used in the data collection due to the nature of qualitative approach. Therefore the key findings can be further validated across a wider population using a mixed method of qualitative and quantitative approaches.

References

1. Cavusoglu, H., Hu, N., Li, Y., Ma, D.: Information technology diffusion with influential, imitators and opponents. J. Manage. Inf. Syst. **27**(2), 305–334 (2010)
2. Eze, S., Dean, Y., Chin, H.: Examining emerging ICT's adoption in SMEs from a dynamic process approach. Inf. Technol. People **27**(1), 63–82 (2014)
3. Latour, B.: Reassembling the Social: An Introduction to Actor-Network-Theory. Oxford University Press (2005)

From Heidegger Onwards – Why Data Science Is Social Semiotics? E-Leadership Takes the Lead

Angela Lacerda Nobre

Escola Superior de Ciências Empresariais do Instituto Politécnico de Setúbal,
ESCE-IPS, Setúbal, Portugal
Angela.nobre@esce.ips.pt

Abstract. Bridging different worlds of meaning, overcoming disciplinary borders and expanding horizons of theoretical and practical knowledge is the task of semiotics, in general, and of social semiotics, in particular. The role of the present paper is to question the emergence of information sciences' new paradigms through the use of philosophically grounded constructs. The argument is: contemporary societies, and the organisations they host, are bounded by thought and action mind frames, which practical philosophy is able to address, to identify and to make explicit. Heidegger's mastery work has set in motion a tradition which enables the design and exploration of the bridges between three different worlds: first, data science and its computing science paradigms; second, social semiotics, and its contribution to the understanding of meaning-making; and third, e-leadership, as a practical application of the fundamental ideas and concepts that are transversal to diverse disciplinary areas and that capture business making fundamentals.

Keywords: Data science · Social semiotics · E-leadership · Organizational information systems · Techno-science

The present poster addresses the links between the business contexts that are being influenced by the emergence of the big data phenomenon and the need to master the potential of e-leadership to the full. This implies explaining how practical philosophy is able to promote a better understanding of the semiotic and language based processes of meaning-making, which are present in every practical circumstance of organisational reality. Three steps, as a summary: (i) To do business is to buy resources in order to sell an idea; (ii) Ideas come in words, which come in sentences that capture information fields; information fields reveal an excess of information, which is captured by sentences in context; consequently, texts leave room for infinite ways of expressing the same idea through a multitude of existent or newly created words; and (iii) Human existence, or human nature, is artificially, that is, culturally created through language, which, in its written form, acquires a life of its own; this means that others may adopt the lessons and insights from written texts and give them new meanings, different from, and richer than, the author's original intentions; meaning-making is constitutive of human nature; through language, new cultural paradigms emerge, which may be captured by ideas, which are transformed in resources that may then be used as a raw

M.C.C. Baranauskas et al. (Eds.): ICISO 2016, IFIP AICT 477, pp. 237–239, 2016.
DOI: 10.1007/978-3-319-42102-5

material for further ideas, that are the backbone of meaning-making; and such is the potential for development of all human made endeavours, including business organisations.

Heidegger's monumental contribution was triggered by a search for ontological and phenomenological quest for new meanings and new interpretations of contemporary societies. According to Heidegger's work, "technicity distorts human nature with an accompanying loss of meaning" [1]. The technological environment imposes complex questions on how to interpret meaning-making. Hegel's Phenomenology [2] enables addressing explicit directions for the design and development of IS, not as an isolated walled garden process, but incorporating end-to-end value creation processes involving the interests of all stakeholders. Ronald Stamper, developed the subfield of organisational semiotics in order to bridge the social world of organisational practices and norms, and the way information is represented through IS. Organized behaviour is norm-governed behaviour. Signs trigger the norms leading to more signs being produced [3]. Semiotics, as the study of signs and of sign systems, has a wide range of applications and of perspectives to be explored. To examine the structural nature of theory in IS, Gregor [4] claims the need to address its form, types and purposes. He argues in favor of the building of integrated bodies of theory that encompasses all theory types. "In the age of big data, ... the emphasis in industry has shifted to data analysis and rapid business decision making based on huge volumes of information." [5]. Computing science uses practical philosophy in order to decode loose strings of meaning. Through this process, computing science continuously creates new cultural paradigms. "Many marketing researchers believe that social media analytics presents a unique opportunity for businesses to treat the market as a "conversation" between businesses and customers instead of the traditional business-to-customer, one-way "marketing"" [6]. Monod [7] argues for the need for epistemological pluralism in IS research. He refers to the importance of the concept of "conditions of possibilities". Baskerville and Myers [8] address the issue of the practical relevance of IS research, and argue in favour of a methodological option for action research as a basis for improved results.

References

1. Dreyfus, H.L., Spinosa, C.: Further reflections on Heidegger, technology, and the everyday. Bull. Sci. Technol. Soc. **23**(5), 339–349 (2003)
2. Hegel, F.: Phénoménologie de l'esprit, Trad. Hyppolite, t. I, p. 178 (original publication: Phänomenologie des Geistes, 1807) (1946)
3. Liu, K., Sun, L., Bennett, K.: Co-design of business and IT systems—introduction by guest editors. Inf. Syst. Front. **4**(3), 251–256 (2002)
4. Gregor, S.: The nature of theory in information systems. MIS Q. **30**(3), 611–642 (2006)
5. Chen, H., Chiang, R.H., Storey, V.C.: Business intelligence and analytics: from big data to big impact. MIS Q. **36**(4), 1165–1188 (2012)
6. Lusch, R.F., Liu, Y., Chen, Y.: The phase transition of markets and organizations: the new intelligence and entre-preneurial frontier. IEEE Intell. Syst. **25**(1), 71–75 (2010)

7. Monod, E.E., Heisenberg, K.: Methodological distinction and conditions of possibilities. Inf. Organ. **14**(2), 105–121 (2004)
8. Baskerville, R., Myers, M.: Action research in information systems: making IS research relevant to practice. MIS Q. **28**(3), 329–335 (2004)

Multicultural Interaction Redesign Using a Semio-Participatory Approach

Jean C.S. Rosa and Ecivaldo Matos

Department of Computer Science,
Federal University of Bahia, Adhemar de Barros Avenue, Salvador, Brazil
{jean.rosa, ecivaldo}@ufba.br

Abstract. This paper presents a research in progress about an interaction redesign of an educational software based on a new semio-participatory approach. Brazil is a multicultural country, and its diversity may affect the educational and interactive processes. With the increase of digital technologies use into classroom, the impact of the people culture on interaction with that technologies should be consider. Particular cultural context makes for the people use solely specific signs of their signification systems, ignoring possible signs that are unknown. Based on the Semiotic Engineering and Participatory Design, this study aims to develop a multicultural interaction design approach which support end-users' diversified needs. An action research is adopted to drive an interaction redesign. Using the Semio-participatory approach is expected to be possible to introduce the cultural and pedagogical characteristics of subject-users on the interface, developing a multicultural interaction.

Keywords: Interaction design · Multiculturalism · Human-computer interaction · Education · Cultural aspects · Participatory design

1 Introduction

Basing this research on Semiotics can understand that interaction is a process of communication and that communication has conducted through the exchange of signs. The Semiotics Engineering theory (a theory of HCI) considers interaction as a communication between a designer and a user. The interface is a collection of signs. Thus, the culture can influence the interpretation of the signs that are in the system interface causing a problem of communication [3].

Our research work adopts a semio-participatory approach of interaction design. The semioparticipativas practices carry messages, highlighting the role of the subjects and their understandings through their effective participation in the design. The first part of the expression, the particle "semio" refers to Semiotics. The "participatory" particle refers to participatory approaches. Participatory approaches have as a principle user participation in the product construction process (e.g. Participatory Design, Metadesign, Design Thinking, Codesign) [1]. The use of this interaction design approach generates two questions: a) the semio-participatory design can contribute to the educational and cultural redesign of the interaction of socio-educational networks; and

© IFIP International Federation for Information Processing 2016
Published by Springer International Publishing Switzerland 2016. All Rights Reserved
M.C.C. Baranauskas et al. (Eds.): ICISO 2016, IFIP AICT 477, pp. 240–242, 2016.
DOI: 10.1007/978-3-319-42102-5

b) given the multicultural context of the school, the semio-participatory role of inter-action (re)design can advantage the school's multicultural profile?

2   Proposed of Semio-Participatory Approach

With the third wave of IHC, researchers have trying to understand the daily life and culture of users. According to Bødker [2], the Participatory Design (PD) can contribute to resolution of these challenges. Participatory practices aim to bring users to center of the product construction process. Thereby, the solution may emerge from users [4]. Baranauskas [1] originated the term "semio-participatory" considering design like a semiotic and social process. According to De Souza [3], the interaction process also is an semiotic process. In our approach, the particle "*Semio*" relates to Semiotic Engineering. The particle "*participatory*" concerns the participation practices. The semio-participatory design approach are participatory practices that carry messages to build the meta-communication by interaction design.

The approach is composed of Communication-Centered Design associated with the Contextual Inquiry, BraiStorm, BrainDraw, and Think-Loud techniques (Table 1). The experiment data showed that use of semio-participatory approach can give voice to users speak out problems in accordance with their experience, enabling the end-user development of the interaction causing the signs of the users' signification systems to be inserted in interface.

Table 1. Methods and Techniques used in the novel approach

Semiotic	Participatory
Communication-Centered Design	Contextual Inquiry
	BrainStorm
Semiotic Inspection Method	BrainDraw
	Think-Aloud

3   Next Steps

In the next steps, we aim to develop a high-fidelity prototypes based on BrainDraw. To do this, students and teachers will be invited to evaluate the interaction of an educational software using Think-Aloud technique.

References

1. Baranauskas, M.C.C.: O modelo semioparticipativo de design. In: Baranauskas, M.C.C., et al. (eds.) Codesign de Redes Digitais: Tecnologia a Serviço da Inclusão Social. Penso, Porto Alegre (2013)

2. Bødker, S.: When second wave HCI meets third wave challenges. In: Proceedings of the 4th Nordic Conference on Human-Computer Interaction Changing Roles - NordiCHI 2006, pp. 1–8. ACM Press, New York (2006)
3. De Souza, C.S.: The Semiotic Engineering of Human-Computer Interaction. MIT Press (2005)
4. Spinuzzi, C.: The methodology of participatory design. Tech. Commun. 52(2), 163–174 (2005)

Optical Wireless Communications
for Ubiquitous Computing

Fabián Seguel, Ismael Soto, Pablo Adasme, and Belarmino Núñez

Department of Electrical Engineering, Universidad de Santiago de Chile,
Avenida Ecuador 3519, Estación Central, Chile
{Fabian.Seguel,Ismael.Soto,Pablo.Adasme,
Belarmino.Nunez}@usach.cl

Abstract. In this paper, we propose resource allocation optimization problems for indoor Optical Wireless Communications uplink. More precisely, a Binary NP-HARD optimization problem together with its relaxation are proposed. Cuckoo Search (CS) and Genetic Algorithms (GA) have been unlikely to find feasible solutions when dealing with the relaxation of the problem. For the binary model, Binary Cuckoo Search outperforms the classical GA achieving better solutions in less computational CPU time.

Keywords: Pervasive computing · Optical wireless communications · NP-hard

1 Problem Formulation and Methods

Ubiquitous Computing collects information from a variety of sources in any location and in any time. Due to the recent advances in wireless communications, integrated digital circuits, micro electro mechanical systems and the mobile technology many devices are now connected through a wireless link. In the recent years, Optical Wireless Communication (OWC) has been subject of study of many researchers. OWC provides many advantages compared to Radio Frequency (RF) making this technology suitable for new generation devices.

The proposed optimization problems referred to as OPT1 and OPT2 are defined next. OPT1 tries to increase the speed of the transmitting information by assigning each device in a pre-defined partition of the channel while OPT2 intends to maximize the bit rate of the wireless link by defining the percentage of the sub channel that will be assigned to each device. The channel link is modeled by the fundamental equations formulated in Komine & Nakagawa [1]. We use Cuckoo Search, Binary Cuckoo Search [2] and Genetic Algorithms [3].

The mathematical model can be formally written as:

$$\max_{\{x_{u,c},P_{u,c}\}} \sum_{u=1}^{U} R_u = \sum_{u=1}^{U} x_{u,c}(\text{B/C})\log_2\Big(1 + \frac{R_{PD}H_{u,c}P_{u,c}}{\sum\limits_{\substack{j\neq u \\ j=1}}^{U}\sum\limits_{\substack{k\neq c \\ k=1}}^{C} x_{j,k}H_{j,k}P^*_{j,k} + \sigma}\Big). \tag{1}$$

© IFIP International Federation for Information Processing 2016
Published by Springer International Publishing Switzerland 2016. All Rights Reserved
M.C.C. Baranauskas et al. (Eds.): ICISO 2016, IFIP AICT 477, pp. 243–245, 2016.
DOI: 10.1007/978-3-319-42102-5

244 F. Seguel et al.

The optimization problem is subject to different limitations. In OPT1 $x_{u,c} \in \{0, 1\}$ while in OPT2 $0 \leq x_{u,c} \leq 1$. For both $P_{u,c} \in \mathbb{R}$, $0 \leq P_{u,c} \leq 10$

$$\sum_{u=1}^{U} x_{u,c} - 1 \leq 0 \ \forall \ c \in C, \ 1 - \sum_{c=1}^{C} x_{u,c} \leq 0, \ \sum_{c=1}^{C} x_{u,c}P_{u,c} - 10 \leq 0 \ \forall \ u \in U. \quad (2)$$

2 Results and Conclusion

It can be seen from Table 1 that the BCS algorithm is faster to compute feasible solutions. GA overcomes BCS in 4 scenarios. Nevertheless GA also provides unfeasible (Unf) solutions in scenarios where BCS provides a feasible one.

Table 1. Objective function values for OPT1 and OPT2 by using BCS, CS and GA

Devices	Channels	R_{OPT1} BCS	R_{OPT2} CS	R_{OPT1} GA	R_{OPT2} GA	BCS Fitness GAP (%)	GA Time Gap (%)
4	32	180.74	Unf	154.15	Unf	17.24	−32.05
8	32	70.45	Unf	79.19	Unf	−11.03	−37.84
12	32	451.54	Unf	518.17	Unf	−12.85	−42.22
14	32	269.03	Unf	Unf	Unf	–	–
4	64	20.54	Unf	29.46	Unf	−30.26	−35.39
8	64	205.49	Unf	Unf	Unf	–	–
12	64	166.77	Unf	Unf	Unf	–	–
14	64	53.14	Unf	Unf	Unf	–	–
	Min	70.45	–	62.70	–	–	–
	Max	668.59	–	732.14	–	–	–
	Average	233.68	–	155.81	–	–	–

In this case, BCS outperforms GA reaching feasible solutions in less computational time. The relaxation proposed cannot find feasible solutions in the searching space. In a future work a decomposition approach will be proposed in order to deal with the binary NP-HARD optimization problem.

Acknowledgments. The authors acknowledge the financial support of the "Center for Multidisciplinary Research on Signal Processing" (CONICYT/ACT1120 Project), the USACH/DICYT 061413SG and 061513VC_DAS Projects and CORFO 14IDL2-2991914.

References

1. Komine, T., Nakagawa, M.: Fundamental analysis for visible-light communication system using LED lights. IEEE Trans. Consummer Electron. **50**(1), 100–107 (2004)
2. Yang, X.S., Deb, S.: Engineering optimisation by cuckoo search. Math. Model. Numer. Optim (2015)
3. Goldberg, D.E.: Genetic Algorithms. Pearson Education (2006)

A Semantically-Based Big Data Processing System Using Hadoop and Map-Reduce

Wang Wanting[1] and Qin Zheng[1,2]

[1] School of Information Management and Engineering,
Shanghai University of Finance and Economics, Shanghai, China
2014311051@live.sufe.edu.cn,
qinzheng@mail.shufe.edu.cn
[2] South University of Science and Technology of China, Shenzhen, China

Abstract. In financial industry, a wide range of financial systems generate vast amount of data in different structures, which change with compliance rules change and hard to manage due to their heterogeneity. This paper introduces a semantically-based big data processing system to integrate the data from different sources, which realizes the query and computation in semantic layer. The system provides a new data management way for the financial industry. With Semantic Web, the information can be managed, integrated, and collaborated in a more fluent way than it in traditional ETL. In order to clear the complex logical relationship among data, the system uses SPARQL to query. Through Map-Reduce, this system, based on Hadoop and Hbase can improve the processing speed for big data.

Keywords: Big data · Semantics · Data integration · Distributed computation

1 Introduction

There are some characteristics in financial big data, which bring lots of problems of data management in financial field, including cross-regional and cross-system distribution [1], multiple structured and non-standardized data formats, and rapid change in the analysis strategy of big data [2]. This paper presents a new semantically-based big data processing system, which connects data through linked data to integrate the heterogeneous data.[1]

2 Model Design

The big data in financial field is so huge-scaled and multi-structured that traditional ETL cannot integrate data efficiently. On the one hand, by using semantic analysis the data can be connected and the system can realize data sharing with RDF based on semantic data queries. On the other hand, distributed computation can provide efficient

---

[1] This research is supported by National Natural Science Fund of China (71302080) and Ministry of Education Research of Social Science Youth Foundation Project (13YJC630149).

M.C.C. Baranauskas et al. (Eds.): ICISO 2016, IFIP AICT 477, pp. 246–247, 2016.
DOI: 10.1007/978-3-319-42102-5

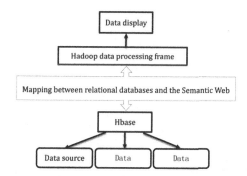

Fig. 1. The semantically-based big data processing system

big data processing [3]. An experiment of distributed semantics queries is tested in order to validate the practicability of semantic mapping of relational data. The semantically-based big data processing system is a vertical structure (Fig. 1), which is based on Hbase storage. The data collected from the data sources are uploaded to central system and permanently stored in Hbase after corresponding conversions. All the data can be connected through Linked Data, and then generate RDF data sets. With Hadoop platform, after semantic analysis and distributed computation, the results can be delivered to every application terminal in cloud.

3 Conclusion

The experiment illustrates that the system based on semantics can solve the problem of the integration of heterogeneous data to some extent. With semantics and distributed computation, the efficient process and integration of complex big data are able to be realized.

References

1. Madnick, S.E.: From VLDB to VMLDB (Very MANY Large Data Bases): dealing with large-scale semantic heterogeneity. In: Proceedings of the 21st International Conference on Very Large Data Bases, Zurich, Switzerland, pp. 11–15 (1995)
2. Rabl, T., Gómez-Villamor, S., Sadoghi, M., Muntés-Mulero, V., Jacobsen, H.A., Mankovskii, S.: Solving big data challenges for enterprise application performance management. Proc. Vldb Endowment **5**(12), 1724–1735 (2012)
3. Bizer, C., Heath, T., Idehen, K., Berners-Lee, T.: Linked Data on the Web (LDOW2008). In: Proceedings of The 17th International Conference on World Wide Web, Beijing, China, pp. 21–25 (2008)

Author Index

Printed in the United States
By Bookmasters